Mark Stover, MAR, MLS, PhD
Editor

Theological Librarians and the Internet: Implications for Practice

Theological Librarians and the Internet: Implications for Practice has been co-published simultaneously as *Journal of Religious & Theological Information*, Volume 3, Numbers 3/4 2001.

Pre-publication REVIEWS, COMMENTARIES, EVALUATIONS . . .

"**A** MARVELOUSLY COMPREHENSIVE PIECE OF WORK. . . . Almost a theological education in itself!"

John D. Murray, BA, MA, MALS
Director
Library & Information Services
Voskuyl Library
Westmont College
Santa Barbara, California

T0172981

The Haworth Information Press
An Imprint of
The Haworth Press, Inc.

Theological Librarians and the Internet: Implications for Practice

Theological Librarians and the Internet: Implications for Practice has been co-published simultaneously as *Journal of Religious & Theological Information,* Volume 3, Numbers 3/4 2001.

The *Journal of Religious & Theological Information* Monographic "Separates"

Below is a list of "separates," which in serials librarianship means a special issue simultaneously published as a special journal issue or double-issue *and* as a "separate" hardbound monograph. (This is a format which we also call a "DocuSerial.")

"Separates" are published because specialized libraries or professionals may wish to purchase a specific thematic issue by itself in a format which can be separately cataloged and shelved, as opposed to purchasing the journal on an on-going basis. Faculty members may also more easily consider a "separate" for classroom adoption.

"Separates" are carefully classified separately with the major book jobbers so that the journal tie-in can be noted on new book order slips to avoid duplicate purchasing.

You may wish to visit Haworth's website at . . .

http://www.HaworthPress.com

. . . to search our online catalog for complete tables of contents of these separates and related publications.

You may also call 1-800-HAWORTH (outside US/Canada: 607-722-5857), or Fax 1-800-895-0582 (outside US/Canada: 607-771-0012), or e-mail at:

getinfo@haworthpressinc.com

Theological Librarians and the Internet: Implications for Practice, edited by Mark Stover, MAR, MLS, PhD (Vol. 3, No. 3/4, 2001). *Assists theological librarians, instructors, researchers, and others in making sense of the vast amounts of religious and theological information available today on the Internet.*

Theological Librarians and the Internet: Implications for Practice

Mark Stover, MAR, MLS, PhD
Editor

Theological Librarians and the Internet: Implications for Practice has been co-published simultaneously as *Journal of Religious & Theological Information*, Volume 3, Numbers 3/4 2001.

The Haworth Information Press
An Imprint of
The Haworth Press, Inc.
New York • London • Oxford

Published by

The Haworth Information Press®, 10 Alice Street, Binghamton, NY 13904-1580, USA

The Haworth Information Press® is an imprint of The Haworth Press, Inc., 10 Alice Street, Binghamton, NY 13904-1580 USA.

Theological Librarians and the Internet: Implications for Practice has been co-published simultaneously as *Journal of Religious & Theological Information* ™, Volume 3, Numbers 3/4 2001.

Cover design by Thomas J. Mayshock, Jr.

Library of Congress Cataloging-in-Publication Data

Theological librarians and the Internet : Implications for practice / Mark Stover, editor.
    p. cm.
    Co-published simultaneously as Journal of religious & theological information, v. 3, no. 3/4, 2001.
    Inlcudes bibliographical references and index.
    ISBN 0-7890-1341-X (alk. paper) -- ISBN 0-7890-1342-8 (pbk. : alk. paper)
    1. Theological libraries. 2. Library information networks. 3. Internet. 4. Religion–Computer network resources. 5. Theology–Computer network resources. I. Stover, Mark II. Journal of religious & theological information.

Z675.T4 T47 2001
025.06'2–dc21
                                            2001024428

Indexing, Abstracting & Website/Internet Coverage

This section provides you with a list of major indexing & abstracting services. That is to say, each service began covering this periodical during the year noted in the right column. Most Websites which are listed below have indicated that they will either post, disseminate, compile, archive, cite or alert their own Website users with research-based content from this work. (This list is as current as the copyright date of this publication.)

(continued)

Special Bibliographic Notes related to special journal issues (separates) and indexing/abstracting:

- indexing/abstracting services in this list will also cover material in any "separate" that is co-published simultaneously with Haworth's special thematic journal issue or DocuSerial. Indexing/abstracting usually covers material at the article/chapter level.
- monographic co-editions are intended for either non-subscribers or libraries which intend to purchase a second copy for their circulating collections.
- monographic co-editions are reported to all jobbers/wholesalers/approval plans. The source journal is listed as the "series" to assist the prevention of duplicate purchasing in the same manner utilized for books-in-series.
- to facilitate user/access services all indexing/abstracting services are encouraged to utilize the co-indexing entry note indicated at the bottom of the first page of each article/chapter/contribution.
- this is intended to assist a library user of any reference tool (whether print, electronic, online, or CD-ROM) to locate the monographic version if the library has purchased this version but not a subscription to the source journal.
- individual articles/chapters in any Haworth publication are also available through the Haworth Document Delivery Service (HDDS).

Theological Librarians and the Internet: Implications for Practice

CONTENTS

ABOUT THE EDITOR

Mark Stover, MAR, MLS, PhD, holds advanced degrees in Library and Information Science from UCLA and Nova Southeastern University, and received his MA in Religion from Westminster Theological Seminary. He has published articles and given presentations on various topics including Web design, electronic publishing, and information ethics. He has worked in the academic and corporate worlds as a consultant, theological librarian, instructor, and information technology professional. Dr. Stover currently serves as Psychology and Behavioral Sciences Librarian at San Diego State University in California.

Internet Shock:
Change, Continuity,
and the Theological Librarian

Mark Stover

SUMMARY. This article discusses information technology and theological libraries. It compares and contrasts the state of the field in 1990 with the current situation. The article describes ways that the Internet is changing the work of all librarians, but also suggests ways in which librarians can continue to find purpose and meaning in the timeless principles and values of librarianship. *[Article copies available for a fee from The Haworth Document Delivery Service: 1-800-342-9678. E-mail address: <getinfo@haworthpressinc.com> Website: <http://www.HaworthPress.com> © 2001 by The Haworth Press, Inc. All rights reserved.]*

KEYWORDS. Theological libraries, Internet, continuity and change

INFORMATION TECHNOLOGY AND THE THEOLOGICAL LIBRARIAN REVISITED

In 1990 I submitted a manuscript to the *Journal of Religious & Theological Information* entitled "Information Technology and the Theological Librarian" (Stover 1993). The article (which for a variety

Mark Stover, MAR, MLS, PhD, is Psychology and Behavioral Sciences Librarian, San Diego State University, 5500 Campanile Drive, San Diego, CA 92182-8050 (E-mail: mstover@mail.sdsu.edu).

[Haworth co-indexing entry note]: "Internet Shock: Change, Continuity, and the Theological Librarian." Stover, Mark. Co-published simultaneously in *Journal of Religious & Theological Information* (The Haworth Information Press, an imprint of The Haworth Press, Inc.) Vol. 3, No. 3/4, 2001, pp. 1-12; and: *Theological Librarians and the Internet: Implications for Practice* (ed: Mark Stover) The Haworth Information Press, an imprint of The Haworth Press, Inc., 2001, pp. 1-12. Single or multiple copies of this article are available for a fee from The Haworth Document Delivery Service [1-800-342-9678, 9:00 a.m. - 5:00 p.m. (EST). E-mail address: getinfo@haworthpressinc.com].

of reasons would not actually be published for three more years) offered theological librarians multiple ways to utilize computer technology in their work. In the present article, I will compare and contrast the main points of my original article with an updated look at the impact of technology on theological librarians. I will describe ways that the Internet is changing the work of all librarians, but I will also suggest ways in which librarians can (and should) continue to find purpose and meaning in the timeless principles and values of our profession.

Little has changed over the last ten years for many of the technologies that I wrote about in 1990. For example, I discussed sources of continuing education for keeping up with computer technology, and listed a number of journals and magazines that might be helpful for theological librarians. Almost all of these periodicals are still published (and read) today, although of course some of them are also available online. Professional conferences were also high on my list of important educational resources. While some continuing education is now available through the Web, most of us still educate ourselves through professional reading, attendance at conferences, and enrollment in traditional courses of study.

In 1990 I wrote about (mostly bibliographic) electronic databases that were important for theological librarians. These included *Religion Index Online* (now called ATLA Religion Database) and *Religious and Theological Abstracts,* both of which were available on CD-ROM (with *RIO* being accessible online as well). These two databases are still available today, and CD-ROM still seems to be the primary medium of distribution, although the ATLA Religion Database is also accessible through other formats by subscription. The two databases have not changed a great deal since 1990, except in size and in their graphical interface. But traditional concepts such as Boolean searching and authority control in indexing continue to play an important role in the idea of the bibliographic database.

I also mentioned a variety of types of electronic tools that were important for librarians to utilize and make available to library patrons. These included CD-ROM databases, word processing software, and database management programs. While these software packages and search engines are certainly more powerful and sophisticated than they were ten years ago, the differences are mostly incremental and not radical. CD-ROM based reference Bibles are still as popular today as they were in 1990. Indeed, these electronic tools (which combine the full text of multiple versions of the Bible with myriad theological reference books) seem to have proliferated exponentially (see, for example, http://www.logos.com).

In addition, the library-specific software that I wrote about (such as circulation systems, serials control software, acquisitions programs, and online public access catalogs) looks very much as it did ten years ago. Many online catalogs have moved to a graphical interface, and there are today some added features in many integrated library software systems, but for the most part the basic underlying concepts have not radically been altered.

So what has changed since 1990? In a word (or perhaps two words), the Web. The Internet was alive and well ten years ago, but it was limited to academics and a few others. Since the early to mid 1990s, when the Web burst onto the worldwide scene in a flash of multimedia and hyperlinks, important changes have taken place which affect theological librarians. I mentioned the Internet in my original article, but it played a small role in my scenario for librarians using information technology. I wrote about the usefulness of listservs and Internet-accessible databases (few as they were at that time), but I did not foresee the great changes that would be wrought by the Web.

E-mail was barely mentioned in my article, but today it is a crucial part of the communication habits of millions (soon to be billions) of people throughout the world. Web sites, whether personal, organizational, religious, commercial, or educational, play an important role in the lives of many of our library clients. Online discussions, including real time chat, instant messaging, and bulletin boards, are becoming more frequently utilized each day.

Full text journals and "e-books" are growing by leaps and bounds. The electronic journal literature for religion and theology has already made significant inroads into the library community, and much more is promised for the near future. E-books for the religious and theological world are offered by the hundreds on various e-bookstores like NetLibrary and FatBrain, and soon this number will undoubtedly increase into the thousands or even tens of thousands. As I noted earlier, there are some important similarities between the information technology world of the theological librarian in 1990 and in the year 2000, but there are also some significant differences. Most of these differences have been occasioned by the Web and its incredible impact on the way we communicate and transfer information.

My original article also discussed the advantages and drawbacks of information technology for theological librarians. I mentioned increased productivity and efficiency in the workplace, and these continue to be important positive aspects of computer usage today. I referred to multitasking, Boolean searching, and blended (or integrated) technology, concepts that most of us take for granted today. But there were two areas that I alluded to in my article that can provide us with an interesting contrast in our retrospective analysis: expert systems and hypermedia. Expert systems (or, to use the broader and more flamboyant term, artificial intelligence), remain at the primitive stage of development. While some attempts have been made to allow "machine-assistance" in the information seeking process, we are still far away from the intelligent agent utopia envisioned by some futurists.

On the other hand, hypermedia (along with its cousin, multimedia) has been brought up to the top tier of emerging technologies by the explosion of the Web. The Web is unthinkable without hypermedia, and hypermedia would undoubtedly still be a minor phenomenon without the Web. The words I wrote in 1990 were optimistic but did not foresee the champion "killer app" that eventually came in the form of the Web:

> Hypermedia is a concept that views computers as analogous to people. That is, computers, even if they cannot "think" like humans, should be programmed in a way that produces a more friendly interaction between the computer and the user than has traditionally been the case. Hypermedia, often using a graphical interface, "intuitively" guides the user down a path that has many crossroads and thus many options. Hypermedia uses a sensory combination of sight (pictures and text) and sound (digitized spoken words and digitized music) to create an atmosphere that is conducive to learning and productivity. (Stover 1993)

My article also referred to the disadvantages of information technology. Included in this discussion were concepts like information overload, the high learning curve of technological applications, and the high cost of computer hardware, software and technical support. Other problems that I brought up included the complexity of electronic copyright issues, computer phobia, and technological triumphalism. These issues still demand our attention. Indeed, with the exception of the high costs of technology (which the Internet seems to have ameliorated to some degree), the advent of the Web has done little to alleviate most of these difficulties. In some cases, such as the issue of information overload, the Web has actually exacerbated the problem.

CONTINUITY

The comparison and contrast between yesterday and today leads me to the conclusion that there is a great deal of continuity between library work then and now. Despite the fact that the Web did not exist, we still carried out a similar mission and we used many of the same tools. In 1990 we had electronic databases for end users (on CD-ROM) and electronic databases for librarians (through Dialog and other vendors). Today we have even more electronic databases, and even though some of them require complex searching skills, the divide between end users and professional librarians has narrowed significantly.

In 1990 we had online public access catalogs, and of course today we continue to use these important tools. We had the Internet in primitive form ten years ago, and we had early versions of hypertext and hypermedia. Some of us used e-mail and listservs from our desktop personal computers. And, as I recall, we also had a few books and a number of librarians in the library of 1990.

These are for the most part technologies that we have utilized for positive ends. But there were also negative aspects of librarianship ten years ago, although it was mostly in the non-technological realm. When I think about the kinds of problems that we librarians experience today, especially those kinds of troubles related to the Internet, I see an unmistakable connection to the previous generation. Take for example the following modern troublesome scenarios and their ancient equivalents. The chart below describes the ancient problem (from 1990) and then translates it into the modern vernacular.

The Original Manuscripts	The Modern Translation
The library is closed	The Server is down
The book is not yet published	This Web site is still under construction
The book is missing	A hacker shut down the site
The book is out of print	The Web site no longer exists
The book has been mutilated	The Web site has been vandalized
You wrote down the wrong Call Number	You typed in the wrong URL
The book must be mis-shelved	The DNS name and the IP address are not synchronized correctly

The Biblical writer stated, perhaps with a little cynicism, that there is nothing new under the sun. The French like to say that the more things change, the more they stay the same. These two axioms well describe the continuity perspective that is illustrated by the above examples.

CHANGE

I have noted some of the similarities between then and now, but clearly the library world has changed a great deal since 1990. I would like to spend the balance of this article describing some of the ways that the Internet (and the Web in particular) has altered the lives of theological librarians. I have divided up my observations about how the Internet has altered our lives under the following headings: Work Habits; Communication; Reference Service; Organization of Information; and Commerce.

Work Habits

Because of the Internet, some of us can now work from home instead of driving to the library. I did this one day a week for three years in the mid 1990s. Telecommuting was not a completely positive adventure for me. To use a theological metaphor, my telecommuting experience was a mixed blessing. While there were fewer disruptions for the most part, there were also many distractions that one simply does not experience at the office. On the other hand, there was also a tendency to become overly involved in my work. Since the home office was already set up, why not check work-related e-mail at home in the evenings or on the weekends? Why not spend a few minutes (read: hours) finishing up those Web pages that didn't get done at the office. In any event, even with the marvels of the Internet, telecommuting will not replace driving to work at the library any time soon. Many of the duties of theological librarians involve face-to-face interaction with both patrons and co-workers, and e-mail often doesn't pass muster on those verbal and non-verbal cues like a shrug of the shoulders or a disappointed facial expression. Perhaps things will improve when everyone is equipped with PCs with video cameras attached, but even then we will probably lose something in the translation.

I also worked as an Internet consultant for several years in the mid to late 1990s. I designed Web pages and performed library technology consulting, and I also spent two years as the "online librarian" for a "virtual campus" online theological college based in the Midwest. Almost all of this work was done through the Internet. I could (and did) work from any location in the world where I could get an Internet connection, and it was an excellent part-time "side job" that supplemented the income from my day job as a traditional librarian. I performed online reference, online bibliographic instruction, and even a bit of online collection development in the form of creating links to relevant Web sites and choosing appropriate databases. The hours were flexible, the work was fun, and I earned extra income. I think that this might be one of the areas that will change the way that theological librarians work in the future. Until the concept of intelligent agents is perfected there will be a need for us to do what we do best: help others find the information they are looking for, and assist them through the complex structure of what we used to call "the body of literature" and what I now call "the Information Infrastructure."

Communication

The Internet has certainly altered our communication habits. We get a great deal of our professional collegiality and continuing education from listservs. And e-mail, of course, is ubiquitous. There are many good things about e-mail and listservs. These tools are quick, efficient, and relatively inexpensive, but there are also drawbacks to these new technologies that have become apparent to most of us in the last ten years.

Listservs can create tremendous information overload problems. For several years I was conflicted about this genre. I belonged to too many listservs, and I would get caught up in the details of each message. On the other hand, I often benefited from reading (and sometimes participating in) the various discussions that took place. I finally resolved the tension by configuring Eudora to filter each listserv discussion into a separate mailbox. Once or twice daily I check my e-mail with one finger poised over the delete key. I receive perhaps 80-100 listserv messages per day, and I delete about 75% of them after quickly glancing at the subject line.

E-mail comes with its own set of problems. I alluded earlier to the loss of non-verbal cues in e-mail, but there are other dangers as well. Using the "blind carbon copy" function can expose the user to multiple perils, and checking one's e-mail can easily become an addictive behavior or an obsessive-compulsive disorder. E-mail is clearly a double-edged sword that has advantages and limitations.

Reference Service

Reference service for theological and religious-oriented questions today is much more complex than it was before the advent of the Web. There is of course much talk today about the potential for e-mail reference and "instant messaging" (or online chat) reference, but these areas have not yet come into full bloom for most theological librarians. More to the point is the knowledge base that librarians must maintain in order to keep up a high standard of service. We must be experts in using many of the same print tools that we had ten years ago, but now we must also be experts (or at least literate and knowledgeable) in using a wide spectrum of online databases, Internet search engines, and other electronic tools. This challenges us to keep active in continuing education and professional development, but it also has the potential to create a massive professional information overload crisis.

Is it a good thing or a bad thing that theological librarians can do most anything now from their desktops? It is not just the Internet that makes this possible, of course; online public access catalogs, databases, and local networks contribute to this armchair librarianship. But are the chairs in religious and theological libraries really so comfortable that this is seen as a good thing? The demise of the card catalog and the loss in popularity of printed indexes may someday be blamed (at least in part) for the sedentary nature of technologically astute librarians and the resulting health problems due to lack of exercise.

Organization of Information

Theological librarians, like most other members of our profession, often consider themselves highly skilled in the art of organizing information. While it is mostly catalogers and indexers who traditionally have been involved in organizing information on a daily basis, reference librarians are becoming more concerned about the problem of the organization of information on the Web. The Internet has opened up new possibilities in this arena, but there clearly are major challenges that need to be addressed.

The first big problem in this area is the fact that the Internet is essentially unorganized. Search engines are wonderful tools, and most of us could not function very well without them, but search engines plainly have not even come close to reaching their potential. There is very little if any controlled vocabulary on the Web, and intellectual access to most of the Internet can only be gained through search engines. Most search engines, unfortunately, leave much to be desired in terms of thoroughness, timeliness, the balance between precision and recall, and relevancy ranking. Information overload is clearly a significant issue for information seekers on the Web.

The second problem is that many users on the Web do not understand that the Internet is in a state of disarray. In some ways this is like the frog which is placed in a pot of slowly boiling water. Both the frog and end users fail to recognize their dilemma until it is too late. The source of the end users' complacency is the existence of search engines. When using search engines, information seekers on the Internet should remember the old platitude that "a little knowledge is a dangerous thing." End users often do not realize that individual search engines cover (at best) 20%-30% of the Web. To add to this dilemma is the recent introduction of "conversational" or "natural language query" search engines like AskJeeves. AskJeeves is, admittedly, a very interesting resource, and it does find the right information (more or less) perhaps 30% of the time. But again, this kind of search tool lulls the end user into a state of complacency. The user believes that she has found everything there is to find on the Internet, and that no special searching skills or techniques are necessary for a successful outcome. Another related issue is the authority of information and the Internet. Search engines often empower end users to the point where other sources of information (such as a subscription database) are considered unnecessary because Infoseek or Google has brought them to Information Nirvana.

The last big problem with organizing information on the Internet has to do with what I call "multiplication of genres." Static Web pages, dynamic Web pages, personal Web sites, organizational Web sites, commercial Web sites, CD-ROM databases, online databases, newsgroups, listservs, Web-based bulletin boards, chat rooms, online auction houses, and other Web genres (new ones seemingly sprouting up every day) make the topic of organizing the Internet even more complex. In addition, marginalized (and often illegal) Web sites that feature online gambling, adult-only content, and marketing scams blur the line between legitimate and illegitimate sources of information. There are many spheres of influence on the Internet, and unsophisticated search-ers often cannot properly distinguish one from the other. But even if one only considers the "legitimate" side of the Internet, one must ask if it is really the job of librarians to organize these diverse segments of the "Internet Industrial Complex" into a coherent whole?

I would submit that it *is* our job to organize the Internet, but on the other hand it is *not* our job. Librarians have always organized information, but more on a "meta" or 2nd order level than on a primary or 1st order level. Primary information organization, such as back-of-the-book indexes and periodical databases, are for the most part created by non-librarians. The main exception is of course library online catalogs and to a lesser degree bibliographies. But while librarians (with some notable exceptions) have never been the primary producers of most organization-of-information projects, the profession at large seems to have the ability to work with these tools on a meta level. Librarians select and purchase these resources, learn how to use them, teach others how to use them, publicize them in different ways, and in general provide access to these 1st order tools. That has always been the gift of the library profession, and it is a contribution of which we can be very proud.

That being said, how can theological librarians continue this tradition in the age of the Internet, especially since it appears that our profession has not been at the forefront of designing search engines or other Internet finding aids? The following suggestions might be useful:

- Learn the search engines well and teach others how to use them
- Organize (and provide descriptions for) your subscription data-bases in a clear and concise manner
- Create Web pages with links to meta sites (which are Web sites that provide links to other sites within one subject area) and li-brary guides on different topics related to religion and theology, and promote these pages to your primary clients as well as to the entire Internet community
- Link your Web pages to other meta sites
- Concentrate on substantial Internet information, and only deal with ephemeral online information if you have plenty of spare time
- Encourage a standard approach to cataloging the Internet (such as the Dublin Core Metadata Initiative) and utilize this approach when creating your own Web sites

Commerce

The World Wide Web brought the Internet into the mainstream. But online commerce has made the Internet the *Main Stream*. Has online commerce made much of a difference in the lives of theological librarians? Probably not, unless you count all the patrons in religious and theological libraries buying airline tickets from library workstations or trying to sell used textbooks through E-Bay on an OPAC terminal. The online bookstores are useful tools for such tasks as overnight book delivery or bibliographic verification. Document delivery is in some ways a form of online commerce, and the CARL Uncover service is a good example of how libraries can utilize this technology through the Internet. But at this point in time, online commerce simply does not impact the professional lives of theological librarians to any significant degree, and it is doubtful that the near future will prove to be much different.

CONCLUSION

There are two important themes running through this article: the theme of "form" and the theme of "content." Form is, of course, *how* we perform our tasks as librarians, and content is *what* we do. Clearly the Internet has transformed the nature of our jobs in terms of form. The larger question, of course, is whether the Internet will change the content of our profession.

The Internet, in my opinion, will not alter a great deal of the content of the work of librarians in the coming years. We will continue to create both static and dynamic guides to information sources. We will continue to provide personal assistance to individuals looking for the right information at the right time. We will continue to teach groups of people how to find necessary data. We will continue to label and categorize knowledge to facilitate information retrieval. These tasks will look very different in ten years than they do now, but I expect that *what* we do–selection, organization, and preservation of information sources, and the provision of personal and group instruction in finding these sources–will not radically change.

As our profession evolves during the next few years and decades, it would serve us well to remember the values that lie behind our professional activities, values like service, scholarship, and intellectual freedom. These are the values that will keep us on the right track, that will help us adapt to different environments and changing technologies without destroying the foundation of our work.

Build on the past, but look toward the Future. Keep the traditions, but be flexible and be ready to change. And when in our most iconoclastic moments we are tempted to cancel all of our print journal subscriptions and spend most of our book budget on electronic "Rocket Books," we should remember the words of the 16th century German reformer Martin Luther. In response to the radical reformation of his day he said, "Man sol das kind nicht mit dem bad ausgiessen." Which being translated is: "Don't throw the baby out with the bath water."

REFERENCE

Stover, M. 1993. Information technology and the theological librarian. *Journal of Religious & Theological Information* 1(1):81-96.

Religious and Theological
Journals Online:
The ATLA Serials Collection Project

Mark Dubis

Near the time this column reaches publication, scholars and students will be able to access electronically the full text of religious and theological journal articles. This development is a result of an initiative by the American Theological Library Association (ATLA) which on January 1, 1999, created the Center for Electronic Resources in Theology and Religion (CERTR). James R. Adair serves as the director for this new center based in Atlanta. CERTR states its purpose as fourfold: "to disseminate electronic texts of interest to scholars of religion, to promote the publication of original scholarly works in formats compatible with online study and distribution, to support other

---

Mark Dubis is Assistant Professor of Christian Scriptures, The George W. Truett Theological Seminary, Baylor University, Waco, TX.

[Haworth co-indexing entry note]: "Religious and Theological Journals Online: The ATLA Serials Collection Project." Dubis, Mark. Co-published simultaneously in *Journal of Religious & Theological Information* (The Haworth Information Press, an imprint of The Haworth Press, Inc.) Vol. 3, No. 3/4, 2001, pp. 13-15; and: *Theological Librarians and the Internet: Implications for Practice* (ed: Mark Stover) The Haworth Information Press, an imprint of The Haworth Press, Inc., 2001, pp. 13-15. Single or multiple copies of this article are available for a fee from The Haworth Document Delivery Service [1-800-342-9678, 9:00 a.m. - 5:00 p.m. (EST). E-mail address: getinfo@haworthpressinc.com].

13

efforts to move the academic study of religion into the information age, and to remain on the forefront of advances in technology through a commitment to research and development."

CERTR's first major project is the ATLA Serials Collection Project (or ATLAS). This project, initially supported by a four million-dollar grant from the Lilly Endowment, aims to provide online access to the full text of fifty key journals in religious and theological studies. This project will be retrospective, providing access not only to recent journal articles but also to the past fifty years of each journal (a scope that will cover the entire print run of most journals). CERTR is working in close cooperation with both the Society of Biblical Literature and the American Academy of Religion. Journals that have already agreed to participate include, among others, the *Journal of Biblical Literature, Journal of the American Academy of Religion, Church History, Interpretation, Semeia, New Eastern Archaeology, Muslim World, International Bulletin of Missionary Research* and the *Journal of Pastoral Care.*

CERTR intends to provide access to these journals in two formats: images and fully searchable text. The initial phase of ATLAS will be to provide digitized images (150 dpi grey-scale GIFs) of all articles in all selected journals. Although users at this stage will not be able to perform full-text searches, limited searches will be possible since CERTR plans to attach basic searchable information (e.g., bibliographical data, keywords, and biblical references) to the image of each page. This image-based phase should be complete by January 2001.

The next phase of ATLAS will be to provide fully searchable XML-formatted text of all journal articles. This text-based phase should be complete by January 2002. While the digitized images produced in the first phase will allow online viewing of articles and limited search capabilities, the fully-searchable text of this second phase will be a particular boon to users since it will allow complex searches of the entire contents of those articles (totaling over 400,000,000 words). Boolean operators, proximity searches, and searches based on XML encoding will all be supported.

Another great advantage of this project is that these electronically accessible journals will be linked to the *ATLA Religion Database* (ARD) the most comprehensive database of religious and theological periodical literature. Thus, after finding a particular article through an ARD search, users will be able to click on a link within ARD to immediately take them to an online version of that article.

The projected subscription cost for access to this resource is as follows: $110-150 per year to individual users, and $2500 per year to institutions for a site license with unlimited users (institutions must already subscribe to the *ATLA Religion Database*).

As for future plans, once ATLAS moves beyond its three-year plan to digitize fifty journals, ATLAS will work to digitize the over 500 other journals that appear in the ARD, adding a minimum of 15 journals per year. ATLAS also plans to incorporate current e-journals into its project (an easy task since these are already in digital format).

One caveat regarding the availability of any given journal is that ATLAS has given publishers the option to establish a "rolling gap" whereby access to the most recent issues of a journal may be restricted to those who are subscribers of the print version. Fortunately for the user, most publishers are not choosing this option but rather are making all of their issues available to the general user. And the publishers that are opting for a rolling gap are usually opting for a gap of not more than one year.

ATLAS promises to be a substantial step forward for those who need to access periodical literature in religion and theology quickly, conveniently, and at a reasonable cost. For further information see CERTR's web site at http://purl.org/CERTR and the additional reading below.

FURTHER READING

Adair, James R. "The ATLAS Project: An Online Religion Journal Collection for Scholars and Teachers." *ATLA Newsletter* (May 1999). Online: http://rosetta. atlacertr.org/CERTR/ATLAS/articles/Diktuon-ATLAS.html.

Adair, James R. "The ATLAS Project of the Center for Electronic Texts in Religion: 50 Years of 50 Journals." Paper presented at the Research Libraries Group Forum. Atlanta, May 20-21, 1999. Online: http://rosetta.atla-certr.org/CERTR/ATLAS/articles/RLG-ATLAS.html.

Adair, James R., Patrick Durusau. "Online Print Journal Collections and the Academic Study of Religion." *Religious Studies News* (February 1999). Online: http://rosetta.atla-certr.org/CERTR/Offline/off64.html.

American Theological Library Association. "ATLA Serials: Fifty Years of Fifty Journals." Proposal for the ATLAS Project. Online: http://rosetta.atla-certr.org/CERTR/ATLAS/articles/ATLAS-proposal.html.

The Function of Web Catalogs in Theological Libraries

John Dickason

SUMMARY. The World Wide Web is an environment in which academic libraries are able to improve and extend their services, and help achieve the goals of their institutions. The Web catalog is one tool that can help advance these goals. Theological libraries are beginning to utilize Web catalogs in order to improve access to their unique collections. This article summarizes a study of 132 theological library Web catalogs in North America, and attempts to identify and interpret the roles these catalogs play. The essay concludes with thoughts on the future shape of Web OPACs, and an identification of the major gateways to these catalogs. *[Article copies available for a fee from The Haworth Document Delivery Service: 1-800-342-9678. E-mail address: <getinfo@haworthpressinc.com> Website: <http://www.HaworthPress.com> © 2001 by The Haworth Press, Inc. All rights reserved.]*

KEYWORDS. OPACs, Web catalogs, Z39.50, theological libraries, library technology

The World Wide Web is an environment in which libraries are able to improve and extend their services.[1] Academic libraries are using the Web to continue their leadership in providing access to information, encouraging and enabling research, acquiring and preserving collec-

John Dickason, ThM, MSLS, is Director of the Library and Associate Professor of Theological Bibliography, Fuller Theological Seminary, 135 North Oakland Avenue, Pasadena, CA 91182 (E-mail: dickason@fuller.edu).

[Haworth co-indexing entry note]: "The Function of Web Catalogs in Theological Libraries." Dickason, John. Co-published simultaneously in *Journal of Religious & Theological Information* (The Haworth Information Press, an imprint of The Haworth Press, Inc.) Vol. 3, No. 3/4, 2001, pp. 17-43; and: *Theological Librarians and the Internet: Implications for Practice* (ed: Mark Stover) The Haworth Information Press, an imprint of The Haworth Press, Inc., 2001, pp. 17-43. Single or multiple copies of this article are available for a fee from The Haworth Document Delivery Service [1-800-342-9678, 9:00 a.m. - 5:00 p.m. (EST). E-mail address: getinfo@haworthpressinc.com].

tions, delivering resources to clientele, and collaborating with teaching and learning. Though a library will implement and coordinate many technologies and products in its computing environment, the online public access catalog (OPAC), when placed on the Internet, is, arguably, the most influential and dramatic component in a library's program. The OPAC has become an indispensable lifeline, which connects a student to local and remote resources, and, in some iterations, offers the ability to request delivery of needed materials. The most recent generation of OPACs are Web-based, and have the potential of providing functionality that cannot be realized in more traditional telnet or dial-access catalog flavors. The Web-based OPAC is widely used among North American college and university libraries.[2] This article will explore the use of Web-based catalogs within theological libraries, and will attempt to project how these catalogs might be shaped to meet the special needs of theological institutions.

THE STRATEGIC IMPORTANCE OF THE WEB FOR THEOLOGICAL LIBRARIES

After a slow start, most North American theological libraries now have a Web presence. These Web sites display a great variety of artistic style and content, which often reflects the rich diversity of these institutions. The content of these Web sites ranges from minimal (no more than a page of catalog copy), to vast offerings of services. In some libraries, though, there appears to be hesitation and confusion about their reasons for being on the Web. This is understandable, because theological libraries tend to be understaffed and under-funded, and Web development is often managed, and controlled, by campus public relations or computing offices that have little understanding of libraries. In some cases, institutional Web sites are implemented for economic reasons, to enable the school to maintain its marketing edge. As our institutions push themselves into each other's backyards, competing against each other for a greater share of the market (financial FTEs), is it any wonder that our libraries are struggling to define their purpose and relevance in this unfamiliar environment?

Why should a library enter the Web? Mark Stover provides the clearest and most persuasive articulation of the mission and role of a library Web site. Unlike commercial Web sites, the academic library Web site serves the three-fold mission of its institution: research, teaching, and public service. Libraries accomplish this by re-engineering, not abandoning, their traditional roles that have always undergirded the academy's mission: selecting resources (linking clientele with relevant material), organizing resources (through local and national indexing and metadata projects), improving access to and delivery of resources (with effective Web catalogs and online services), and preserving these resources (through various storage and digitizing strategies).[3] Minimalist, static Web pages will not be sufficient, because our students and faculty are already using other Web pages to obtain the services that they expected from us. Libraries must use available technology to promote, coordinate, and deliver information and services to their clientele.

How does the Web-based OPAC fit into this picture? Web catalogs have the potential of assisting institutions in their educational, research, and service activities. Most of the major library automation vendors have developed Web versions of their online catalogs, or Web capabilities built into their OPACs. Some of the most impressive, though, are produced outside this sector, such as the University of California's Melvyl® Catalog and OCLC's SiteSearch Web Z software.[4] Though a vendor evaluation, or a feature-by-feature comparison of various products, is beyond the scope of this article,[5] libraries, regardless of how far technology has penetrated their services, should review and leverage the major advantages and potentials of Web catalogs, as well as their limitations.[6]

The Web catalog, unlike other components in an automated system (e.g., serials control, circulation, cataloging and authority control), is the visible and public architectural space in which local and remote scholars utilize the library's collections. Like the physical design of the material library facility, the architecture of this virtual library space has the potential for encouraging research, and providing visual, intuitive clues about how information is organized and accessed. Though early Web interfaces to library catalogs lagged far behind the functionality and displays of most OPACs, the new generation of Web catalogs show great improvement over their predecessors. There are several characteristics of Web catalogs that may help a library build this virtual environment.

- A Web-based online catalog meets the user on his or her turf. Most Internet users flourish in a graphical environment, within that sector of the Internet we call the Web. If our constituencies do not work in the esoteric world of telnet and dial-access, then it is becoming increasingly more difficult to state with credibility that character-based OPACs are accessible to off-campus users.

- Web-catalogs take advantage of tools such as hypertext, providing nonlinear access to information.
- Software on the user's end (a Web browser) is free of charge, readily available, and widely used. Both users and libraries are beneficiaries: there is a minimal learning curve for clientele, and the implementation of this technology is less complicated for libraries because there is no need to distribute and license software to each user, or to train users in telnet connections.
- Libraries are able to integrate some of their services with the Web catalog, such as interactive interlibrary lending, self-renewals, and access to electronic reserves.
- Web catalogs give the user a single starting point and interface for accessing multiple catalogs and databases simultaneously, or in sequence. The Z39.50 protocol embedded in most Web catalogs enables libraries to provide a seamless access to disparate resources.[7]
- A Web catalog is perhaps the easiest way for a library to take full advantage of recent enhancements of the MARC format. With the ability to embed Internet Resource Locators (URLs) into a cataloging record, libraries have an opportunity to change the character of the catalog: an online catalog is not merely a passive resource that displays document surrogates; it can deliver text and multi-media content through the cataloging records.
- At this critical period in library history, when our relevance and future is shrouded in doubt, libraries must employ effective tools that will push our services, resources, and value to those whom we serve, and those who determine our budgets. The Web catalog is one of many tools that can enhance the visibility and impact of libraries.

CHARACTERISTICS OF THEOLOGICAL LIBRARIES

The dramatic changes in information technology and scholarly communication raise questions on the future of libraries and the role of professional librarians. As librarians and libraries retool themselves to face uncertain futures, the historic core values of librarianship remain relevant and critical, even in the specialized field of theological librarianship. Stephen Peterson's *Project 2000* report identified five critical roles that theological libraries are undertaking: (1) representing the tradition of theological thought and practice, (2) reflecting the intellectual and cultural pluralism of theological investigation, (3) extending the curriculum of theological institutions, (4) shaping new knowledge and research, and (5) teaching ministerial students the patterns and skills necessary for lifelong learning.[8]

Since this landmark study in 1984, many seminary libraries find themselves facing new challenges, which impede their progress in fulfilling these important roles. First, student demographics have changed: our student bodies tend to be older, commuting, part-time, and somewhat disconnected from the ethos and programs of the traditional "cloister." Second, many ATS schools are launching new educational delivery systems, such as satellite campuses, distance learning, and online courses, which often lack credible library support. Third, the rapid infusion of technology on seminary campuses threatens library development–not by causing the demise of print, but by requiring substantial financial resources that are no longer available to libraries. Successful library programs will seek to harness technology, in order to fulfill these mission-critical roles, and reinvent services for their new constituencies.

METHODOLOGY

The purpose of this study is to explore the function of Web catalogs in theological libraries, identify broad trends and paths that these libraries have taken, and to suggest possible areas of growth. Does the current generation of online catalogs merely replicate the traditional functions of card catalogs, or do they exhibit a fundamental change in paradigms? Have any patterns or trends emerged that might be of help to those theological libraries that have not yet been able to implement this technology? Is it possible to document the progress libraries are making? Have theological libraries taken advantage of this technology by pushing their catalogs in new directions, and how might their catalogs be developed in the near future?

The author undertook a study of the Web catalogs used in the theological libraries of the Association of Theological Schools (ATS). The study was (a) unobtrusive, based on the actual function and behavior of Web catalogs, rather than upon how vendors or librarians wish them to work, (b) drawn from live Web connections to these catalogs, rather than upon data collected from surveys, and (c) restricted to accredited ATS members. As of March 2000, the ATS embraced 208 accredited members; for various reasons, 203 of these were included in this study.[9] A review of relevant literature supplemented this investigation.

The method of locating these Web catalogs turned out to be more complicated than expected. The first task was to identify specific institutions to be included in the study, using the ATS online Membership Directory. Then, the search for each theological school's home page began with the URLs included in this directory. If the links proved to be broken or missing (which was often the case), the Theological Schools of North America gateway was used as an alternate path to institutional home pages.[10] Each home page was probed in order to reach library Web sites. In the absence of links, large search engines, such as Northern Light, were used to locate the home pages of theological libraries. Each available online catalog was explored. Most web catalogs were easy to locate; some were inexplicably hidden from view. Every attempt was made to locate the more elusive catalogs, including the use of web catalog gateways, and the scanning of regional, statewide, and province-wide library consortia, in order to find the missing links. It is possible, however, that some catalogs remain undiscovered.

This study does not undertake formal comparisons of library automation vendors, function by function review of vendor products, or an examination of issues in system selection or implementation. Much of this information is available elsewhere, and becomes dated very quickly.[11] Instead, the following questions were used to evaluate each site.

1. Does the theological school have a presence on the Web?
2. Does the library have a Web site?
3. Does the institution's home page provide a link to the library?
4. Does the library have a Web catalog?
5. If not, does the library provide an alternate access to its catalog, such as telnet?
6. Does the library's home page provide a link to this catalog?
7. Does the institution's home page point to this catalog?
8. Which vendor supplied the Web catalog?

9. Does the catalog appear to be the product of a consortium?
10. Is the Web catalog part of a larger system (e.g., college, university, or an affiliated school)?
11. Can other databases be searched within the OPAC?
12. Can the catalogs of other libraries be searched within the OPAC, or through the front pages of the catalog?
13. Does the Web catalog provide access to the reserve collections?
14. Does the catalog provide any form of patron empowerment (review of circulation records, online renewals, holds, etc.)?
15. Does the catalog provide a "new titles" list?
16. Does the library provide additional or alternate versions of the catalog?
17. Are there any other special features implemented in this catalog?

FINDINGS

The Penetration of Technology into Theological Schools

Web identity. Ninety-seven percent of ATS accredited schools (196 in all) have an institutional Web site, and 78% of theological libraries have a Web presence. An institutional Web presence, particularly one that offers interactive services of several departments, presupposes some measure of a campus networking, computing infrastructure, and technological planning.

Online catalogs. Theological libraries have made substantial progress in implementing online catalogs. This study determined that 65% of theological libraries have Web-based catalogs, accessible via the Internet. Twenty-three percent of the schools that do not provide a Web catalog offer a telnet version of their OPAC.

Three earlier studies help provide benchmarks that mark the technological progress of theological libraries over the past 25 years: the *Project 2000* report (1984), James Pakala's survey of theological library automation (1995), and the ATS survey of educational technology (1998).[12] In 1984, only 6 libraries (4%) had online catalogs and 17 others were using microfiche (COM) catalogs. By 1995, online catalogs were used in 43% of theological libraries. Within three years, according to the ATS survey, this figure rose sharply to at least 60% (this is the figure reported for the remotely accessible catalogs, and does not include those online catalogs that provide internal access only). However, true progress must be measured by means of additional factors. For example, the value of these catalogs is determined, in part, by the range of resources they represent.

Over the past twenty-five years, theological libraries made minimal progress in the retrospective conversion of older cataloging records. Peterson reported that this agenda was "not being pursued aggressively" among these libraries: intensity ranged from very selective (44%), active on some basis, such as use (16%), targeting only certain sub collections (5%), and comprehensive (35%). Ten years later, Pakala concluded that only 41% of theological libraries had completed their catalog conversion. In the recent ATS survey, this figure dropped to 29%. These projects are clearly underway in many theological libraries, but seem to have taken on the weight of a Sisyphean rock.

Access to Resources

Are we falling behind? As noted above, theological libraries have not kept pace with the Web development of their parent institutions, and this limits access to important resources. The question of access is significant, and needs further study. The *Project 2000* report predates the Internet. Curiously, Pakala's study does not include any specific question on the use of the Internet, including the Web, nor does it address the issue of remote, external access to library resources. The ATS survey explored some questions relating to external access, and found that theological libraries appear to be trailing their parent institutions in implementing technology. Computer networks are installed in 78% of theological schools; Internet availability and networked access to academic resources are found in 78% and 68% of these institutions, respectively. In contrast, only 60% of libraries offer remote access to their catalogs, and 58% provide access to remote databases. This is surprising, because, historically, theological libraries have typically been the first department on campus to make use of networked resources and services. The lack of adequate human and financial resources in many of our theological institutions may account for some of this underdevelopment.

Moving Webward. The Web is becoming the primary environment in which libraries offer some of their services. With only sixteen libraries offering a telnet catalog as their only Internet accessible OPAC, the Web catalog has become the catalog of choice in the networked environment. This confirms the findings of the earlier ATS study.

Barriers to access. One of the most disturbing findings of this study was the number of elusive theological library Web sites and catalogs. Ironically, some theological libraries are hidden and inaccessible with the very technology that should make them ubiquitous. Forty percent of institutional home pages do not provide a link to their respective library page, and 20% of theological library Web sites do not provide a link to their own online catalogs. Though these missing links are widely dispersed throughout the ATS membership, the highest concentration tends to occur with accredited departments and schools of religion, whose Web pages are "dead end" program descriptions, and in those Roman Catholic institutions whose only Web presence is found on the pages of a regional diocesan Web site. This is bound to create substantial difficulty, since some of these institutions have off-campus programs. If experienced database searchers have difficulty finding these resources on the Internet, then surely the off-campus student is doomed. One particular theological library Web catalog is inaccessible because it lies behind a tight firewall managed by a consortium of corporate libraries. In another case, an accredited ATS institution that has a telnet catalog does not acknowledge the existence of this resource in any of its Web content. Its existence can be discovered only by stumbling upon a province-wide library network, which contains instructions for connecting to this catalog.

In the words of Beatrice Agingu, "a Web site that cannot be found is as good as one that does not exist."[13] This situation is bound to improve, however, as librarians begin to accomplish in their Web sites what they have done in their libraries: provide guidance and navigation in the discovery of information.

Vendors

Six library integrated library system vendors captured 87% of the theological library marketplace. Some of the smaller vendors, who appealed to theological libraries with limited resources, are now out of the picture. Though some standards and protocols (e.g., Z39.50) may give librarians more options in integrating solutions from different vendors, it appears that most theological libraries have not exploited this potential. Libraries seem content with the "out of the box" Web solution offered by their primary system vendor. Table 1 summarizes this data.

TABLE 1. Web Catalog Vendors Used by North American Theological Libraries

Vendor	Number of Libraries (n = 132)	Percentage
Data Research Associates	25	19%
Innovative Interfaces, Inc.	24	18%
Endeavor Information Systems	23	17%
epixtech, Inc.	19	14%
Sirsi Corporation	14	11%
The Library Corporation	10	8%
Others	17	13%

Partnerships

There is very strong evidence that many theological libraries are taking advantage of existing networks in order to deliver their Web-based OPACs. Sixty-three libraries (48%) use a consortium's Web catalog, and 61 libraries (46%) use the Web catalog of a college, university, or other affiliated institution. There is some overlap, as a library may load its records in both local and regional systems. Building strategic partnerships will permit smaller libraries to reap the benefits of existing infrastructures and share their resources more broadly.

Functionality

The capabilities of Web catalogs are improving and give theological libraries the opportunity to offer services to clientele with diverse computing platforms, geographies, and needs. The most common added values that theological libraries give to their Web catalogs are: the ability to search other databases and library catalogs with the same interface and search engine of the OPAC, access to the reserve collection through search indexes built on professors' names and course titles, the ability of authenticated library users to access their circulation account (to review books checked out, notices, fines, and to initiate holds and online renewals), and new title alerting services. Table 2 summarizes these findings, and indicates that, in most cases, libraries have not taken full advantage of the technology at hand.

Emerging Models of Web Catalogs

The Web sites of theological institutions differ radically in their content and purpose. These Web pages range from those with rich

TABLE 2. Selected Features of Web Catalogs in Theological Libraries

Features	Number of Libraries (n = 132)	Percentage
Catalog provides interface for other databases	22	17%
Catalog provides interface for other library catalogs	60	45%
Catalog allows access to reserve collections	76	58%
Catalog offers patron empowerment (e.g., online renewals)	92	70%
Catalog provides new book lists	20	15%
Catalog available in another format (telnet, dial access)	42	32%

content, professional appearance, and many interactive services, to others that have nothing more than a static, isolated front page. A virtual tour of theological schools is fascinating, and the traveler will discover a variety of roles that these Web sites play: public relations, marketing, evangelism, apologetics, hagiography, information, spiritual enrichment, fundraising, and research. Some theological schools, typically smaller institutions and some departments of religion, are currently deferring Web development to an affiliated college or parent institution. This may be expedient for the time being, but the practice may tend to further marginalize the theological community.

Theological libraries are implementing Web catalogs in different ways, across a broad continuum. The following models are an attempt to interpret these implementations; they are not necessarily mutually exclusive.

Model 1: The catalog reinvented. In this model, the Web catalog functions as an innovative transformation of the traditional card catalog. Like the catalog it replaces, it is an index to the local collection, containing document surrogates–i.e., conventional cataloging records that represent materials shelved in the library. Because it is accessible via the Web, this resource is not restricted by the limits of time and space (operating hours and geographical location) or the limitations of traditional card files. If such a catalog represents the entire collection, eliminating the need for multiple searches in older files, and if the collection is specialized, as is the case with most theological libraries, then this model is impressive, and constitutes a profound contribution to theological bibliography.

The recent debut of Sophia is a major milestone in theological bibliography. Created by the librarians of the Burke Library of Union Theological Seminary in New York and St. Mark's Library of General Theological Seminary, this Web catalog provides seamless access to one of the most comprehensive theological collections in the world and the specialized collection of the oldest Episcopal seminary in the United States. The designers did their homework (consulting the Yale Web style guide, as well as analyzing the catalog at Brown University) and have given the scholarly community a resource that is both rich and aesthetically pleasing.[14] It is also a union catalog.

Model 2: The Web catalog as a union–and unifying–catalog. The National Union Catalog is a hard act to follow, but, on a smaller scale, some theological libraries have joined cooperative linked cataloging projects that are impressive in their own right. Union catalogs have exerted an enormous impact on resource sharing among libraries.

Theological libraries participate in several forms of union catalogs. The single-type library union catalog, comprising libraries of similar size and profile, may lack collection breadth and diversity, but provides a cost-effective way for smaller libraries to automate their services. OPALL, the Oregon Private Academic Library Link, illustrates this type, unifying the catalogs of Concordia University, Mount Angel Abbey Library, Multnomah Bible College & Biblical Seminary, Northwest Christian College, Warner Pacific College, Western Baptist College, Salem, and Western Seminary.[15]

The multi-type union catalog represents the collections of diverse libraries (e.g., academic, public, special) and can become the basis for significant resource sharing projects at local and regional levels. Two consortia illustrate the wealth of information available in these networks. The Galileo Project embraces the University System of Georgia Libraries, as well as Georgia's public libraries, technical institutes, and private academic libraries, including Emory University, and provides access to databases. The unique collections of the Interdenominational Center and the Atlanta University Center are available through the Web interface of WebPals.[16]

Some union catalogs are built from merged cataloging records and holdings data; as an alternative, Web technology enables a consortium to simulate a union catalog by providing a single interface for searching multiple databases simultaneously and returning the results to the user.[17]

Model 3: The Web catalog as an aggregation of local resources. A number of theological libraries are using their Web catalogs to merge local resources into a single interface. In earlier years, library clients relied on several catalogs and listings to determine what was held by their libraries: card catalogs, periodical lists, new book shelves, printed indexes to reserve collections, etc. The merging of local resources into a single catalog is a major step forward.

The United Library (of Seabury-Western Theological Seminary and Garrett-Evangelical Theological Seminary) participates in the automated system of Northwestern University. NUCatWeb, the shared catalog, provides access to the collections of the University and the seminaries, as well as special local files, such as the Africana Conference Paper Index, and the Africana Vertical File Index.[18]

The integration of resources into a single Web interface, however easy it may be for the user, can make life difficult for librarians and systems administrators. David Fox provides helpful and candid comments, from the perspective of a complex university setting.[19]

Model 4: The Web catalog as a gateway to external resources. Libraries are beginning to change fundamental paradigms in library theory. In dramatic contrast to Model One, some theological catalogs do not merely represent what is held in a local collection; rather, they re-direct the user to external databases and resources. This can take the form of broadcast searching mechanisms within Web catalogs that query several databases simultaneously: MARC records with embedded URLs that point to full-text resources, external databases loaded into local library catalogs, and cataloging records in a local system that describe, and link to, Internet resources not owned by the library. In this model, the catalog is not merely a representation of the collection–it is the gateway through which users reach needed material.

However desirable a single, "one stop" gateway may be, this model raises significant issues for libraries. How does a library begin cataloging the Internet, when faced with substantial local backlog? How are these sites selected and evaluated? Are the cataloging conventions girding this gateway understood by our users? How authoritative and stable is the content that we provide?[20]

Two libraries, differing radically in their levels of funding, offer encouraging examples. The Web catalog of Princeton Theological Seminary includes the MARC records of the ATLA Religion Database. When the data load problems are resolved, the OPAC should provide a seamless access to both databases, using the search screens of the Web catalog software. Even though its Web catalog software is modest, the Evangelical School of Theology's Web catalog enables a user to invoke an online interlibrary loan request form that can be shared across a network.[21]

The conclusion we may draw from this is that the quality and function of a given Web catalog flows more from the vision, initiative, and enterprise of the library, than from the vendor. This conclusion is admittedly subjective. However, having used over 200 Web catalogs during this study, the author is convinced that an "out of the box" installation of a high-end Web catalog is not as functional or impressive as a less-sophisticated catalog, customized by librarians to meet the specific needs of their constituencies. Given the fact that theological libraries have specialized and unique research materials that must serve a rapidly changing constituency, a catalog, however impressive its features are, has not matured until it provides access to *all* of the library's holdings and offers solutions created by the librarians, rather than the vendor, in response to the needs of the communities served.

A Concern

Some ATS institutions may not have the financial or human resources necessary to sustain technological initiatives. Several theological libraries have fallen far behind the product development of their own vendors.[22] The point here is not to suggest that only the newest technology is good, or that libraries must install the first built of every new product, or that libraries should keep up with their vendors out of blind loyalty. Instead, *libraries must keep up with their clientele*, who expect and demand more from them. In addition, as vendors must assign their developers and support staff to the most important projects, it is not likely that obsolescent software will be supported–or understood–by customer support teams.

Web sites of theological institutions provide more evidence of the lack of adequate resources: broken links between internal pages and URL "rot" throughout the sites. Do we really have adequate staff for basic Web site mechanics and maintenance? Ongoing development of library technology will demand substantial human and financial resources.

THE FUTURE OF WEB CATALOGS

Howard Strauss has observed that we cannot predict what will replace the Web, but it keeps reinventing itself and reestablishing its worth.[23] We also do not know how vendors will develop their systems, yet it might be possible to suggest where librarians might be pushing their Web catalogs in the near future. I would like to suggest seven prospects, based on the framework of the Library and Information Technology Association (LITA). LITA's Top Technology Trend Committee attempts to identify the top technology trends that will have the greatest impact upon libraries. Their focus is not on specific vendors, products, "killer apps," or the latest processor;[24] rather, the committee attempts to identify those technology trends that will have the greatest impact upon libraries. The ongoing revision of these themes provides focus for national conferences, as well as ongoing guidance for libraries overloaded or overwhelmed by the complex landscape of information technology. To date, LITA has identified seven "Top Technology Trends."[25] A review of these trends might help us think more creatively about how our libraries shape their catalogs.

A Catalog for the User

Why not provide a catalog that satisfies the customer, rather than the systems administrator or chief cataloger–a catalog that is personalized, customized by the user, interactive, and supported, when assistance is needed?

> *TREND 1: Library users who are Web users, a growing group, expect customization, interactivity, and customer support. Approaches that are library-focused instead of user-focused will be increasingly irrelevant . . .*[26]

Many of the clients who search our Web catalogs have also recently searched the catalog at Amazon.com, where they were greeted by name, presented with materials that fit their interests, given the opportunity to customize their delivery plan, and thanked at the end of their visit. If the client happens to be our Provost or President, we may have to explain again–with considerably more discomfort–the rationale behind our expensive technical services infrastructure that does not seem to "sense" or "care" if the time spent in our catalog was successful. Writing within the context of the public library system, Michael Schuyler warns,

> Putting up a library Web site and placing community links on it is not going to cut it. Sorry. That was last year. We must establish a "presence" in cyberspace that matches anything an e-commerce site can do and is absolutely as state of the art as can be.[27]

As of March 2000, most of the Web catalogs in theological libraries tended to be "out of the box" products. This will change, as librarians begin listening to the user. Some of this change is taking place now. One of the most exciting examples outside of theological libraries is the MyLibrary@NCState project,[28] which gives the user the ability to customize a personal Web page portal to local and remote resources. This personal library page enables the user to create a list of favorite databases, display daily messages from the librarians regarding these resources, and choose which catalogs, local resources, databases, links, and current awareness services that are most important to him or her. A user connecting to MyLibrary@NCState is greeted by name and by a personalized search screen containing only those options needed. The California Polytechnic State University at San Louis Obispo has designed a similar service for its faculty. Their MyLibrary research page is customized by faculty, providing resources and update services relevant to their disciplines.[29]

There is no crystal ball that depicts what our OPACs will look like in five years. However, some clues may be discerned in two arenas: the major search engines and corporate Intranets. The Internet search engine is now the "OPAC" of choice for most Internet users. According to Ran Hoch, different categories of search tools, such as search engines and Web directories, are merging the best characteristics of each for more useful results pages. "Search engine functionality is being integrated into Web directories, Web directory results are being automatically integrated into search engine results [and] the Web portal concept integrates tools on a single screen."[30] There are many examples of very impressive Web interfaces that give specialized clients the resources and competitive intelligence they need. These are found in corporate Intranets. Though they are often behind firewalls, some of their achievements are described in specialized library conferences and literature. The Web portal at the Los Alamos National

Laboratory is but one example of integrating all relevant resources into a single Web page.[31]

Strauss identifies three major advances in Web technology. Static, "read-only" Web pages (designed to share documents and images) gave way to "entity-centric" Web sites, which were more developed and interactive. In both types, the Web sites focus on the corporation and provide the same information to every user. The next major shift will be a move to "user-centric" vertical portals, in which each validated user has direct access to relevant information–the actual data, not merely links to that data. The end of the home page may not be far behind.[32] Libraries will need to position their customized services into this framework.

The Evaluative and Selective Catalog

Given the sheer mass of mediocrity on the Web, libraries must give the user resources that are relevant and high quality, without sacrificing those tools that provide comprehensive bibliographic control of disciplines.

> *TREND 2: In dealing with electronic information resources, what librarians bring to the table is evaluative guidance. Comprehensive lists and catalogs aren't possible anymore . . .*

Long before the Web and GUI, libraries provided guidance and graphical clues that assisted users in the search for information; there is no visual or human guidance for Internet users who discover thousands of documents that look the same and appear to have equal value and authority.

> As users move to online catalogs and "virtual shelves," they also sacrifice the spatial and appearance clues that help people locate and identify the information they need. Just as we expect an encyclopedia not to look like a romance novel, so we must be able to understand at a glance what an online system does, and how to use it.[33]

We are beginning to see efforts at local and national levels that attempt to address this issue. Taking advantage of their new Web catalog, librarians at the University of Notre Dame selected high quality Internet resources that supplemented the library's material collections, cataloged these Web sites, and loaded these records, with linking

URLs, into their local system. Including these resources in the catalog, though laborious, enhanced library collections (including Catholic theology).[34]

Humanizing Our Catalogs

Can our OPACs begin to reflect some personal and personalizing qualities, and move beyond the "cookie cutter" look determined by the vendor?

> TREND 3: *It's time to put a human face on the virtual library. What's the critical factor in the success of the nonvirtual library? The people who work there and serve the user!*

Perhaps the online catalog might be one of the most difficult library services to humanize, but catalogs of the future will have made the attempt. The earliest catalog cards were handwritten, reflecting the labor and craft of librarians and reminding the user that there was a human face behind the cataloging superstructure, much like the medieval cathedrals exhibit the artistry and idiosyncrasies of effort of anonymous, faithful builders. Eric Morgan argues that, by studying the characteristics of commercial online catalogs, "we can make our catalogs more interactive, user centered, customizable, and proactive, and we can provide users with value added services."[35]

The *Alex Catalogue of Electronic Texts,* which Morgan maintains, is an excellent example. The user of *Alex* searches MARC records, selects a specific group of documents, creates a concordance that identifies words and their specific locations, and manufactures an annotated and publishable bookcase containing these chosen texts.

One of the most refreshing and attractive examples of library "handwriting" (i.e., a home-made OPAC), reflecting the human artistry behind the interface, is Southeastern Baptist Theological Seminary's Web catalog. Its sidebar is present at each stage of the search, linking the user to several services.[36] By showcasing the artistry of various library departments that weave services for their users, and increasing the visibility and accessibility of librarians, our catalogs can begin to exhibit the warmth and hospitality of some of our nonvirtual services.

The Collaborative Catalog

It will not be easy to customize and humanize our catalogs, and each library must find a balance between the need for individual expression, and the need to keep pace and capitalize on the pioneering work of others.

> *TREND 4: Why re-invent the wheel? Co-opt existing technologies that haven't been used in libraries, and take advantage of cooperative efforts in information access . . .*

The OCLC Cooperative Online Resource Catalog (CORC) is just underway. In this collaborative project, libraries will assume a major role in evaluating, selecting, cataloging, and organizing high quality Internet resources; participants may download CORC records into their local systems, or create Web pathfinders that guide users to resources of high quality.[37] In the outstanding "Paper on Theological Cataloging," Eileen Crawford describes the unique knowledge, expertise, and contribution that theological catalogers may bring to other collaborative programs, such as the Program for Cooperative Cataloging, and suggests that we have underestimated the value that "hundreds of invisible employees" have given to our local catalogs.[38]

Web Catalogs That Provide Resources to Several Tiers

Depending upon how we position our libraries, the traffic coming to our Web sites will either crush us, force us to close the door, or provide the opportunity to extend services to new clientele.

> *TREND 5: The isolated scholar is out there, and she wants your resources! That widespread distributive tool, the Web, is making library resources available to more people than ever before and blurring the lines between audiences . . .*

The easiest solutions will be the most unsatisfactory: prohibiting access to everyone except the initiated, primary clientele, or, valiantly attempting to give everything to everyone. The former is self-destructive (as clientele will meet their needs without the use of libraries); the latter is self-defeating. Versioning is a middle road worth exploring. In a penetrating analysis of the information marketplace, Shapiro and Varian suggest offering product lines, giving distinct user groups options, in terms of price, quality, turn around time, etc.[39]

Catalogs as Gateways and Gatekeepers

Without sacrificing hospitality and ease of use, Web catalogs will need to become not only gateways, but gatekeepers.

TREND 6: Authentication and rights management: who has the right to use this, but not that, and how much will they be charged? And is that document the real thing?

If libraries continue to acquire and network licensed databases, and integrate these with their Web catalogs, then librarians and vendors will need to collaborate more closely on user validation and authentication. The most prevalent solution offered by vendors is IP recognition, which authenticates users based on a unique range of IP addresses within an institution. The classic problem with this model is that it does not take into account the demographics of academic institutions (including scholars in transit and on sabbaticals, commuting students, and those involved in distance learning and online courses). Other methods of authentication are equally problematic. The issues have become so complex that Clifford Lynch established database authentication as a priority when he became Executive Director of the Coalition of Networked Information.[40]

In the course of researching this article, the author found several theological libraries that provide unrestricted access to licensed databases through their Web sites. Even the ATLA Religion Database is accessible, with no authentication required, in at least one theological Web catalog. Libraries will need to invest substantial staff time and energy into balancing the conflicting needs of users, librarians, publishers, and authors, and managing responsible and responsive access to needed resources.

A Farewell to Telnet and CD/ROM Catalogs

How can we make a credible case that our telnet catalogs provide access, when our constituencies clearly do not live in this arcane, character-based world? With incompatible menus, screen forms, and commands, the telnet application, which cannot be integrated with emerging resources, is an island–isolated, and rarely visited.[41]

TREND 7: Don't run aground on submerging technologies! Often just as important to libraries as emerging technologies are submerging technologies . . .

It may be too early to write the obituary columns, but one of our profession's best experts on databases, Peter Jacsó, recently announced the close of his CD/ROM column,[42] based on his diagnosis of a technological solution that is fading fast. Though CD/ROM products may continue to have a place in our libraries over the next 3-5 years, Marshall Breeding advises against the installation of any new CD/ROM networks, and recommends the creation of a Web-based environment that can integrate electronic resources and deliver them to remote users.[43]

Most theological libraries have very limited resources and will need to re-direct these away from technologies that served their needs over the past decade, but do not address our users' preferred environment or their need for current information. The point here is not to suggest that the Web catalog is the wave of the future, and that it will endure throughout the 21st century. The future should give us solutions that are far better than what we can implement today. However, the Web is where our users live today, and this is where libraries need to invest, at least through the near future.

CONCLUSION

In a beautifully written essay, chronicling a search for "the catalog of catalogs," Jamie Metzl describes a journey from the catalogs of the Bodleian ("the gargantuan, elegantly leather-bound tomes that contain listings glued on thickly textured paper") to the "disharmonious" catalog rooms at Harvard (where "the computer terminal room pulsates with the busy sounds of clicking keys and rhythmically-gliding printer jets . . . [in contrast] the long rows of mahogany cabinets languish, antique-like in a completely silent and almost empty room nearby") and, finally, to Westlaw, which usually met legal research needs more efficiently than did print indexes. However impressive the new catalogs are, Metzl laments that they cannot preserve the fleeting electronic information that decays as rapidly as it streams.[44] The "catalog of catalogs" may never be found, but the journey is worthwhile, and will require courageous decisions along the way.

As Charles Willard reminded us, in his essay on winning in the game of academia, many railroads went bankrupt because they thought they were in the railroad business, not the transportation business. Librarians are not in the business of managing repositories, insulated from the users we serve. Initiative, and some risk, will be required to listen to our constituencies, and deliver what their research process requires.[45] Libraries can assume a central role in the academic life of our institutions, in part, through visible, creative and aggressive development of Web-based services. However we develop our catalogs, we must keep in mind our core values, and remember that technology is not the end, but a means to strengthen our role in the life of our institutions.

GATEWAYS TO WEB CATALOGS OF THEOLOGICAL LIBRARIES IN NORTH AMERICA

This study did not anticipate user difficulty in locating theological libraries on the World Wide Web. However, many theological institutions, as well as their libraries and resources, were virtually hidden from the "view" of the largest search engines. Presumably this situation will improve over time. Until then, there are several gateways that may be helpful in locating theological libraries in North America.

Gateways to theological library catalogs. There are four ambitious Internet sites that provide links to religious and theological library catalogs. (1) *The Wabash Center Internet Guide: Libraries and Librarianship,*[46] maintained by Charles Bellinger, includes links to the online catalogs of theological libraries. It is not limited to North America, and appears to be the largest compilation of such links on the Web. (2) Marshall Breeding's *Lib-Web-Cats,*[47] a directory of Web catalogs, employs a database, rather than a static list of links. Breeding's database permits a search by library type, including "Religion/ Theology." Each entry provides brief information about the library and its automated system, and URLs. (3) *Library Web-Based OPACS,* maintained by Peter Scott,[48] includes a gateway to "religious" library Web catalogs, under its "Library-Types" index. (4) The Tennessee Theological Library Association's *Theological Online Catalogs,*[49] maintained by Eileen Crawford, provides links, as well as information on each library's denominational affiliation, classification system, and collection strengths.

The user must bear in mind that these gateways are limited in their coverage, and rely, in part, on the willingness of libraries to contribute information. As of March 2000, the number of theological libraries included were 89 (Bellinger), 69 (Breeding), 54 (Scott) and 43 (Crawford). This study identified 136 theological libraries of accredited ATS institutions with Web catalogs.

Additional gateways. Other resources proved helpful in tracking down the more elusive theological Web sites. (1) Fuller Theological Seminary's *Theological Schools of North America*[50] provides links to institutional home pages, and includes many schools that are not part of ATS. (2) The ATS *Member Directory*[51] includes links to the home pages of the theological institutions that are full members, as well as schools that are associates and candidates for membership in the Association of Theological Schools. (2) Both institutional and library URLs are found in many of the entries of the ATLA *Institutional Directory*.[52] (3) Theological libraries that participate in shared cataloging programs can usually be found through *Links to OCLC Library Web Sites*,[53] and (4) Berkeley's *Libweb*[54] is gradually including theological libraries and will become an indispensable gateway, particularly for international sites.

NOTES

1. For an early inventory of how libraries used the Web, see: Jim Whalen, "A Study of Library Web Sites," (Manchester, Eng.: John Ryulands University Library of Manchester, 1996) <*http://rylibweb.man.ac.uk/pubs/libraries/html*>. For an impressive overview, description, evaluation, and rating of over 2,000 library Web sites, see: Gwen Turecki, ed., *Cyberhound's Guide to Internet Libraries* (Detroit, MI: Gale, 1997).

2. In preparing her OPAC directory, Bonnie Nelson notes "the explosive growth in the number of libraries offering a World Wide Web interface to their OPACs." Bonnie R. Nelson, *OPAC Directory 1998: A Guide to Internet-Accessible Online Public Access Catalogs* (Medford, NJ: Information Today, 1998): xiii. More than a compilation of sites, this directory provides a useful subject guide to OPACs, as well as specific instructions for working with the telnet catalogs of each vendor.

3. Mark Stover, "Library Web Sites: Mission and Function in the Networked Organization," *Computers in Libraries* (Nov/Dec 1997) 17, No. 10: 55-57, as well as Stover's *The Construction and Validation of an Evaluative Instrument for Academic Library World Wide Web Sites* [Ph.D.dissertation] (Nova Southeastern University, School of Computer and Information Sciences, 1997): 12-18.

4. The University of California catalog provides access to the holdings of all libraries within the statewide university system, the Graduate Theological Union, digital projects, and other resources <*http://www.melvyl.ucop.edu/*>, and OCLC's Site-Search links the resources of both GALILEO (Georgia Library Learning Online) <*http://www.galileo.peachnet.edu/*> and MIRLYN (Michigan Research Library Network) <*http://mirlyn.web.lib.umich.edu:80/*>.

5. For the evaluation of Web catalog content and display, see the Bibliographic Elements and Displays Project, Faculty of Information Studies, University of Toronto <*http://www.fis.utoronto.ca/research/displays/index.htm*>, Ralph W. Kopak and Joan M. Cherry, "Bibliographic Displays and Web Catalogs: User Evaluations of

Three Prototype Displays," *The Electric Library* 16, No. 5 ((1998): 309-323, Joan M. Cherry, "Bibliographic Displays in OPACs and Web Catalogs: How Well Do They Comply with Display Guidelines?" *Information Technology and Libraries* 17, No. 3 (1998): 124-137, Walt Crawford, "Webcats and Checklists: Some Cautionary Notes," *Information Technology and Libraries* 18, No. 2 (1999): 100-103, Martha M. Yee, "Response to 'Webcats and Checklists: Some Cautionary Notes'" *Information Technology and Libraries* 18, No. 4 (1999): 225-226, and Walt Crawford's "Response to Martha Yee's Letter," *Information Technology and Libraries* 18, No. 4 (1999): 226-227.

6. Web catalogs are still limited by the inflexibility and irrelevance of certain aspects of the MARC format. See Virginia Ortiz-Repiso and Purificación Moscoso, "Web-Based OPACs: Between Tradition and Innovation," *Information Technology and Libraries* 18, No. 2 (June 1999): p. 68-77.

7. For an overview of the Z39.50 protocol, see the two technical briefings by Peter Evans, "Z39.50: Part 1–an overview," and "Z39.50: Part 2–Technical Details," in *Biblio Tech Review: Information Technology for Libraries* at *<http://www.biblio-tech.com/html/z39_50.html>* and *<http://www.biblio-tech.com/html/z39_50_part_2.html>*, respectively; both pages updated as of March 7, 2000.

8. Stephen L. Peterson, "Theological Libraries for the Twenty-first Century: Project 2000 Final Report," *Theological Education* 20, No. 3, Supplement (1985): 23-29.

9. Though there are some discrepancies concerning membership numbers in the pages of the ATS Web site, the membership total of 208 is based on the "1999-2000 Member Directory," *<http://www.ats.edu/sets/membfst.htm>*, accessed March 18, 2000. Of these 208, 5 member Web sites could not be included in the study because of apparent system downtime, over a period of several weeks; another 2 institutions were excluded because they are part of larger institutions and cannot be discretely studied at this time.

10. Fuller Theological Seminary, *Theological Schools of North America*, maintained by Grant Millikan (Pasadena, CA: Fuller Theological Seminary, 1996) *http://www.fuller.edu/provost/seminaries/*.

11. For overviews of vendors and products see the *Library Journal's* annual "Review of the Library Automation Marketplace" (April 1 issue), and Pamela Cibbarelli's *Directory of Library Automation Software, Systems, and Services 2000-2001 Edition* (Medford: Information Today, 2000).

12. Peterson, op. cit.:1-114; James Pakala, "Theological Library Automation in 1995," *The American Theological Library Association: Essays in Celebration of the First Fifty Years* (Evanston, IL: The American Theological Library Association, 1996): 196-206; and the Association of Theological Schools' "Educational Technology Survey," summarized in Mary Martin's "ATS Surveys and Theological Libraries," *Summary of Proceedings: Fifty-third Annual Conference of the American Theological Library Association*, ed. by Margret Tacke Collins (Evanston, IL: The American Theological Library Association, 1999): 133-138. Though the surveyed institutions varied slightly depending upon the methodology, and the questions were posed in different ways, these instruments are useful benchmarks.

13. Beatrice O. Agingu, "Library Web Sites at Historically Black Colleges and Universities," *College & Research Libraries* 61, No. 1 (January 2000): 36.

14. The URL for Sophia is: *<http://128.59.143.18/search/>*.

15. OPALL's URL is: *<http://opall.mtangel.edu/webvoy.htm>*.

16. WebPals URL is: *<http://www.auctr.edu/webpals/home.html>*.

17. Dominick J. Grillo, "Creating a Web-Simulated Union Catalog," 19, No. 9 (1999): 56-60.

18. NUCatWeb's URL is: *<http://nucat.library.nwu.edu/>*.

19. David Fox, "U-SEARCH: The University of Saskatchewan Library Web," in *The Library Web,* ed by Julie M. Still (Medford, NJ: Information Today, 1997): 11-20.

20. For a good discussion on embedding URLs in cataloging records, especially on the problem of how to maintain their currency, see Frank Knor, "Using MARC Tag 856 for URLs and Keeping Them Current," a Virtual Conference Presentation, June 19, 1998, for the Canadian Library Association Conference (June 17-21, 1998) *<http://www.lib.bcit.bc.ca:80/tab_856.htm>*.

21. The URLs for Princeton Theological Seminary and Evangelical Theological Seminary are: *<http://library1.ptsem.edu/>* and *<http://rostad.library.net/>*, respectively.

22. For example, there are several theological libraries that use the Dynix (epixtech) character-based telnet online catalog, though a Java-based Web catalog has been available for several years.

23. Howard Strauss, "Web Portals: A Home Page Doth Not a Portal Make," *The Edutech Report: The Education Technology Newsletter for Faculty and Administrators* 15, No. 11 (February 2000): 1.

24. Garlock and Pointek define the future of library Web sites in terms of additional software applications and plug-ins. Kristen L. Garlock and Sherry Pointek, *Designing Web Interfaces to Library Services and Resources* (Chicago, The American Library Association, 1999): 84-93.

25. For details and commentary on LITA's ongoing work in exploring these trends see Library and Information Technology Association. "Top Tech Trends: January 1999 ALA Midwinter." American Library Association, 1999 *<http://www.lita.org/committe/toptech/trendsmw99.htm>*.

26. Ibid. In this, and the next few paragraphs of this article, the exact text of each trend is quoted in italics, and in each case the bibliographic reference is identical to the above endnote.

27. Michael Schuyler, "Better Service through Creativity and Technology," *Computers in Libraries* 20, No. 3 (March 2000): p. 52.

28. Eric Lease Morgan, "MyLibrary@NCState: The Implementation of a User-centered, Customizable Interface to a Library's Collection and Information Resources," (North Carolina State University Libraries, 1999) *<http://my.lib.ncsu.edu/about/sigr-99/>*. LITA also identified the University of Washington's MyGateway as another example of a user-customized interface to resources.

29. Paul T. Adalian, Jr. and Judy Swanson, "Beyond Basic HTML: Creating Dynamic Pages for a Web Site and a Web Pac," in *IOLS '99: Proceedings of the Fourteenth National Conference on Integrated Online Library Systems, New York, May*

19-20, 1999, comp. by Pamela Cibbarelli (Medford, NJ: Information Today, 1999): 8-9.

30. Ran Hoch, "Web Finding Tools: Choosing and Using the Right One": Workshop Presented at: *Internet Librarian,* San Diego, CA, October 7, 1999 (Vienna, VA: Online Strategies, 1999): 2.

31. Mona L. Mosier et al., "aha!–Portal to a Corporate Intranet," in *Internet Librarian '99: Proceedings of the Third Internet Librarian Conference, San Diego, California, November 8-10, 1999* (Medford, NJ: Information Technology, 1999): 121-126.

32. Strauss, op. cit.: 1,3,6,7.

33. Susan Feldman, "The Key to Online Catalogs that Work? Testing: One, Two, Three," *Computers in Libraries* 19, No. 5 (May 1999): 16.

34. The project explored the feasibility of providing access to Internet resources through a new Web catalog. See Margaret G. Porter and Laura Bayard, "Including Web Sites in the Online Catalog: Implications for Cataloging, Collection Development, and Access," *The Journal of Academic Librarianship* 25, No. 5 (September 1999): 390-394.

35. Eric Lease Morgan, "Catalogs of the Future," *Computers in Libraries* 19, No. 9 (October 1999): p. 39. The Alex Catalogue of Digital Texts, which he maintains, is located at *<http://sunsite.berkeley.edu/alex>.*

36. The direct link to this catalog is: *<http://ezekiel.sebts.edu/prophet/search/shtml>,* but at the time of this writing, the sidebar did not appear via this direct connection. Connection via the library's home page will provide this view: *<http://library.sebts.edu/>.*

37. For a project description, see the CORC Web site: OCLC Online Computer Library Center, "Cooperative Online Resource Catalog" (Dublin, Oh.: OCLC, Inc.) at: *<http://www.oclc.org/oclc/corc/index.htm>,* as well as "OCLC CORC Project," *OCLC Newsletter* No. 259 (May/June 1999): 27-41.

38. Eileen Crawford, Bill Hook, "Paper on Theological Cataloging," (Tennessee Theological Library Association, 1997) *<http://divinity.library.vanderbilt.edu/ttla/ts/chapintro.htm>.*

39. Carl Shapiro and Hal R. Varian, *Information Rules: A Strategic Guide to the Network Economy* (Boston, MA: Harvard Business School Press, 1999): 53-81.

40. For background on the issue of authentication, see Clifford Lynch, "A White Paper on Authentication and Access Management Issues in Cross-organizational Use of Networked Information Resources," available at the Web site of the Coalition for Networked Information: *<http://www.cni.org/projects/authentication/authentication-wp.html>.*

41. Virginia Ortiz-Repiso and Purificación Moscoso, op. cit. : 69.

42. Peter Jacsó, "The End of an Era . . . or a Column, at Least," *Computers in Libraries* 19, No. 9 (October 1999): 44-45; this is his final "CD-ROM Currents" column.

43. Marshall Breeding, "Does the Web Spell Doom for CD and DVD?" *Computers in Libraries* 19, No. 10 (November/December 1999): 74.

44. Jamie Frederic Metzl, "Searching for the Catalog of Catalogs," in *Books, Bricks, & Bytes: Libraries in the Twenty-first Century,* ed. by Stephen R. Graubard and Paul LeClerc (New Brunswick, NJ: Transaction Publishers, 1999): 149-151, 159.

45. Louis Charles Willard, "The Only Thing," *The American Theological Library Association: Essays in Celebration of the First Fifty Years,* ed. by M. Patrick Graham, Valerie R. Hotchkiss, Kenneth E. Rowe (Evanston, IL: American Theological Library Association, 1996): 217-227.

46. Charles K. Bellinger, *Wabash Center Internet Guide: Libraries and Librarianship,* a subsection of *The Wabash Center Guide to Internet Resources for Teaching and Learning in Theology and Religion* (Wabash Center for Teaching and Learning in Religion and Theology) *<http://www.wabashcenter.wabash.edu/Internet/library.htm>*.

47. Marshall Breeding, *Lib-Web-Cats: Library Web Pages, Online Catalogs, and Profiles: a Directory of Over 4,500 Libraries Worldwide.* (Vanderbilt University Library) *<http://staffweb.library.vanderbilt.edu/breeding/libwebcats.html>*.

48. Peter Scott, *Library Web-Based OPACS* (hosted by Northern Lights Internet Solutions) *<http://www.lights.com/webcats/>*.

49. Eileen Crawford, *Theological Online Catalogs* (Tennessee Theological Library Association, 1998) *<http://divinity.library.vanderbilt.edu/ttla/ts/technical.htm>*.

50. Fuller Theological Seminary, *Theological Schools of North America,* maintained by Grant Millikan (Pasadena, CA: Fuller Theological Seminary, 1996) *<http://www.fuller.edu/provost/seminaries/>*.

51. Association of Theological Schools, *Member Directory* (Pittsburgh: Association of Theological Schools) *<http://www.ats.edu/sets/membfst.htm>*.

52. American Theological Library Association, *Institutional Directory* (Evanston, IL: American Theological Library Association) *<http://www.atla.com/membserv/dirinst.html>*.

53. OCLC Online Computer Learning Center, *Links to OCLC Library Web Sites* (Dublin, Ohio: OCLC Online Computer Learning Center, Inc.) *<http://www.oclc.org/oclc/menu/libs.htm>*.

54. Berkeley Digital Library SunSITE, *Libweb: Library Servers via WWW* (Berkeley, CA: The Library, University of California, Berkeley) *<http://sunsite.berkeley.edu/Libweb/>*.

Electronic Journals in Religious Studies: Theological Libraries Prepare for the Digital Future

Marshall Eidson

SUMMARY. A number of factors have kept scholarly religious studies journals from having a significant presence on the Internet. This paper examines two projects that are addressing these barriers, the American Theological Library Association Serials project and the Association of Peer-Reviewed Electronic Journals in Religion, and offers theological librarians an overview of the advantages, disadvantages, issues, and trends associated with online journal delivery as they plan for the future. *[Article copies available for a fee from The Haworth Document Delivery Service: 1-800-342-9678. E-mail address: <getinfo@haworthpressinc.com> Website: <http://www.HaworthPress.com> © 2001 by The Haworth Press, Inc. All rights reserved.]*

KEYWORDS. Electronic journals, theological librarianship, American Theological Library Association, religious studies journals

Scholarly journals in the field of religious studies have yet to exploit cyberspace the way journals in other disciplines have. Perhaps, as Quentin Schultze (1999, 178) suggests: "Religious periodicals are waiting for the dust to settle, hoping to learn from the success or

Marshall Eidson, MLIS, MA, is Reference Librarian, Iliff School of Theology, 2201 South University Boulevard, Denver, CO 80210.

[Haworth co-indexing entry note]: "Electronic Journals in Religious Studies: Theological Libraries Prepare for the Digital Future." Eidson, Marshall. Co-published simultaneously in *Journal of Religious & Theological Information* (The Haworth Information Press, an imprint of The Haworth Press, Inc.) Vol. 3, No. 3/4, 2001, pp. 45-67; and: *Theological Librarians and the Internet: Implications for Practice* (ed: Mark Stover) The Haworth Information Press, an imprint of The Haworth Press, Inc., 2001, pp. 45-67. Single or multiple copies of this article are available for a fee from The Haworth Document Delivery Service [1-800-342-9678, 9:00 a.m. - 5:00 p.m. (EST). E-mail address: getinfo@haworthpressinc.com].

failure of mainstream media in the digital world." More probably, however, two primary factors explain the dearth of religious studies journals available online. First, the publishers of most religious periodicals are single-title publishers. Of the more than 600 journals indexed in the American Theological Library Association's *Religion Index One*, 84 percent are the products of single-title publishers (ATLA CERTR 1999). As a result, they lack the political clout, financial resources, and organizational wherewithal to attempt large-scale digitization projects. Second, "pure" electronic journals, or those religious studies periodicals published exclusively online, continue to be eschewed by leading scholars as lacking the legitimacy and staying power of the print medium.

While these factors are currently inhibiting the Web presence of the field's periodical literature, all this is about to change. Two important projects, the American Theological Library Association's Serials Project (ATLAS) and the Association of Peer-Reviewed Electronic Journals in Religion (APEJR), are addressing these barriers in significant ways. This paper examines how ATLAS and APEJR will dramatically influence the way in which theological libraries use the Internet to provide their patrons with electronic journal scholarship. These projects represent initial steps toward realizing Tomney and Burton's (1998, 420) claim that "electronic journals, and what they evolve into, will be at the heart of scholarly communities that are created tomorrow." In addition, this paper offers theological librarians an overview of the advantages, disadvantages, issues, and trends associated with online journals in religious studies, theology, and related disciplines.

DEFINITIONS

Any discussion about electronic journals begs the question of definition. What do we mean when we talk about an electronic, or online journal? For instance, Lancaster (1995, 520) claims that electronic journals should be publications "created for the electronic medium and available only in that medium." However, the term electronic journal is also used to describe, particularly in regard to digitization projects, electronic *versions* of print journals. Carol Tenopir (1999, 142) identifies five different categories of electronic journals, ranging from traditional print journals that make contents lists or excerpts of their publications available online to "full electronic journals, without print equivalents."

Because the ATLAS project will result in full-text electronic versions of print journals, and because APEJR is especially geared toward journals available only online, these types of e-journals form the basis of the present discussion. Specifically, this paper is concerned with religious studies e-journals, with or without print counterparts, that deliver in full text and maintain a policy of blind, scholarly peer-review. However, other categories of e-journals, such as those offering contents only or partial editions online, form the bulk of the field's current online presence and should not be overlooked. Many of these journals appear in the selected Webliography included here as Appendix C.

AMERICAN THEOLOGICAL LIBRARY ASSOCIATION SERIALS PROJECT (ATLAS)

The American Theological Library Association (ATLA) formed the Center for Electronic Resources in Theology and Religion (CERTR) on January 1, 1999. Headquartered in Stone Mountain, Georgia, CERTR's purpose, according to its director, James Adair (1999, par., 1), is to:

> Disseminate electronic texts of interest to scholars of religion, to promote the publication of original scholarly works in formats compatible with online study and distribution, to support other efforts to move the academic study of religion into the information age, and to remain on the forefront of advances in technology through a commitment to research and development.

ATLAS, CERTR's first significant undertaking, was awarded a $4 million grant from the Lilly Foundation in May of 1999. The primary goal of the ATLAS project is to digitize 50 years' worth of 50 journals in the field of religious studies and make them accessible via the World Wide Web. Under the direction of James Adair, ATLAS will work with the Wabash Center for Teaching and Learning in Theology and Religion to select outstanding journals in six areas:

- Bible Archaeology and Antiquities
- Theology, Philosophy and Ethics

- Religions and Religious Studies
- Pastoral Ministry
- History, Missions, and Ecumenism
- Human Culture and Society

Thus far, the publishers of 22 journals have committed to the project, including such journals as *Church History, Theological Studies, The Journal of Biblical Literature,* and *The Journal of Pastoral Care* (see Appendix A for a complete listing). Unlike other digitization projects in the humanities, e.g., JSTOR or Project Muse, the ATLAS project intends to digitize full runs of journals and link to the primary indexer in the field, ATLA's *Religion Index One.* Moreover, initial plans call for working closely with scholarly societies, particularly the Society of Biblical Literature (SBL) and the American Academy of Religion (AAR), and creating an electronic research environment that is not cost prohibitive (ATLA CERTR 2000, Project Update). The project team expects to begin beta testing in August 2000 and hopes to "go live" with the full-text versions by January 2001 (ATLA CERTR 2000, ATLAS FAQ).

Funding for ATLAS expires after three years, though its developers are optimistic that the project will be self-sustaining. By the end of the third year, the project team hopes to have an adequate subscription base to allow for the continued digitization of 20 to 30 journals per year (Adair 1999). A number of ATLA member libraries have also pledged their commitments to assist in subsequent digitization efforts. (See Appendix B for a list of libraries that have agreed to sponsor the digitization of one title per year.)

ATLA, through CERTR, is uniquely positioned to undertake such a massive digitization project. One reason is that ATLA librarians are themselves distinct. Theological librarians are the only group of special librarians that produce their discipline's primary bibliographic tool, the *ATLA Religion Database.* To wit, medical librarians do not produce *Medline*; nor do law librarians produce *Lexis* or *Nexis.* Secondly, ATLA will make it possible for ATLAS to link electronic journal images directly to the field's primary indexing tool, *ATLA Religion Database,* a feat no other electronic journal collection can claim. Finally, the ATLAS project proposal aims to include full runs of journals, thus realizing the historical import of theological research. Most active digitization projects, conversely, have planned their electronic efforts around current and future journals issues, while ignoring earlier volumes (ATLA CERTR 1999).

ASSOCIATION OF PEER-REVIEWED ELECTRONIC JOURNALS IN RELIGION (APEJR)

APEJR was established in the fall of 1998 with the purpose of "promoting the development of electronic journals . . . and setting high standards for academic quality and longevity . . . " (APEJR, par. 1). Currently, seven journals participate in the Association:

- *Hugoye: Journal of Syriac Studies*
- *Journal of Buddhist Ethics*
- *Journal of Christian Theological Research*
- *Journal of Hebrew Scriptures*
- *The Journal of Southern Religion*
- *TC: A Journal of Biblical Textual Criticism*
- *Women in Judaism: A Multidisciplinary Journal*

At present, none of these journals are indexed in ATLA's *Religion Index One*, though *Religious & Theological Abstracts* indexes five electronic journals, all of which are members of APEJR.

APEJR will work with periodical publications that are "primarily an electronic journal" (APEJR, par. 5, no. 7). By this, they mean that a journal's first electronic issue must have appeared before or at the same time as its first printed issue; that all subsequent issues appear online at the same time as the print edition; that no significant portion of the print journal is omitted in the electronic version; and that access to the electronic journal is available online free of charge (APEJR).

One of the Association's goals has been to convince standard indexing and abstracting services, particularly ATLA's *Religion Index One,* to include electronic journals in their portfolios. Their advocacy appears to have paid dividends, as ATLA planned to begin indexing selected e-journals sometime in 2000. In contacts with editors of APEJR journals, some noted that their journals were indexed elsewhere–for instance, *Women in Judaism* is indexed in *Ulrich's International Periodicals Directory* and *Contemporary Women's Issues*–but most agreed that increasing e-journal coverage in the major indexing and abstracting literature is essential to long-term success.

Another goal of APEJR is to confront the attitude of resistance toward e-journals that is prevalent among religious studies scholars. APEJR has been proactive in this regard, developing an extensive list of criteria for membership. For one, they require that the journal have recognized scholars on its editorial board. Second, APEJR requires prospective member journals to practice blind, scholar peer-review. Third, in order to be considered for inclusion in the association, journals must have a year's worth of issues under their belts and a registered ISSN number (APEJR).

The digital road that is being paved by ATLAS and APEJR will clearly have an affect on theological libraries. The magnitude of these affects, and whether such affects are productive or limiting, will depend in large part on how theological libraries prepare for the arrival and proliferation of digital media. Theological librarians, therefore, should seriously consider the strengths and weaknesses inherent in electronic journals and electronic versions of journals so their constituencies might be best served.

ADVANTAGES OF ELECTRONIC JOURNALS

There are a number of advantages associated with the publication of electronic journals and e-versions of journals. The key question, in determining the usefulness of the digital medium, is to ask what it is that electronic journals can do that print journals cannot. With that question in mind, there are at least four important advantages of the electronic format.

One obvious advantage of the electronic medium is speed. For fully electronic journals, the speed factor is evident in the area of distribution as well as in access and retrieval. Both Hickey (1995) and Lancaster (1995) have analyzed the efficiency and speed associated with electronic journal publication, and they have noted that publishers can distribute their e-journals more quickly because they are not bound by traditional printing and mailing processes. James Adair (1997), editor of the e-journal *TC: A Journal of Biblical Textual Criticism*, remarks that it takes only two to three months for his journal to publish an article after it has been received. He compares this time-frame with the average production cycle of a year or more for print journals.

In addition to production and distribution, Rodgers (1993) points out that electronic formats enable scholars around the world to comment more quickly on their colleagues' scholarship. As Adair (1997) notes, by the time print journals go to press, the authors contributing to these volumes may have modified their original positions. Therefore, e-journals may actually enhance the scholarly process by making it more efficient and encouraging more timely feedback.

At the consumption level, persons experience increased speed in retrieving electronic journal articles when compared to traditional retrieval methods. Typically, persons interested in particular articles have had to spend valuable time physically tracking down hard copies in libraries' periodical stacks or waiting days, or even weeks, for materials from interlibrary loan to arrive. Electronic journal articles, on the other hand, can usually be downloaded and printed in a matter of seconds.

Another advantage of e-journals is their accessibility. Users of ATLA's *Religion Database*, provided that they also subscribe to AT-LAS, will be pleased to discover that all the journals to which their library subscribes are available to them in full text on the Internet. Journals publishing exclusively online or moving their print operations to the digital medium will also increase their visibility and accessibility. Once online, a journal's potential audience is virtually unlimited. For instance, in 1996, its first year on the Web, the home page of *TC: A Journal of Biblical and Textual Criticism* received an average of 145 hits per day, a number far outpacing anything it could have expected if it were to produce in print (Adair 1997). Similarly, the *Journal of Buddhist Ethics*, an award-winning online journal, receives 50,000 hits per year to its Web site (Prebish, e-mail).

The accessibility of electronic journals is further enhanced when one considers that e-journals are not under spacial or temporal constraints. Respondents to a survey conducted by Ashcroft and Langdon (1999) indicate that twenty-four hour availability of periodical literature is perhaps the most important advantage of e-journals from a user's standpoint. Moreover, Hawbaker and Wagner (1996) rightly point out the electronic medium allows multiple users to simultaneously access and print the same journal article.

A third advantage of electronic journals is that they can incorporate Internet technologies such as multimedia and linking functionalities. Interactive segments, audio, and even video, are all enhancements available to electronic journals in addition to traditional textual and visual features. For instance, *Mennonite Life*, which recently eschewed print for cyberspace, explains how the flexibility of digital media will appeal to different learning styles: "We will now include . . . brief audio segments. In the future we hope to add video segments as well" (Bethel College 1999, par. 2).

In addition to multimedia, electronic journals can accommodate internal as well as external linking. For example, hypertext links within a journal article allow users to reference footnotes, as well as other relevant sections within the article, with the click of a button. Such functionality can also be used to link to other parts of the journal, other Web sites, e-mail contacts, etc. Chan (1999) reports on the usefulness of strategically placing electronic mail links so that users may contact authors, publishers, or other groups and institutions for further information, interaction, and general queries.

A fourth benefit of the electronic format is an economic one. In fact, the Internet may well be the only feasible medium for sustaining the kind of narrowly focused journals often found in religion and theology. Extremely specialized journals, whose readership is small, and subscription base even smaller, may find that cyberspace is a more amenable medium to the journal's long-term viability. Societies and university presses often produce religious studies journals at cost, or even at a loss, due to the expense of paper and printing. By converting their operations to the electronic medium, they can substantially reduce their costs. Dina Eylon, editor of the e-journal *Women in Judaism*, notes that her periodical achieves economic independence by going digital. "It does not cost us anything," she remarks, "to publish the journal" (Eylon, e-mail).

The economic benefits of e-journals and e-versions of journals extend to theological libraries as well. First, storage costs are reduced as electronic journals require no storage space, and in some cases the option of e-versions eliminates the need for future storage considerations. Second, reducing the number of print subscriptions reduces operating costs associated with ordering, cataloging, and binding. Finally, fewer items will require shelving and e-journals cannot be damaged, stolen, or mis-shelved.

DISADVANTAGES OF ELECTRONIC JOURNALS

Though the advantages of electronic journals are compelling, this format has not arrived without its obstacles. In fact, certain aspects of e-journals, such as accessibility and economic impact, are both a blessing and a curse. For instance, though e-journals may in theory offer greater accessibility, in practice there are precious few indexing and abstracting journals that include fully electronic journals in their offerings. Thus, authors interested in ensuring that their work can be found, and students, scholars, and others who need to locate such materials, may find their efforts frustrated. While this problem is currently being addressed by APEJR and will not be an issue for ATLAS subscribers, there are a significant number of online journals in disciplines related to religion and theology that will not find their way into indexing and abstracting services. Moreover, of the online religious studies journals producing in full text, none have adequate searching capabilities within their Web sites. As Adair (1999) notes, having online access to images of journal articles is beneficial, but the images themselves are insufficient unless specific pages can be accessed rapidly and unless some form of searching is possible. ATLAS has confronted this problem by making the *ATLA Religion Database* its search engine. In other words, the *ATLA Religion Database* will generate the bibliographic data and provide a link to the full text article in ATLAS.

Just as accessibility is both strengthened and threatened in the electronic medium, the economic impact of e-journals is likewise a double-edged sword. E-journals may relieve a theological library of some of its storage and ordering costs, but they also initiate new technological and economic demands. In order for electronic journals to be accessed, theological libraries and academic communities must have the necessary hardware and infrastructure in place to support e-journal access. Harrison and Stephen (1995) have noted that the issue of accessibility may divide academic communities into "have" and "have-nots" because the equipment required for displaying, storing, and printing electronic journals is expensive. Moreover, Wills and Wills (1996) point out that graphics quality is still poor on many machines, and network connections may be too slow for downloading large files. Furthermore, as ubiquitous as Internet connectivity seems to persons and libraries in the west, there are many places throughout the world where access to the Internet is not yet a live option. For these areas, electronic journals cannot be accessed, and the loss of a print journal to the digital format represents a complete loss of access.

Another economic issue is subscription fees, which many e-journals charge. According to Ashcroft and Langdon (1996) 86 percent of the academic libraries in their survey list site license arrangements as a major barrier to accessing e-journals. Fortunately, for the time being, APEJR requires member journals to make all of their issues available free of charge through the Internet. ATLAS will be available by institutional subscription to libraries and by individual subscription to members of AAR and/or SBL. Libraries subscribing to *ATLA Religion Database* on CD-ROM or from online vendors may subscribe to AT-LAS for $2500 annually for unlimited simultaneous users at a single site. As well, members of AAR and SBL may subscribe to ATLAS for $110 per year. Other individuals may subscribe for $150 annually (ATLA CERTR 1999).

Though more affordable than most other electronic journal collections, the ATLAS business model contains some features of which potential subscribers should be wary. For instance, the publisher of a journal participating in ATLAS may restrict access, in the form of a five-year rolling gap, to ATLAS subscribers who are not also subscribers to their journals. In these cases, the publisher may choose to offer a document delivery service, for an as yet undetermined fee, so that ATLAS members not subscribing to a particular journal may nonetheless obtain restricted articles (ATLA CERTR 1999).

A third disadvantage of e-journals is the reluctance of scholars to embrace electronic publishing. The legitimacy of the electronic format for scholarly production has been a topic of some debate (e.g., Cronin and Overfelt 1995; Kling and Covi 1995; Tenopir 1995; Warkentin 1997). Though this stumbling block will not affect ATLAS subscribers, it will continue to impinge on APEJR journals and especially fully electronic religious studies journals not associated with APEJR. Warkentin (1997) explains that e-journals are perceived by many in academia as vehicles without rigorous refereeing processes that publish what print journals will not accept. Furthermore, Kling and Covi (1995, 266) have shown that electronic publishing is largely perceived by the academy as experimental. Their research elicited comments indicating that e-journals reside "in a ghostly netherworld of academic publishing," where standards are lower and quality is lacking. This perception exists, they argue, primarily because faculty "sense something insubstantial and transient" in electronic publications. As a result tenure committees may look askance at articles published in online journals (Tenopir 1995). Adair (1997) recounts how his attempts to entice a leading textual scholar to contribute to *TC* were met with remarks implying that online journals could not represent serious scholarship. Theological librarians can be aware of their faculties' perceptions of electronic journals and use this information to determine how much energy they need to expend in organizing online guides for religious studies journals and/or educating their constituents about developments in electronic media that strengthen its scholarly value.

Finally, James Adair and Patrick Durusau (1998) warn of two other potentially harmful results inherent in electronic journal publication. First, they point out that journals of poor quality may be able to successfully promote their products due to the ease of online publishing and the lack of evaluative controls on the Internet. Second, they fear that authors may be tempted, because of the speed that is now possible with Internet technologies, to rush their manuscripts to publication.

ISSUES FOR THEOLOGICAL LIBRARIES

A primary issue facing libraries concerns permanence. Ashcroft and Langdon (1999) report that libraries have been afraid to cancel print subscriptions because they fear that the continuity of their periodical collections may be compromised. Permanence will not be a significant issue for ATLAS subscribers, since the journals in the project's e-version collection already have proven track records. ATLAS subscribers will want to remember, however, that they will most likely need to subscribe, either in print or online, to any ATLAS journal for which they desire access to full runs of full text. On the other hand, theological librarians will want to pay special attention to permanence issues for fully electronic journals. The APEJR membership requirements certainly increase the likelihood of a journal's continued presence online, but librarians should evaluate these and other online journals on a case-by-case basis in determining whether or not to subscribe and/or maintain access links to these journals.

Archiving is a related issue with which librarians must be concerned. Adair and Durusau (1998) note that archived material must be accessible (i.e., properly indexed), refreshed periodically, and exist in multiple copies at more than one physical location. One way to archive e-journals is to create "mirror sites" around the world. The

Center for Research Libraries (http://wwwcrl.uchicago.edu/info/cic) is an example of an institution committed to archiving electronic journals. Originally, the idea for ATLAS developed in the context of discussions about creating a digital archive for paper journals (Adair 1999), and the project has not lost sight of this early goal. All journals participating in the ATLAS project will be archived in a high-resolution format (600 dpi TIFF images) from which microfilm as well as future preservation formats may be generated.

A third issue facing libraries is one of collection development. Harloe and Budd (1994, 83) note that "collection managers should focus on the content of the scholarly information provided, regardless of the actual form in which the information arrives." Focusing on content means using the same set of criteria for judging both e-journals and print journals. Gabriel (1998) articulates several considerations, including high quality, expected longevity, and evidence of peer review. Furthermore, Ashcroft and Langdon (1999) have found that many university libraries are dealing with the issue of e-journal collection development by consulting with their faculties. Simpson and Seeds (1998) also recommend that libraries consider the interest level in a particular title, which can be determined by the number of recommendations, user inquiries, or document delivery requests it receives. Theological libraries must also remember that even if the e-journals are "free," they still represent a cost to the library in terms of maintaining the collection, providing technical support and user education, and cataloging.

The cataloging of e-journals is another issue confronting theological librarians. Simpson and Seeds (1998, 129) argue that "the purpose of the library catalog must be extended beyond the traditional inventory of physically held items to include remotely accessed items that have been selected by the subject bibliographer as appropriate for the particular collection." Theological librarians may indeed create useful e-journal guides as part of their Web page offerings, but they should also include electronic periodicals in the library catalog by means of an appropriate MARC record, including 856 lines which provide Internet access points to electronic journals. One benefit of creating catalog records for e-journals, outside of promoting Internet resources to patrons, is to prevent unnecessary article requests through interlibrary loan or document delivery services (Simpson and Seeds 1998).

A few theological libraries have been experimenting with cataloging electronic resources and creating hyperlinks to these journals. Yet, questions remain as to which electronic resources to catalog, how to create and display bibliographic records, and how to maintain records for items whose URL and content may change at a moment's notice (Ford and Harter, 335). The Heard Divinity Library at Vanderbilt University is an exemplary model for seeing how e-journals can be effectively incorporated into an online public access catalog. (One may search their catalog, ACORN, for specific e-journal titles at http://acorn.library. vanderbilt.edu/uhtbin/cgisirsiDpohs6a620/28751145/60/69 or visit the Library's electronic journal page at http://divinity.library.vanderbilt.edu/relig.html.) Despite their efforts, even Vanderbilt's online catalog contains a number of dead-end URLs for e-journals. To help prevent these access problems, Adair and Durusau (1998) emphasize the need for libraries to agree on a set of standards for accessing electronic journals. One way, he suggests, would be to create standards whereby an e-journal's home page is accessed by its ISSN number through a Persistent URL (e.g., http://purl.org/ISSN/1762-4545). Because ISSN numbers are unique and PURLs remain static, librarians can be sure that their time spent cataloging electronic journals will not be wasted.

Access concerns pose yet another issue for theological libraries. Above all, libraries must ensure that their users are aware of what electronic journal titles are available, and how to access and evaluate them. Ashcroft and Langdon (1999) encourage libraries to practice promotional techniques, such as developing printed user guides, leading workshops and class presentations, and/or promoting their electronic journal collections on library Web pages. These methods will help ensure that patrons make full use of a library's online periodical offerings.

In examining access issues, theological libraries should also consider whether additional technical staff would be necessary to provide troubleshooting and daily maintenance for computers and printers. Furthermore, theological libraries will need to plan for an adequate number of computer workstations and decide whether/how much to charge for printing. Finally, the access issue becomes most critical when libraries consider the potential for downtime at the local, institutional, or Internet level. Some theological librarians have suggested printing off a hard copy of each electronic journal issue (or each issue of an electronic version if the print subscription was cancelled). While in some ways this would defeat the ecological advantage of e-journals, it would nonetheless hedge against system failures and, as Hawbaker and Wagner (1996) suggest, allow patrons to continue browsing in the periodicals stacks.

TRENDS

Where the digital revolution will ultimately lead us in regard to electronic periodical publication is open to speculation. Nonetheless, at least three trends are emerging that deserve attention. First, electronic journals will not eliminate their print counterparts, at least not in the foreseeable future. Tenopir (1997, 37) has argued that e-journals "can't replace print journals yet because only a fraction of scholarly materials is available electronically. What is available varies in quality, accessibility and price." However, one may expect the proliferation of highly specialized journals in cyberspace where the electronic medium makes narrowly focused periodicals more accessible to potential users and cost-effective to produce. *Mennonite Life*, which moved its operations online in early 2000 after 53 years of print publication, epitomizes this trend. Its publishing body explains that the Internet allows *Mennonite Life* to reach out

> to youthful readers who are attuned to the new technology. We have also learned that our more senior subscribers . . . are rapidly becoming computer literate and web-connected . . . (and) the cost of printing out an entire issue on a printer will be less than the old cost of a subscription. (Bethel College 1999, par. 4)

One question to be answered, according to Adair and Durusau (1998) is whether or not publishers of e-journals that also appear in print will be able to get away with charging for access to online articles. Web culture, they argue, staunchly resists paying for access to information, so for-profit publishers will likely need to figure out how to recover costs in some way other than charging readers of their articles.

Another trend to look for is the increased use of XML, or Extensible Markup Language, to encode electronic journal articles. Presently, electronic journal delivery is dominated by two formats: Portable Document Format (PDF) and Hypertext Markup Language (HTML). PDF, though inexpensive to create, results in large files with little structural flexibility and no search features–navigation is limited to turning pages. HTML is also popular because its coding is relatively simple and HTML browsers are free. However, the simplicity of HTML makes it an unlikely method for delivering complex information types over the long haul (Pope 1999). XML, on the other hand, is a much more flexible tool for marking article content. For example, dates, names, or scripture references, can be "tagged" with XML codes, and XML-compatible browsers will have built-in indexing and searching functions. Such functionality will allow online researchers to search for, say, a scripture reference, throughout a complete journal issue or over the entire run of a journal (Adair and Durusau 1998).

A third trend will be the advent of what Adair and Durusau (1998, par. 16) call "smart articles." In the near future, they predict, authors will be able to produce articles with which readers can interact. This interaction may include "entering sample data into an embedded program to demonstrate a theory proposed or allowing the reader to choose from a variety of options to generate graphs or charts on the fly." Smart articles will also be able to administer reader surveys and evaluate responses or dispense quizzes and tabulate test scores.

CONCLUSION

The primary obstacles that have inhibited the online presence of religious studies journals are being met head on, and credit in large measure is due to the work of persons and organizations associated with ATLAS and APEJR. By negotiating with publishers and creating a business model that seeks to protect publishers' interests as well as those of scholars and researchers, CERTR has turned the dream of a large-scale digitization project into a reality. If ATLAS can maintain its momentum, academic and theological communities will soon share in the fruits of an electronic journal collection unparalleled in terms of affordability and accessibility. As the project moves forward, the AT-LAS board may want to consider implementing a sliding-scale subscription fee based on an institution's F.T.E. enrollment. Otherwise, ATLAS may be a fiscal impossibility for smaller seminary libraries.

While ATLAS addresses the issues associated with digitizing leading religious studies journals, APEJR continues to counter scholars' concerns about the legitimacy of exclusively electronic journals. The stringent membership criteria instituted by the APEJR cannot help but influence those who would discriminate based on delivery medium.

By the end of 2000, most, if not all, of the APEJR member journals should have been indexed in the *ATLA Religion Database*. Theological librarians can assist in this educational process by making sure faculty, students, and researchers are aware of peer-reviewed e-journals in their fields and by beginning to catalog selected e-journals.

The journal literature of any discipline is vital to teaching and learning in the classroom. Academic and theological libraries are becoming more and more dependent on electronic resources, and it is increasingly important for religious studies journals to be available to library users. As these users discover the virtual world of electronic information, they will begin making demands to which theological libraries must respond. In the early 1990s, Ruth Pagel articulated these demands as they impinged on academic libraries. These same demands define the task of theological libraries as they move into the twenty-first century:

> No longer do users think that the ability to get a list of citations online is a wondrous thing, and getting a summary of the article is no longer a miracle but a nuisance. Users now want the full-text, and they want it now, at their terminals, with graphic image output capability–and of course searchable as well. (1993, 8)

REFERENCES

Adair, J. 1997. "A Modern Experiment in Studying the Ancients." *The Journal of Electronic Publishing* 3 (September) <http://www.press.umich.edu/Jep/03-01/TC.html> (21 January 2000).

_____. 1999. "The ATLAS Project of the Center for Electronic Texts in Religion: 50 Years of 50 Journals." Paper Presented at the Research Libraries Group Forum, Emory University. <http://rosetta.atla-certr.org/CERTR/ATLAS/article/RLG-ATLAS.html> (24 February 2000).

Adair, J., and P. Durusau. 1998. "Offline 63: Electronic Journals Make Their Move." *Religious Studies News*. (November) <http:rosetta.atla-certr.org/CERTR/Offline/off63.html> (20 January 2000).

APEJR. 1999. "Association of Peer-Reviewed Electronic Journals in Religion." <http://purl.org/apejr> (22 December 1999).

Ashcroft, L., and C. Langdon. 1999. "Electronic Journals and University Library Collections." *Collection Building* 18: 105-113.

ATLA CERTR. 1999. "ATLA Serials: Fifty Years of Fifty Journals: Full-Text Electronic Editions of Journals in Religion, Indexed by and Accessed Through the *ATLA Religion Database*." (May). <http://rosetta.atla-certr.org/CERTR/ATLAS/articles/ATLAS-proposal.html> (24 February 2000).

_____. 2000. "ATLAS Frequently Asked Questions." (January) <http://rosetta. atla-certr.org/CERTR/ATLAS/FAQ.html> (15 February 2000).

_____. "Project Update for October 15, 1999." (January) <http://rosetta.atla-certr. org/CERTR/ATLAS/NEWS/oct15.html> (24 February 2000).

Bethel College. 1999. "*Mennonite Life* to Publish Electronically." (September). <http://www.bethelks.edu/mennonitelife/electronic.html> (3 February 2000).

Chan, L. 1999. "Electronic Journals and Academic Libraries." *Library Hi Tech* 17:10-16.

Cronin, B., and K. Overfelt. 1995. "E-Journals and Tenure." *Journal of the American Society for Information Science* 46: 700-703.

Eylon, D. <dina.eylon@utoronto.ca> "Women in Judaism." 23 January 2000. Personal E-mail (24 January 2000).

Ford, C. E., and S. P. Harter. 1998. "The Downside of Scholarly Electronic Publishing: Problems in Accessing Electronic Journals Through Online Directories and Catalogs." *College & Research Libraries* 59: 335-346.

Gabriel, J.A. 1998. "Managing and Coping with Electronic Serials: A Report from the ACRL New England Chapter Serials Interest Group's Fall 1996 Program." *Managing Library Finances* 11: 14-17.

Harloe, B., and J.M. Budd. 1994. "Collection Development and Scholarly Communication in the Era of Electronic Access." *The Journal of Academic Librarianship* 20: 83-87.

Harrison, T.M., and T.D. Stephen. 1995. "The Electronic Journal as the Heart of an Online Scholarly Community." *Library Trends* 43: 592-608.

Hawbaker, A.C., and C.K. Wagner. 1996. "Periodical Ownership versus Fulltext Online Access: A Cost-Benefit Analysis." *The Journal of Academic Librarianship* 22: 105-109.

Hickey, T.B. 1995. "Present and Future Capabilities of the Online Journal." *Library Trends* 43: 528-543.

Kling, R., and L. Covi. 1995. "Electronic Journals and Legitimate Media in the Systems of Scholarly Communication." *The Information Society* 11: 261-271.

Lancaster, F.W. 1995. "The Evolution of Electronic Publishing." *Library Trends* 43: 518-527.

Pagell, Ruth A. 1993. "Reaching for the Bottle, not the Glass: The End-User Factor of Electronic Full Text." *Database* 16: 8-9.

Pope, L. 1999. "Emerging Trends in Journal Publishing." *The Serials Librarian* 36: 163-174.

Prebish, C. <csp1@psu.edu> "APEJR." 20 January 2000. Personal E-mail (24 January 2000).

Rodgers, D. 1993. "Maintaining Scholarly Quality in Electronic Journals." *Proceedings of the 1993 International Conference of Refereed Electronic Journals.* Winnipeg: University of Manitoba Libraries.

Schultze, Quentin J. 2000. "Lost in the Digital Cosmos." *Christian Century,* 117(5) 178-179.

Simpson, P., and R.S. Seeds. "Electronic Journals in the Online Catalog: Selection and Bibliographic Control." *Library Resources and Technical Services* 42: 126-132.

Tenopir, Carol. 1995. "Authors and Readers: The Keys to Success or Failure for Electronic Publishing." *Library Trends* 43: 571-591.

_____. 1997. "The Complexities of Electronic Journals." *Library Journal* 122: 37-38.

_____. 1999. "Should We Cancel Print?" *Library Journal* 124: 138, 142.

Tomney, H., and P.F. Burton. 1998. "Electronic Journals: A Study of Usage and Attitudes Among Academics." *Journal of Information Science* 24: 419-429.

Warkentin, E. 1997. "Consumer Issues and the Scholarly Journal." *Canadian Journal of Communications* 22: 39-47.

Wills, M., and G. Wills. 1996. "The Ins and Outs of Electronic Publishing." *Internet Research* 6: 10-21.

APPENDIX A

As of March 1, 2000, publishers of the following journals had signed agreements with ATLA CERTR to participate in the ATLAS project:

Church History
Cross Currents: The Journal of the Association for Religion and Intellectual Life
The Ecumenical Review
Interpretation: A Journal of Bible and Theology .
International Bulletin of Missionary Research
The International Review of Mission
Journal for Preachers
The Journal of Biblical Literature
Journal of Ecumenical Studies
The Journal of Pastoral Care
Journal of Pastoral Theology
The Journal of Ritual Studies
Journal of the American Academy of Religion
The Muslim World
Near Eastern Archaeology (a.k.a. Biblical Archaeologist)
Novum Testamentum
Numen
Religious Education
St. Vladimir's Theological Quarterly
Semeia: An Experimental Journal for Biblical Criticism
Theological Studies
Vestus Testamentum

For an update, see http://rosetta.atla-certr.org/CERTR/ATLAS/FAQ.html

APPENDIX B

ATLA member libraries indicating their willingness to sponsor the filming of one journal annually, as indicated in the ATLAS project proposal (http://rosetta.atla-certr.org/CERTR/ATLAS/articles/ATLAS-proposal.html):

Princeton Theological Seminary
Concordia Seminary
Hartford Theological Seminary
University of St. Mary of the Lake
Austin Theological Seminary
Asbury Theological Seminary
St. Paul Seminary (at the University of St. Thomas)
University of the South
Harvard Divinity School
Christian Theological Seminary
Lancaster Theological Seminary
Virginia Theological Seminary
Associated Mennonite Biblical Seminary
Pitts Theological Library (at Emory University)
Vanderbilt University
Union Theological Seminary (Virginia)
Trinity College Library
Luther Theological Seminary
Andover Newton Theological Seminary

(Source: http://rosetta.atla-certr.org/CERTR/ATLAS/articles/ATLAS-proposal.html)

APPENDIX C

Selected Webliography of religious studies journals publishing online in whole or in part. "Search" indicates that there is a search engine embedded in the Web site; "ATLA" indicates whether the journal is indexed in *ATLA Religion Index One*; "RTA" indicates whether the journal is indexed in *Religious & Theological Abstracts*; "Years" indicates the time period for which journal contents, text, etc., are available online. It does not designate the years in which a journal has been in operation.

Journal Name	URL/PURL	Full Text	Contents	Abstract	Reviews	Search	ATLA	RTA	Years
Al-Tawhid	http://www.al-islam.org/al-tawhid/	selected	no	no	no	no	no	yes	?
American Journal of Philology	http://www.press.jhu.edu/journals/american_journal_of_philology/	yes	yes	no	no	no	no	no	1996-
American Missionary	http://moa.cit.cornell.edu/MOA/MOA-JOURNALS2/AMIS.html	1878-1901	yes	no	no	no	no	no	archive
Amer. Sch. Of Oriental Rsrch Newsl.	http://www.asor.org/NEWSLETTER/ASORNHP.html	yes	yes	no	no	no	no	no	1995-
Ancient History Bulletin	http://ivory.trentu.ca/www/cl/ahb/	back iss.	yes	no	no	no	no	no	1987-
Anglican Journal	http://www.anglicanjournal.com/	yes	yes	no	no	yes	no	no	1998-
Animus	http://www.mun.ca/animus/	yes	yes	yes	no	no	no	no	1996-
Anistoriton	http://users.hol.gr/~dilos/anistor/cover_en.htm	yes	yes	no	no	no	no	no	1997-
Arachnon	http://www.cisi.unito.it/arachne/arachne.html	no	yes	no	no	no	no	no	1995-
Asian Journal of Pentecostal Studies	http://www.apts.edu/ajps/	yes	yes	no	2000-	no	no	no	1998-
Australian Humanities Review	http://www.lib.latrobe.edu.au/AHR/	yes	yes	no	yes	no	no	no	1996-
Biblica	http://www.bsw.org/project/index.htm	1998-	1990-	yes	no	no	yes	no	1990-
Biblical Studies on the Web	http://www.bsw.org/	1998 only	yes	yes	no	yes	no	no	1998-
Biblical Theology Bulletin	http://academic.shu.edu/btb/	no	yes	yes	no	no	yes	yes	1995-
Bridges: A.J. for Jewish Feminists	http://www.pond.net/~ckinberg/bridges/index.html	no	yes	no	no	no	no	no	1990-
Bryn Mawr Classical Review	http://ccat.sas.upenn.edu/bmcr	no	yes	no	yes	yes	no	no	1990-
Bull. Amer. Sch. Oriental Rsrch	http://www.asor.org/BASOR/BASORHP.html	no	yes	yes	yes	no	no	yes	1994-
Bulletin for Contextual Theology	http://www.unp.ac.za/UNPDepartments/theol/BCT.HTM	1994-96	yes	no	no	no	no	no	1994-
Catholic World	http://moa.umdl.umich.edu/moa_browse.html	1865-1901	yes	no	no	yes	no	no	archive
Chafer Theological Seminary Journal	http://www.bible.org/chafer/ctsjrnl/ctsjrnl.htm	no	yes	no	no	no	no	no	1995-
The Christian Activist	http://www.tca1.org	yes	yes	no	no	no	no	no	1996-
Christian Scholar's Review	http://www.hope.edu/resources/csr/	no	yes	yes	no	no	yes	yes	1999-
Christianity Today	http://www1.christianity.net/ct/ct_main/issues.html	back iss.	yes	no	no	yes	yes	yes	1996-
Contra Mundum	http://www.visi.com/~contra_m/cm/	yes	yes	no	yes	no	no	no	1991-
Cross Currents	http://www.crosscurrents.org/	no	yes	no	some	no	yes	yes	1996-

Journal Name	URL/PURL	Full Text	Contents	Abstract	Reviews	Search	ATLA	RTA	Years
Crux	http://www.gospelcom.net/regent-bookstore/crux/crux_home.html	no	yes	no	no	no	yes	yes	1997-
Cyberjournal for Pentec/Charis. Rsrch	http://www.pctii.org/cyberlab.html	yes	yes	no	no	no	no	no	1997-
Denver Journal	http://www.gospelcom.net/densem/dj	no	no	no	yes	no	no	no	1998-
Didaskalia	http://didaskalia.berkeley.edu/	no	no	no	no	no	no	yes	1994-
Diskus	http://www.uni-marburg.de/fb03/religionswissenschaft/journal/diskus/	yes	yes	yes	no	no	no	no	1993-
East-West Church & Ministry Report	http://www.samford.edu/groups/global/ewcmreport/	back iss.	yes	no	no	no	no	no	1993-
Elec. Journal of Vedic Studies	http://www1.shore.net/~india/ejvs/	yes	yes	no	no	no	no	no	1995-
First Things	http://www.firstthings.com/menus/index.html	yes	no	no	no	yes	yes	yes	1992-
Gouden Hoorn	http://www.geocities.com/Athens/Parthenon/5157/index.htm	yes	yes	no	no	no	no	no	1993-
Gravitas	http://aquinas.gtu.edu/library/Gravitas/	unk	unk	unk	unk	unk	no	no	new
Harvard Theological Review	http://divweb.harvard.edu/htr/	no	yes	no	no	no	yes	yes	1998-
Hebrew Linguistics	http://www.biu.ac.il/js/linguistics/	no	yes	no	no	no	no	no	1996-
Hindu Studies Review	http://www.csuchico.edu/rs/hsr/hsr.html	no	yes	no	yes	no	no	no	1995
History of Religions	http://www.journals.uchicago.edu/HR/home.html	no	yes	no	no	no	yes	yes	1996-
Histos	http://www.dur.ac.uk/Classics/histos/	yes	yes	no	yes	no	no	no	1997-
Hugoye: J. of Syriac Studies	http://syrcom.cua.edu/Hugoye/	yes	yes	no	yes	yes	no	no	1998-
Int'l Journal of Hindu Studies	http://web.clas.ufl.edu/users/gthursby/ijhs/	no	yes	yes	yes	no	no	no	1997-
Int'l Journal of Tantric Studies	http://www.asiatica.org/publications/ijts/default.asp	no	yes	yes	no	no	no	no	1995-
Internet Archaeology	http://intarch.york.ac.uk/	yes	yes	no	no	yes	no	no	1996-
Interpretation	http://www.interpretation.org/	no	yes	no	no	yes	no	yes	1980-
IOUDAIOS Review	http://listserv.lehigh.edu/lists/ioudaios-review/	yes	no	no	yes	no	no	no	1994-
Jain Journal	http://www.cba.uiuc.edu/doogar/www/Other/Jain/Jainjour/toc.html	no	yes	no	yes	no	no	no	1994-
J. for the Study of Rhet. Crit. of the NT	http://newton.uor.edu/FacultyFolder/Hester/Journal/JSRCNTintro.html	no	no	no	yes	no	no	no	1999
Journal of Applied Missiology	http://www.bible.acu.edu/missions/Journals/jam/default.htm	yes	yes	no	no	no	no	no	1990-
J. of Arabic & Islamic Studies	http://www.uib.no/jais/	yes	yes	yes	no	no	no	no	1996-
Journal of Asian Missions	http://www.apts.edu/jam/	yes	yes	no	no	no	no	no	1999-
Journal of Biblical Ethics in Medicine	http://capo.org/jbem/intro_pa.htm	1987-92	yes	no	yes	no	no	yes	1987-
Journal of Buddhist Ethics	http://jbe.la.psu.edu/	yes	yes	no	yes	no	no	yes	1994-

65

APPENDIX C (continued)

Journal Name	URL/PURL	Full Text	Contents	Abstract	Reviews	Search	ATLA	RTA	Years
J. of Christian Theological Research	http://home.apu.edu/~CTRF/jctrnf.html	yes	no	no	no	no	yes	yes	1996-
Journal of Cuneiform Studies	http://www.asor.org/JCS/JCSHP.html	no	yes	no	yes	no	yes	yes	1991-
Journal of Early Christian Studies	http://muse.jhu.edu/journals/journal_of_early_christian_studies/	yes	no	yes	yes	no	yes	yes	1996-
The Journal of Hebrew Scriptures	http://www.arts.ualberta.ca/JHS/	yes	no	yes	no	no	no	no	1996-
Journal of Higher Criticism	http://www.depts.drew.edu/jhc/	select	yes	no	no	no	no	no	1994-
Journal of Maronite Studies	http://www.mari.org/jms/	yes	yes	no	no	no	no	no	2000-
Journal of Near Eastern Studies	http://www.journals.uchicago.edu/JNES/home.html	no	yes	no	no	no	yes	yes	1996-
Journal of Religion	http://www.journals.uchicago.edu/JR/	no	yes	no	no	no	yes	yes	1996-
Journal of Religion & Film	http://www.unomaha.edu/~wwwjrf/	yes	yes	no	yes	no	no	no	1997-
Journal of Religion & Society	http://purl.org/JRS	yes	yes	yes	yes	no	no	no	1999-
Journal of Religious Ethics	goher://gopher.lib.virginia.edu/11/alpha/jre	no	1990-94	no	no	no	yes	yes	1990-4
Journal of Semetic Studies	http://www3.oup.co.uk/semitj/contents/	no	yes	no	no	no	yes	yes	1996-
Journal of Southern Religion	http://jsr.as.wvu.edu/index.html	yes	yes	no	yes	no	no	no	1998-
J. of the Center for Buddhist Studies	http://ccbs.ntu.edu.tw/FULLTEXT/cfb_cbsj.htm	yes	yes	no	no	no	no	yes	1996-
Journal of Theological Studies	http://www3.oup.co.uk/theolj/	no	yes	no	no	no	yes	yes	1996-
Jouvert	http://152.1.96.5/jouvert/	yes	yes	yes	yes	no	no	no	1997-
KMT: A Modern J. of Ancient Egypt	http://www.egyptology.com/kmt/	no	yes	yes	no	no	no	no	1995-
Literature and Theology	http://www3.oup.co.uk/litthe/	no	yes	yes	no	yes	yes	yes	1996-
Living Tradition: J. of R. Cath. Theology	http://www.rtforum.org/lt/index.html	yes	yes	no	yes	yes	no	no	1987-
Magistra	http://www.benedictine.edu/mount/magistra/magistra.html	no	yes	no	no	no	no	no	1995-
Marburg Journal of Religion	http://www.uni-marburg.de/fb03/religionswissenschaft/journal/mjr/	past iss.	yes	no	no	no	no	no	1996-
The Master's Seminary Journal	http://www.mastersem.edu/journal.htm	1990-95	yes	yes	no	yes	yes	yes	1990-
McMaster J. of Theology & Ministry	http://www.mcmaster.ca/mjtm/	yes	yes	no	no	yes	no	no	1998-
The Medieval Review	http://www.hti.umich.edu/b/bmr/bmr.html	yes	yes	no	yes	yes	no	no	1993-
Mennonite Life	http://www.bethelks.edu/mennonitelife/	yes	yes	no	yes	no	yes	no	1998-
Mennonite Quarterly Review	http://www.goshen.edu/mqr/	yes	yes	no	yes	no	yes	yes	1997-
Near Eastern Archaeology	http://www.asor.org/BA/BA-HP.html	no	yes	no	yes	no	no	no	1994-
Newsletter on African OT Scholarship	http://www.misjonshs.no/publikasjoner/ot_afr/	yes	yes	no	yes	yes	yes	no	1996-
The North Star: J. of Afr-Amer Rel Hist	http://cedar.barnard.columbia.edu/~north/	yes	yes	no	yes	no	yes	no	1997-

Journal Name	URL/PURL	Full Text	Contents	Abstract	Reviews	Search	ATLA	RTA	Years
Nova Religio	http://www.novareligio.com/	no	yes	no	no	no	no	no	1998-
The Other Side	http://www.theotherside.org/	yes	yes	no	no	yes	yes	yes	1997-
Peace & Conflict Studies	http://www.trenton.edu/~psm/pcs/	yes	yes	no	no	yes	no	no	1994-7
Perspectives on Science & Xn Faith	http://asa.calvin.edu/ASA/PSCF.html	no	yes	no	no	no	yes	no	1998-
Philosophia Christi	http://asa.epsociety.org/journal.htm	no	yes	no	no	no	no	no	1991-
Philosophy East and West	http://ccbs.ntu.edu.tw/FULLTEXT/cfb_phil.htm	partial	yes	no	no	no	no	yes	1954-
Quaker Theology	http://www.quaker.org/quest/	yes	yes	no	no	no	no	no	1999-
Radical Philosophy	http://www.ukc.ac.uk/secl/philosophy/rp/index.html	no	yes	no	yes	no	no	no	1972-
Religion & the Arts	http://www.bc.edu/bc_org/avp/cas/relarts	no	yes	no	no	no	no	no	1997-
Religion & Theology	http://www.unisa.ac.za/dept/press/onjourn.html	no	yes	yes	no	no	yes	yes	1995-7
Religious Studies News	http://www.jv-site.org/topic/RSN/rsnhome.html	yes	yes	no	no	no	no	no	1997-
Renaissance: A Monthly Islam Journal	http://www.renaissance.com.pk/	yes	yes	no	no	no	no	no	1995-
Research on the Contemplative Life	http://140.190.128.190/merton/RCL.html	yes	yes	no	no	no	no	no	1994
Review Biblique	http://www.op.org/op/ebaf/revue-fr.htm	no	yes	yes	no	no	no	yes	1996-
Revue d'Histoire et de Philosophie	http://perso.wanadoo.fr/rhpr/en/rhpr.html	no	yes	yes	no	yes	yes	yes	1996-
Review of Biblical Literature	http://www.bookreviews.org/	yes	yes	no	yes	yes	no	yes	1996-
Scandanavian J. of the Old Testament	http://www.scup.no/journals/en/toc/j-124/j-124.html	no	yes	no	no	no	no	no	1997-
Scholia Reviews	http://www.und.ac.za/und/classics/reviews.html	no	yes	no	yes	no	no	no	1992-
Science of Religion Abstracts	http://www.uni-marburg.de/fb03/religionswissenschaft/journal/sor/	no	no	some	no	no	no	no	1992-
Scottish Bulletin of Evangelical Theol.	http://www.rutherfordhouse.org.uk/sbetback.htm	v.14-15	yes	no	no	no	yes	no	v.14-15
Semper Reformanda	http://members.aol.com/SemperRef/	yes	yes	no	no	no	no	no	1999-
Sojourners	http://www.sojourners.com/	back iss.	yes	no	no	no	yes	no	1994-
Soundings: An Interdisciplinary J	http://svhe.pdx.edu/page6.html	no	yes	no	no	no	yes	yes	1997-
Southwestern J. of Theology	http://www.swbts.edu/journal/	no	yes	no	no	no	yes	yes	1961-
Stromata	http://www.calvin.edu/seminary/pubs/stromata/	yes	yes	no	no	no	no	no	v.40
Studia Theologica	http://www.scup.no/journals/en/toc/j-134/j-134.html	no	yes	no	no	no	yes	yes	1993-
TC: A J. of Bib. Textual Criticism	http://rosetta.atla-certr.org/TC/TC.html	yes	yes	yes	yes	no	no	yes	1996-
Textual Reasoning	http://www.bu.edu/mzank/Textual_Reasoning/	yes	yes	no	no	no	no	no	1991-
Theological Gathering	http://private.fuller.edu/~talarm/	yes	no	no	no	no	no	no	current
Wesleyan Theological Journal	http://wesley.nnc.edu/theojrnl/	1966-93	yes	no	no	no	yes	yes	1966-
Westminster Theological Journal	http://wts.edu/publications/wtj/wtjcontents.html	no	yes	no	no	no	yes	yes	1995
Women in Judaism	http://www.utoronto.ca/wjudaism/journal/index.html	yes	yes	yes	no	no	no	no	1997-
Zygon	http://www.blackwellpublishers.co.uk/asp/journal.asp?ref=0591-2385	no	yes	yes	yes	no	yes	yes	1997-

Theological Distance Education:
A Librarian's Perspective

Dave Harmeyer

SUMMARY. Theological institutions accredited by the Association of Theological Schools with distance education courses or programs continue to increase. Theological librarians, although often overlooked, play a significant role in their use of technology to meet the needs of distance students with the support of national library guidelines and accreditation standards. The current state of support to seminary distance programs includes traditional interlibrary loans, consortium relationships, proprietary full text journals, and free Internet resources. Distance learning for graduate theological education is here to stay. The continuing efforts of pioneering distance seminary librarians will guarantee quality, passionate service to students of tomorrow. *[Article copies available for a fee from The Haworth Document Delivery Service: 1-800-342-9678. E-mail address: <getinfo@haworthpressinc.com> Website: <http://www.HaworthPress.com> © 2001 by The Haworth Press, Inc. All rights reserved.]*

KEYWORDS. Theological distance education, library services, student learner

---

Dave Harmeyer, MA (Theological Studies), MA (Pastoral Studies), MLS, is Chair of the Marshburn Memorial Library, Assistant Professor, Liaison for Electronic Resources to the Library's Collection Development Team, Library Liaison to the Department of Biology and Chemistry, and Chair of the Program Review Committee of the Graduate Studies Council, Azusa Pacific University.

Address correspondence to: Dave Harmeyer, Marshburn Memorial Library, Azusa Pacific University, 901 East Alosta Avenue, Azusa, CA 91702 (E-mail: dharmey@apu.edu).

The author would like to acknowledge the generous contributions of the following individuals not already mentioned in the article: Kitty Amos, Paul Gray, Sheli Harmeyer, Liz Leahy, Alan Padgett, Mark Stover and Roger White.

[Haworth co-indexing entry note]: "Theological Distance Education: A Librarian's Perspective." Harmeyer, Dave. Co-published simultaneously in *Journal of Religious & Theological Information* (The Haworth Information Press, an imprint of The Haworth Press, Inc.) Vol. 3, No. 3/4, 2001, pp. 69-86; and: *Theological Librarians and the Internet: Implications for Practice* (ed: Mark Stover) The Haworth Information Press, an imprint of The Haworth Press, Inc., 2001, pp. 69-86. Single or multiple copies of this article are available for a fee from The Haworth Document Delivery Service [1-800-342-9678, 9:00 a.m. - 5:00 p.m. (EST). E-mail address: getinfo@haworthpressinc.com].

BACKGROUND

Providing quality theological education at a distance has been a passion of mine for a number of years. Beginning in 1981-1985 and then 1989-1997, I was a member of the library staff at the International School of Theology, a small but entrepreneurial seminary with a global focus, accredited by the Association of Theological Schools and located, at that time, in San Bernardino, California. After being appointed Library Director in the mid 1990s, I was privileged to design and direct the school's first Web site as well as experiment with a prototype, full text online theological library (*www.leaderu.com/cyber/index.html*). I gained a vision for what technology could do for distance library services.

In May of 1995, the Southern California Area Theological Librarians Association coordinated a three-member panel seminar entitled "Theological Distance Education: Its Promises and Problems for Library Services." The members represented three categories of people involved in distance learning in southern California: an Intercultural Studies Ph.D. student focusing on distance education at Fuller Theological Seminary, an Associate Dean teaching distance courses (also from Fuller) and the Director of Off-Campus Library Services at the University of La Verne. The issues discussed revolved around current practices of distance education/learning technologies, the techniques used to deliver extended library services, the "Association of College and Research Libraries Guidelines for Extended Campus Library Services" (1990), and the opinions of regional and national accreditation bodies as they related to distance education.

This article will attempt to update and expand beyond the May 1995 seminar and provide an historical plumb line on the state of library services to theological distance education/learning patrons at Association of Theological School (ATS) institutions. Although greatly influencing innovations in distance theological education, non-ATS accredited non-residential institutions like Trinity Theological Seminary (*http://www.trinitysem.edu/*) based in Newburgh, Indiana, will not be discussed in this paper.

INTRODUCTION

At the cusp of the twenty-first century, the so-called virtual university, delivered via the World Wide Web, is here to stay. Dees Stallings,

Director of Academic Programs for VCampus Corporation in McLean, Virginia, reports that distance higher education has gained acceptance in and endorsements from critical segments of the American society including accreditation associations, boards of education, government bodies and foundations in an environment where there is "an unprecedented global and permanent demand for distance education and training."[1] This is becoming true even in the distinctive academic discipline of theological education.

Some North American institutions actively marketing ATS accredited distance theological courses or programs include: Bethel Theological Seminary, Covenant Theological Seminary, Fuller Theological Seminary, Gordon-Conwell Theological Seminary, New Orleans Baptist Seminary, Reformed Seminary, Regent University School of Divinity, St. Stephen's College (now in association with St. Andrew's College in Saskatoon, Saskatchewan) and Vancouver School of Theology. Distance (also entitled "distributed"[2]) education is defined here as more than a traditional correspondence or extension model. A correspondence course typically involves a student "corresponding" with a faculty member via the mail as assignments and exams are sent back and forth between learner and educator. An extension course can be many things but, in general, it is a faculty-to-student lecture, which takes place at a location other than (or in addition to) the main campus. Distance education can involve elements of both models but is enhanced with the opportunities of educational technology including student-to-student/student-to-instructor collaboration, electronic resources and the use of the Internet (electronic mail) and the World Wide Web (browsers).[3]

Theological distance education continues to have its skeptics and critics. Among distance learners there is a high attrition rate.[4] Students need to be highly self-motivated. There are questions of how seminary programs can maintain quality levels of both academic rigor and, particularly, spiritual formation. How are moral and ethical dimensions of spiritual training measured and inculcated with any sense of reliability in an online environment? And because of theological education's distinct sensitivity to a person's calling and vocation, a higher percent of older adults are attracted to and enroll in these programs. Merely being outside a learning environment, sometimes for decades, academically (and technologically) challenges these distance students.

Arguably these are legitimate, bothersome challenges. However, the growing technology-savvy end of the theological academe is successfully addressing these and other distance education issues.[5] In contrast to an earlier breed of techno-tinkers, these technology leaders are more seasoned, pragmatic and careful in their approach to this educational paradigm shift. The shift is a radical, centuries old divergence from a face-to-face teaching/learning model to an online electronic synchronous (communicating at the same time but different locations) as well as asynchronous (different time and location) pedagogy. The theological librarian, although often sadly overlooked, is a major stakeholder in the process of providing pragmatic answers to these challenges. And, as will be demonstrated, theological librarians, serving their part as distance educators, play a large role in implementing successful information services to students and faculty in the ever-changing environment of theological distance education.

NATIONAL LIBRARY AND ACCREDITATION STANDARDS

In order to gain a foundational understanding of distance librarianship it is important to review the progress of recently approved national library and accreditation standards for distance education. The Association of College and Research Libraries' (ACRL) Distance Learning Services Executive Board mandated a revision of the 1990 "Guidelines for Extended Campus Library Services" during its final 1996 Midwinter meeting. This action resulted in the new "Guidelines for Distance Learning Library Services" approved by the ACRL Board of Directors at the 1998 Midwinter Meeting and by the American Library Association Standards Committee at the 1998 Annual conference. The Guidelines provide high standards of excellence calling on librarians to:

> . . . meet the needs of all their faculty, students, and academic support staff wherever these individuals are located, whether on a main campus, off campus, in distance education or extended campus programs, or in the absence of a campus at all; in courses taken for credit or non-credit; in continuing education programs; in courses attended in person or by means of electronic transmission; or any other means of distance education.[6]

The Association of Theological Schools (ATS), at the time of this writing, is revising accreditation standards to meet the exponential growth and demand for theological distance education. ATS is addressing the changes of nontraditional forms of communication and transmission. The current (older) *General Institutional Standard 10: Extension Education* most closely addresses the issue of distance education as "external independent study" where it states:

> This type of extension education provides for-credit courses for individuals engaged in external independent study, which includes any form of individualized study where regularly scheduled, in person conversations with faculty or other students are unlikely to occur. Such courses typically employ printed, audio, video, computer, or electronic communication as primary resources for instruction. Because of the formational requirements of most ATS degree programs, and the perceived relationship between intentional community and formation, not more than one-third of the total credits required for completion of an ATS-approved basic degree can be earned by external independent study.[7]

However, with the proposed changes in Standard 10, there is a new sense of purposeful commitment and understanding of what distance education can and is doing to theological programs. The proposed standard no longer refers to distance education as an "external independent study" with its requirement that no more than one-third of a program's credits be completed via distance education. The proposed revised standard will include a much larger section on distance learning including a section on library and information resources and educational qualities. The statement appears to reflect some of the ideas addressed in ACRL's 1996 guidelines by holding up a standard that strongly encourages appropriate library resources be comparable to those provided on campus in sufficient amounts and qualities. The "ACRL Standards for College Libraries 2000 Edition" and the "ACRL Standards for University Libraries" provide additional direction regarding access to collections for master and doctorate degrees.[8] These standards can be seen as wonderful leverage tools with seminary administration during the budgetary process as theological librarians implement new technological strategies to meet the resource needs of distance learners. It could open up a new vista for distance theological education like never seen before.

CURRENT STATE OF THEOLOGICAL LIBRARY SERVICES TO DISTANCE STUDENTS

Even before the change of Standard 10, theological librarians and their constituencies have been remarkably innovative in serving distance-learning patrons. According to Elizabeth Paterson, formerly with Fuller Theological Seminary, "professional theological librarians are often on the cutting edge of educational technologies."[9] In an effort to provide a meaningful slice of what theological librarians are doing currently, the following seven categories attempt to organize the types of services available to meet the needs of distance learners. The categories, although informative, are not intended to be exhaustive. However, these groupings are representative of the kinds of services one could expect, given current technologies and accreditation standards.

Consortium Relationships

Denise Pakala is Technical Services and Research Librarian at Covenant Theological Seminary in Saint Louis, Missouri. One method used by Covenant and other seminaries to meet distance patron needs is formal contractual borrowing agreements with other university or seminary libraries.[10] Parent institutional students are given access to collections relatively close to their location. These surrogate libraries provide varying degrees of service, some based on a courtesy patron card fee or other charges. Covenant library personnel advise their distance learners which libraries to go to including public and community colleges. One practice that is strongly discouraged by distance librarians is the sending of students to libraries without contractual or reciprocal agreements. The offended institution should not tolerate this flagrant misuse of tuition-supported libraries and appropriate steps should be taken to prevent reoccurrence. Public libraries, although a wealth of generous information for community constituencies, should not be expected to meet the stringent scholarly needs of seminary students. General, popular religious works are usually available in public libraries but not the language tools, theological sets and pastoral guides generally needed to support graduate theology programs. However, the public library might be a good place to request a few "difficult-to-access" journal articles or books via their interlibrary loan service.

Theological Electronic Resources–Introduction

Jack Lindberg, Executive Vice President of Gordon-Conwell Theological Seminary, was one of 3 members that drafted the proposed new ATS standards. Although he acknowledges that careful, purposeful development of theological book and journal collections will continue, Lindberg advocates an emphasis on access to resources through win-win partnerships.[11] One of the most profound partnerships between libraries and resource vendors at the end of the twentieth century has been the access and delivery of electronic records. Theological information, although one of the last academic disciplines to move to the electronic medium, is nevertheless a booming enterprise.

During this migratory period from ink and paper to digital full text via the Web, theological electronic resources will be at different levels of completeness and price. Some theological resources are full text records while others are citations with brief subject headings. Prices range from too costly except for consortium rates to free to anyone accessing the Internet without decreasing reliability. The following discussion represents some of the theological digital players and, again, is not intended to be exhaustive.

Theological Electronic Resources–Fee Oriented Databases

Today, few seminary programs can succeed without electronic products made available from the American Theological Library Association (ATLA) (*http://www.atla.com/*). ATLA's scholarly topical coverage as well as historical depth is unmatched. Most of its database records are in citation/subject heading format with a few providing brief contents but no full text (presently). The *ATLA Religion Database* has one-million-plus records, dates from 1949 to the present (with some records back to 1818) and contains 1,460 titles with 600 journals currently being indexed. The database can be purchased as a stand-alone or as a networked CD-ROM, uses USMARC coding (compatible with most library automation systems) and, in recent years, is available via the Web from such vendors as: OCLC (Online

Computer Library Center, Inc.) (*http://www.oclc.org/*) with its added values including local library holdings information and some full text titles; SilverPlatter (*http://www.silverplatter.com/*), EBSCO Publishing (*http://www.epnet.com/*) and Ovid (*http://www.ovid.com/*).

With a look to the future, ATLA is currently working on a full text project called Atlas. Jimmy Adair oversees the ambitious digitization (GIF images) of approximately 50 religion titles dating back 50 years (from the mid-1940s to the present). By January 2001, these titles will be linked from the ATLA Religion Database and searchable by embedded metadata. By 2002, Adair projects that most records will be fully encoded XML files, meaning the entire full text of each record will be searchable. Other features will include Scripture tags (click on any Scripture and the passage will appear in English as well as Greek and Hebrew) and links from cited works will bring up full text items.[12]

One proprietary database currently containing full text religion journals as a separate category is ProQuest Religion Database (Bell & Howell Information and Learning formally UMI) (*http://www.proquest. com*). Although several of these full text titles have been available from Bell & Howell's ProQuest Direct database in past years, the religion database, introduced in late 1999/early 2000, has over 90 full text titles including: *Christian Century, Journal of Biblical Literature, Journal of Woman and Religion, Old Testament Abstracts, Sojourners and Trinity Journal*. Some titles go back to 1992 but the majority of runs lack historical depth, covering only a few years.

Another vendor that provides a good number of abstract and some full text theological journal titles is EBSCOhost (*http://www.epnet.com/*) through two products: Academic Search Elite and EBSCOhost Online. EBSCOhost Online, a relatively new creation, links to full text records for a limited number of paper journals that one's institution subscribes to through EBSCO's subscription service.

UnCover (*http://uncWeb.carl.org/*) out of Denver, Colorado, has for many years been (and continues to be) a standard free citation database with over 18,000 journal titles with coverage back to 1988. UnCover is one distance-learner source recommended by John Dickason, Library Director at Fuller Theological Seminary, because of its free accessibility and full text document delivery service (mostly fax and some "desktop image delivery" direct to one's computer) at reasonable per-article prices. Dickason also suggests distance students use Northern Light (*http://www.northernlight.com/*) because of its free search engine, special collection emphasis (20 million documents) and low cost document delivery service ($1.00 to $4.00) for full text journal articles.[13]

Another kind of proprietary vendor that is just beginning to serve the distance learner market is full text digital "book" libraries that do contain a few religious titles. Some electronic libraries just building their collections include: netLibrary (*http://www.netLibrary.com/*)–a repository of free public-domain and for-fee proprietary e-books–and Booklocker.com (*http://www.booklocker.com/browse.html*) which has a limited number of religion e-books under their "Spiritual" category.

Among the more scholarly ancient full text electronic services and products that have theological implications are Thesaurus Linguae Graecae and the Perseus Project. Thesaurus Linguae Graecae (or TLG) (*http://www.tlg.uci.edu/*) was founded as a research center at the University of California, Irvine in 1972 with the goal of digitizing the entire corpus of Greek literature from Homer (8th century) to the present era. To date the center has digitized all ancient texts from Homer to 600 A.D. as well as a large number of texts from A.D. 600 and the fall of Byzantium in A.D. 1453. TLG text materials are available in CD ROM format with the newest release containing 76 million words of text (6,625 works from 1,823 authors). Software to read the CD must be ordered separately from secondary vendors listed on the TLG Web site.

The Perseus Project (*http://www.perseus.tufts.edu/*) is a remarkable free site that contains a variety of digital resources designed to help users study the textual and visual images of the Archaic and Classical Greek (and other) worlds. Some of the materials include: Renaissance records, Roman items, Greek lexicography, interactive period maps, sculptures, coins, buildings, 420+ works from 31 authors in Greek and English (including Aristotle, Plato, Plutarch, Josephus, the Greek New Testament, commentaries and Latin authors), Liddel-Scott-Jones Greek-English Lexicon, the Lewis and Short Latin dictionary and much more. The English to Greek/Latin word search provides dictionary entry searches, word frequencies, morphological analysis and a synonym tool for Greek and Latin.

Two additional full text journal projects that have relevance to theological distance education are JSTOR and Project Muse. An acronym for "journal storage," the relatively new (mid-1990s) JSTOR database (*http://www.jstor.org*) should be mentioned because of its remarkable Web-based, full-text runs from first issues (several in the 19th century) and also because it appears to be a pace-setter in the areas of fair pricing structure, commitment to long-term archiving and customer relations (they listen to their user base). JSTOR has an agreement with publishers called a "moving wall" which is a fixed period of time (2-5 years) that defines the gap between JSTOR's most recent issue and the most recent published issue. By not supplying the most recent 2-5 years of issues, JSTOR is a good example of a digital partnership. They focus on their own successful distinctive allowing other vendors to carry on with their strengths without the threat of lost revenues. Some of JSTOR's titles that might have relevance to religious studies include those under Anthropology: *Annual Review of Anthropology* (1972-1994), *Current Anthropology* (1959-1994), History: *American Historical Review* (1895-1994), *William and Mary Quarterly* (1892-1994) and Philosophy: *Ethics* (1890-1994), *Philosophical Review* (1892-1996).

Project MUSE (*http://muse.jhu.edu*) provides 110 plus titles in the humanities and social sciences and is seen as a pioneer in online scholarly publishing. Beginning in 1995 by Johns Hopkins University Press, Project MUSE now collaborates with nine other university presses that have more than doubled the number of full text journals. Project MUSE has also partnered with several other full text vendors including EBSCO Online, OCLC FirstSearch Electronic Collections Online, and SilverPlatter SilverLinker. However, institutions must still maintain a separate Project MUSE subscription to access the full text. Some titles that are relevant to theological studies include *American Jewish History, Buddhist-Christian Studies* and *Kennedy Institute of Ethics Journal*.

One final area of fee-based theological electronic resources is CD-ROMs. Networked or stand-alone CD-ROM products can have limited benefit to distance education applications. In truly distance programs, CDs are not an ideal delivery medium unless the distance learner has access to networked products geographically near them. Or, distance students and faculty can purchase CD-ROMs individually with high prices being a limiting factor. The suggested answer is that eventually migration of most theological CD products to a Web-based medium should take place. Then, distance students can take advantage of these very powerful products through the parent institution where consortium prices and economies of scale can provide both fair price and a revenue stream for product improvement. Examples of CD-ROM based software available for seminary education include: (1) biblical language and theological studies tools like Logos Research Systems *Scholar's Library* (*http://www.logos.com/*), *Bible Works* for Windows (*http://www.bibleworks.com/*), *Bible Windows* (*http://www.silvermnt.com/bwinfo.htm*), *Anchor Bible Dictionary* and *Word Biblical Commentary* 54 volumes (both from *http://www.logos.com/*), *Soncino Classics Collection* (including the *Talmud, Midrash Rabbah,* and *Zohar* in Hebrew and Aramaic) and the *Encyclopedia of Judaica* (both from *http://www.eisenbrauns.com/*), (2) church history titles like Logos *Early Church Fathers*; and (3) church management software like Parson Technology's *New Membership* and *Bible Illustrator* (both from *http://quickverse.com/*) and *Worship Studio.*

Theological Electronic Resources–Free Oriented Databases

Certainly one of the most active areas of theological and religious electronic resources in the past decade has been the overwhelming amount of free materials accessible on the World Wide Web. The free-for-all nature of the Web has produced a mixture of reliable and questionable quality information, not the least being the field of religious studies. However, today, for the distance theological student, there are many excellent free areas on the Web that have been created by deeply dedicated, self-sacrificing religion scholars. The following is merely an attempt to represent academic theological sources that are available for free online and is not exhaustive.

One of the earliest (1971!) free Internet-based "electronic texts" (Etexts) endeavors that included religious works was Project Gutenberg (*http://promo.net/pg/*) started by its Executive Director Michael Hart at Illinois Benedictine College. Using the lowest common denominator of ASCII-based files and delivering them via FTP (File Transfer Protocol), full text records of major scholarly religious public domain works have been made available including the *Bible,* Milton's *Paradise Lost,* Dante's *Divine Comedy,* works by Reformer Philip Melanchthon (1497-1560), works by G.K. Chesterston and many more. By the end of 2001, the Project Gutenberg Electronic Public Library hopes to finish its 10,000th item (but perhaps more realistically between 3,000 and 4,000).

Harvey Plantinga's (now professor of computer science at Calvin College) Christian Classics Ethereal Library (*http://www.ccel.org/*) is a real labor of love. This digital full text library includes, among hundreds of Christian classics, the complete 38 volumes in English of the Ante-Nicene, Nicene and Post-Nicene Fathers (the most important writings from the first 800 years of the church) and is fully searchable by a search engine. One cannot help but note the passion of this work-in-progress, dedicated to providing free access to some of the world's most profound Christian classics to the masses abroad.

Having many full text theology and religion books for free on the Web, it is no surprise that there are also many scholarly theological journals available, some full text. The "Religious Studies Electronic Journals" site maintained by Saundra Lipton (*http://www.acs.ucalgary. ca/~lipton/journalss.html*) lists over 150 titles in such categories as Bahai, Biblical Studies, Buddhism, Christianity, Hinduism, Islam, Judaism and Philosophy. About a third of the links appear to go to full text records while others go to selected articles or contents only and some sites require subscription before the full text is made available. Another site that links about 200 free electronic religion publications (with varying degrees of quality and completeness) is the Wabash Center Guide to Internet Resources for Teaching and Learning in Theology and Religion (*http://www.wabashcenter.wabash.edu/Internet/ front.htm*). The Guide will be more fully described below.

The Association of Peer-Reviewed Electronic Journals in Religion (*http://purl.org/apejr*) was established in 1998.[14] At the time of this writing, there are six participating journals. All six journals are available only in an electronic format (there are no print editions), are religion oriented, blind peer-reviewed and available for free. APEJR's unique initiative is motivated by the need to confront resistance to electronic-only scholarly journals, to develop better archiving strategies and to recognize the value of electronic publications for tenure and promotion. The six participating journals are *Hugoye: Journal of Syriac Studies, Journal of Buddhist Ethics, Journal of Christian Theological Research, Journal of Hebrew Scriptures, The Journal of Southern Religion, TC: A Journal of Biblical Textual Criticism* and *Women in Judaism: A Multidisciplinary Journal.*

The Wabash Center Guide to Internet Resources for Teaching and Learning in Theology and Religion (*http://www.wabashcenter.wabash. edu/Internet/front.htm*) is, without apology, one of the best gratis sites on the Web which intelligently annotates "about 95% of the high quality academic [Internet] sites in religious studies in English" according to the site's Web developer Charles Bellinger (Ph.D. in Theology, Ethics & Culture, and Public Services Librarian at Regent Carey Library in Vancouver, British Columbia).[15] Bellinger, under the leadership of the director of the Wabash Center for Teaching and Learning in Theology, Raymond Williams, has done a remarkable job as consultant during late 1998 and throughout 1999 "setting up a Website which would provide guidance for faculty and students in theology and religious studies who are seeking to locate [free] Internet resources that have academic value."[16] The mere organization of the Wabash site says something about the current state of Internet sources in religious studies. Each of the 45 subject heading sections (such as World Religions: Islam, History of Christianity: Medieval, Philosophy and Theology: Postmodernism and Practical Theology: Pastoral Counseling) is broken further into six subsections: syllabi, electronic texts, electronic journals, Web sites, bibliographies and listserv discussion groups. Wabash director Williams explained that the underlining philosophy of the site was to counter "disintermediation." He means that most conventional Web search engines seek and find information with no intermediary, no human intelligence, but computer algorithms and markup language. The Wabash site is mediated by the expertise of Bellinger, who acts as a kind of intermediary between faculty and/or students and the Internet through his annotated categories that focus on teaching and learning in theology and religion.[17] This site should be a link on every theological distance education Web site.

Theological Electronic Reserves

One final area of electronic services to distance theological students is electronic reserves. A hot issue in the mid 1990s and pioneered at San Diego State University by Dick Goodram and Don Bosseau, electronic reserves help meet the high demand for materials over a short period of time.[18] Garrett-Evangelical Theological Seminary and Seabury-Western Theological Seminary have a long history of sharing resources with one another and with Northwestern University, all located north of Chicago, Illinois. Dianne Robinson, Circulation Administrator for United Library (which serves as the library for both Garrett and Seabury), collaborated with Northwestern to create United's first electronic reserves in spring 1999 as part of the library's online catalog (NUcatWeb). Robinson proactively reached out to seminary faculty members by asking what materials from previous courses might benefit students on electronic reserves. Robinson supervised the scanning of documents (mostly articles but occasionally whole books broken down by chapters) into PDF files that were linked (via the 856 field) to newly created MARC records and added to the library's NUcatWeb system as part of the electronic reserves section. One faculty member took the process to another level by linking to the electronic reserved items from his course Web page. Robinson usually has a lead-time of 4-5 weeks to process an electronic request. The library secures copyright permissions and a clear "copyright warning" notice is displayed at the beginning of each record. According to Robinson, one of the biggest barriers to the success of electronic reserves is patron equipment requirements; older computers make the process impractical.[19]

Interlibrary Loan and Document Delivery

Interlibrary loan and document delivery are undoubtedly not new services to libraries. But the added effort to deliver items to distance students is somewhat novel. Sandra Oslund, Reference Librarian at Bethel Theological Seminary (with campuses in St. Paul, Minnesota and San Diego, California) explains that the library is ready to mediate interlibrary loan requests (in addition to their traditional seminary students) to the approximate 150 students from thirty-seven states enrolled in the distance "In Ministry" program.[20] As part of the unique program, "In Ministry" students attend on-site campus sessions four weeks per year (two in February and two in August). When they return home, students requesting interlibrary loans via email or by phone identify themselves as enrolled at Bethel Seminary. Filled requests are sent by mail. In the future, there are plans to scan documents and send as email attachments to quicken the process.

Gerald Turnbull, Librarian at Vancouver School of Theology (VST), explains that the library provides interlibrary loan request for all VST students living in Canada including those 600 miles north who are enrolled in VST's Native (American) Ministries Program. The service is free because the national government subsidizes a Library postal rate. Up to four books can be loaned for a six-week period. Requests, including literature searches and document deliveries, are received by phone (via a Canada-wide 800 number) and, increasingly, by email. VST also offers similar provisions as a contracted service to distance students attending St. Steven's College (now amalgamated with St. Andrew's College in Saskatoon, Saskatchewan).[21] St. Steven's, with thirteen Internet courses posted on its Web site, "is one of the pioneers in Internet theological education in Canada."[22]

Helping Build Personal Libraries

Theological students and faculty frequently ask librarians for standard bibliographies and cost effective ways for building personal library collections. For the distance as well as traditional student, the methods for acquiring personal theological libraries have become easier, and, depending on the source, less expensive. Some annotated bibliographies that can be suggested to students as guidelines are listed at the end of this article.[23] With or without the help of a librarian, one can go online and purchase theological books from a variety of sources. There are the discounted vendors like Christian Book Distributors (*http://www.christianbook. com/*)–largely evangelical, strong in Scripture study which also offers an academic catalog–or Dove Booksellerss (*http://www.dovebook.com/*)–sells in the area of biblical studies, ancient history and theology. Used books can be purchased for significant discounts at places like Half.com (*http://www.half.com/*), Advanced Book Exchange (*http://www.abe books.com/*) and Books & Book Collecting (*http://www.trussel.com/ f_books1.htm*). One could also go to the more general retail online booksellers like Amazon.com (*http://www.amazon.com*) or Barnes & Noble (*http://www.barnesandnoble.com*). The Wabash Center (*http://www. wabashcenter.wabash.edu/Internet/front.htm*), described above, also has an extensive list of online religious scholarly bibliographies and booksellers.

FUTURE THEOLOGICAL LIBRARY SERVICES: A PERSONAL GLIMPSE

With the continued expansion of educational technologies, the revisions in accreditation standards at the Association of Theological Schools and a strong market demand, the number of programs and students attending accredited theological distance courses will increase. In the near future what are the possibilities for servicing these distance students? What follows is merely one librarian's idea. My hope is that these thoughts might help the field of theological librarianship "think outside the box" in strategic planning regarding meeting the needs of the next generation of distance users.

Stephen Abram, vice president of product management at Micromedia Limited in Toronto, Ontario with an MLS from the University of Toronto, writes about planning for the next wave of technology convergence as it relates to online distance education and libraries. In short, information will converge with voice, personal real-time interaction, real-time video and sound.[24] One key outcome will be the increased ability to do real-time collaboration. Geographical destinations will become even less defined or even necessary.

The application of Abram's ideas for the theological librarian who is deeply committed to meeting the needs of distance users, institutions, programs and libraries is closer to a 24-7-365 model. For example, with the application of something like NetMeeting (*http://www.microsoft.com/windows/NetMeeting/default.ASP*) or Blackboard.com (*http://www.blackboard.com/*) librarians can serve distance users in real time. SUNY Morrisville College Library (*http://www.morrisville.edu/library/*) for example, uses AOL Instant Messenger (*http://aim.aol.com/*) and calls it "Talk to a Librarian" as a way to assist distance (and traditional) students in a synchronous computer chat environment. Couple this technology with proprietary databases and the possibilities are empowering. Students making online appointments (or contacting librarians during regularly scheduled reference desk hours) can get the same help as traditional students. What the librarian sees and does on their computer screen is duplicated on the distance user's screen anywhere in the world. When this is added to an organized collaboration with seminary librarians from the east to west end of the North American continent, it becomes possible to serve students almost any time of the day or night in any time zone. Much like the managed health care industry, which has an 800 number that members use to call a 24-hours-a-day nurse, so theological distance students would contact a library help desk through a clearinghouse Web site. Here students can secure reference information or conduct a "live" online inquiry chat with a seminary librarian on theological topics from some of the best electronic religion resources available.

To end on a more sober, pragmatic note, the seminary librarian serving distance students will need to be more proactive in the future. Over the next few years, larger numbers of class syllabi will be added to distance faculty Web pages. These Web syllabi will link to electronic reserves, proprietary electronic full text resources and free religion Web sites, unintentionally by-passing the expertise of the seminary librarian. Following and understanding the path of educational technology can reverse such a trend. Librarians will need to maintain involvement in the collaborative 24-7-365 model with faculty, students and administrators. There will continue to be many opportunities to apply the expertise of seminary librarianship through the medium of tomorrow's educational technology. Plan to be a part of that revolution.

NOTES

1. Dees Stallings, "The Virtual University: Legitimized at Century's End: Future Uncertain for the New Millennium," *Journal of Academic Librarianship* 26 (January 2000): 3.

2. Jennifer Ricketts, "Multimedia: Asynchronous Distributed Education" A Review and Case Study," *Social Science Computer Review* 18 (1 May 2000): 132-146.

3. For a more complete definition of theological distance education see the Autumn 1999 issue of *Theological Education* and for a comparison see Elizabeth Patterson, "The Questions of Distance Education," *Theological Education* 33 (Autumn 1996): 60-74.

4. Sarah Carr, "As Distance Education Comes of Age, the Challenge is Keeping the Students," *Chronicle of Higher Education* (11 February 2000), A39.

5. For a review of one successful distance seminary program see Melinda R. Heppe's article on Bethel Theological Seminary's five-year old In Ministry M.Div. program in "On line Campus: How Real is the Virtual Community?" *In Trust* 11 (Autumn 99). [Online]. Available: *http://www.intrust.org/magazine/autumn99/autumn99_online.htm.* Also, Regents College (a distance-based school in Albany, New York) teamed up with librarians from John Hopkins University to create the Regents College Virtual Library when it was determined that students needed more than Internet courses to succeed. "Online," *Chronicle of Higher Education,* 12 May 2000, A45.

6. Association of College and Research Libraries, "Guidelines for Distance Learning Library Services" (1998). [Online]. Available: *http://www.ala.org/acrl/guides/distlrng.html.* [2000, April 12].

7. Association of Theological Schools, "General Institutional Standard 10: Extension Education," *Bulletin 43, Part 1, 1998 . . . Standards of Accreditation, Policy Statements,* [Online]. Available: *http://www.ats.edu/accredit/ac10.htm.* [2000, May 29].

8. Association of College and Research Libraries Standards for College Libraries 2000 Edition [Online]. Available: *http://www.ala.org/acrl/guides/college.html*; Standards for University Libraries [Online]. Available: *http://www.ala.org/acrl/guides/univer.html.*

9. Elizabeth Patterson, "The Questions of Distance Education," *Theological Education* 33 (Autumn 1996): 70.

10. Denise Pakala, Interview, 18 April 2000.

11. Jack Lindberg, Interview, 17 April 2000.

12. Jimmy Adair, Interview, 25 May 2000.

13. John Dickason, Interview, 18 May 2000.

14. Note that this is the only URL in this article that utilizes the PURL (Persistent Uniform Resource Locator) protocol. URLs change but PURLs do not. For more information see *http://purl.org/*.

15. Charles Bellinger, "Wabash Center: Guide Home: Religious Studies and the Internet: A 1999 Status Report," 10 April 2000 [Online]. Available: *http://www.library. regentcollege.Ubc.ca/Wabas/report.htm*. [25 April 2000].

16. Ibid.

17. Raymond Williams, Interview, 3 May 2000.

18. Brett Butler, "Electronic Course Reserves and Digital Libraries: Progenitor and Prognosis," *Journal of Academic Librarianship* 22 (March 1996): 124-7.

19. Dianne Robinson, Interview, 18 May 2000.

20. Sandra Oslund, Interview, 13 April 2000.

21. Gerald Turnbull, Email correspondence, 25 April 2000.

22. Bob Bettson, "Limitless Horizons? Education via Internet Extends Opportunities for Learning," *In Trust* 11 (Autumn 1999): 8.

23. Examples of annotated bibliographies that can be helpful for building personal religious and theological libraries (in no particular order) include: William M. Johnston, *Recent Reference Books in Religion: A Guide for Students, Scholars, Researchers, Buyers & Readers* (Chicago: Fitzroy Dearborn Publishers, Incorporated, 1998); D. A. Carson, *New Testament Commentary Survey,* 4th ed. (Grand Rapids, MI: Baker Book, 1993); Eugene H. Peterson, *Take and Read: Spiritual Reading: An Annotated List* (Grand Rapids: Eerdmans, 1996); James E. Bradley and Richard A. Muller, *Church History: An Introduction to Research, Reference Works, and Methods* (Grand Rapids: Eerdmans, 1995); Frederick W. Danker, *Multipurpose Tools for Bible Study* (Minneapolis: Augsburg Fortress Press, 1993); Cyril J. Barber, *The Minister's Library* (Chicago: Moody Press, 1997); Don Thorsen, *Theological Resources for Ministry: A Bibliography of Works in Theological Studies* (Nappanee, IN: Evangel Publishing House, 1996); Robert J. Kepple and John J. Muether, *Reference Works for Theological Research: An Annotated Selective Bibliographical Guide,* 3rd ed. (Lanham: University Press of America, 1992).

24. Stephen Abram, "Planning for the Next Wave of Convergence." *Computers in Libraries* 20 (April 2000): [Online]. Available: [EBSCOhost] [13 April 2000].

The Creation
of the Wabash Center Internet Guide

Charles K. Bellinger

SUMMARY. This article describes the process through which the Wabash Center Guide to Internet resources in religion was conceived and developed. The resulting structure of the Guide is described, and comments are made concerning possible ways in which the Internet can contribute to the learning process in theology and religious studies. A vision for the future of this Guide or other similar efforts is also outlined. *[Article copies available for a fee from The Haworth Document Delivery Service: 1-800-342-9678. E-mail address: <getinfo@haworthpressinc.com> Website: <http://www.HaworthPress.com> © 2001 by The Haworth Press, Inc. All rights reserved.]*

KEYWORDS. Internet, guide, religion, theology, teaching

A SUMMARY OF MY ACTIVITIES

In September 1998 I began working for the Wabash Center for Teaching and Learning in Theology and Religion as a consultant. I was given the task of setting up a website which would provide guidance for faculty and students in theology and religious studies who are

Charles K. Bellinger, MA, MSLS, PhD, is Theological Librarian, Brite Divinity School, Texas Christian University, Fort Worth, TX 76129 (E-mail: c.bellinger@tcu.edu).

[Haworth co-indexing entry note]: "The Creation of the Wabash Center Internet Guide." Bellinger, Charles K. Co-published simultaneously in *Journal of Religious & Theological Information* (The Haworth Information Press, an imprint of The Haworth Press, Inc.) Vol. 3, No. 3/4, 2001, pp. 87-96; and: *Theological Librarians and the Internet: Implications for Practice* (ed: Mark Stover) The Haworth Information Press, an imprint of The Haworth Press, Inc., 2001, pp. 87-96. Single or multiple copies of this article are available for a fee from The Haworth Document Delivery Service [1-800-342-9678, 9:00 a.m. - 5:00 p.m. (EST). E-mail address: getinfo@haworthpressinc.com].

seeking to locate Internet resources that have academic value. My work was framed as a sixth month pilot project to determine the current state of the resources available on the Internet in religious studies, and to consider how those resources could be incorporated into teaching situations.

The first question which I faced concerned the overall shape of my efforts during the six month period. Three basic possibilities presented themselves. (1) I could produce cataloging records for the websites I had selected similar to those traditionally produced for books; (2) I could attempt to create records in conformity with Dublin Core standards for Internet metadata; (3) I could create an organized and annotated collection of links to the selected resources. In consultation with the director of the Wabash Center, Raymond Williams, I decided that the third option was the most feasible one for directing my efforts. The first option would be advisable for a full-time permanent cataloging librarian who would be able to incorporate the results of his or her efforts directly into an institution's library database. Since I am not a cataloging librarian, and was not in a position to incorporate the results of my efforts into a library database, this was clearly not a viable option for my efforts. Furthermore, certain key members of the American Theological Library Association had been meeting during the previous year to formulate a plan for cataloging electronic resources. I was aware of these plans, which made it clear that my time would be more effectively spent working in another direction. Concerning the second option, the Dublin Core standards for metadata are intended to provide a means for the creators of websites to "catalogue" their own materials to make the use of Internet search engines more efficient. These standards are not intended, however, to provide a way for an external visitor to a site to catalogue it. I have incorporated Dublin Core metadata into the guide that I created, but this avenue of resource description was not a viable option for my efforts. The third option clearly emerged as superior to the others because it gave me a high degree of flexibility in being able to adapt my work to suit the goals for which I was aiming. My principal goal was to create a guide which would allow users to avoid the often time consuming and inefficient process of locating resources through an Internet search engine. In my own use of the Internet, I have found that the most efficient way of finding resources is to use a subject guide which has been created and maintained by a knowledgeable human being. Others I have spoken with have echoed this observation. Creating a set of annotated links has the additional benefit of enabling the results of my efforts to be made immediately available to anyone in the world who has Internet access, rather than only being available to those connected with a particular institution.

The next question that I faced concerned the overall structure of the site that I would be creating. What subject area pages should I create, and how should each page be organized? The answers to these questions evolved gradually over a period of months, rather than appearing at the outset. (This corresponds with the literature concerning web-page design, which speaks of many iterations of a site leading to gradual refinements.) In terms of subject areas, I used the program areas of the American Academy of Religion annual conference, combined with my own knowledge of the courses which are being offered in religious studies departments and seminaries, to set up a basic framework. This framework was filled out as I proceeded to investigate the Internet to discover what has been made available there. In other words, the existence of a substantial body of material on the Internet relating to a certain subject sometimes led to the creation of a page for that subject, even though I was not aware at the outset of that body of material. Thus, the shape of this guide mirrors to a large degree the shape of that portion of the Internet which relates to religious studies materials. In this sense, this guide is different from a guide, which might be created at a particular institution to support the particular courses that are offered at that institution.

The organization of each particular page also evolved gradually. Since I was given the task of setting up a guide to assist in the incorporation of Internet materials into teaching, I decided to segregate resources according to their type or genre. This would enable a professor to find relevant resources which relate to the various aspects of a course: syllabi (for overall course organization), electronic texts (for primary reading materials), electronic journals (for secondary reading materials), websites (for other supplementary and introductory materials), bibliographies, and listserv discussion groups (for possible dialogue with others who are studying a particular subject). To this list the category of liturgical resources was added when appropriate. This basic structure proved to be valuable in establishing a large number of "cubby holes" in which to place resources as I came across them. I have allowed this structure to be flexible rather than rigid, as circumstances warrant. For instance, the page on the visual arts provides links to digital images in the subsection that corresponds to electronic texts on most of the other pages.

My task was to locate Internet resources that would be of use to the academic community. This led me to emphasize selectivity over comprehensiveness. I decided to add an "NB" to the sites which appeared to me to have the highest quality, rather than developing a more elaborate "5 star" rating system. The simpler approach struck me as being more feasible because it is impossible for me to envision how valuable a given site might be or not be to all of the different persons who could conceivably visit it. I decided that the "NB" symbol would be sufficient to indicate that a particular site should be among the first that a person visits to determine if the resources available there are appropriate for their needs. Approximately half way through the sixth month period of employment, I was able to articulate the main criteria that were guiding my efforts in selection. This was also a gradual process of discernment, leading to this list of criteria for website selection: useful, significant content; institutional origin; active maintenance; free access; good webpage design; correct spelling and grammar; English language. This last point is not an absolute, of course, since many resources linked to in the guide provide texts in languages other than English. This point also serves to indicate that the vast majority of the sites linked to have their origin in North America, so I have made no special effort to organize materials in languages other than English.

After approximately four months of full-time (40 hours per week) site construction, I began to feel that I had become aware of about 95% of the high quality academic sites in religious studies in English. I received this impression when visits to pre-existing guides to religious resources on the Internet led almost exclusively to sites I was already aware of. It became harder and harder for me to locate sites in that other 5% which I speculated were probably in existence. This result is interesting because it contradicts the mistaken notion at work in some people's thinking that the Internet is already a limitless source of information, or that "the entirety of the Library of Congress" is on the Internet, or something to that effect. In reality, even though the Internet contains many millions of documents, images, homepages, etc., the amount of high quality material in a particular academic field is clearly finite. It is a challenge to remain on top of this situation, from the perspective of the librarian who is organizing material for the academic community, but it is not an impossible challenge. The dynamic, growing, changing, transient nature of the Internet adds to the challenge, but this also is only a minor obstacle. I will speak further on the topic of "staying on top" of religious studies resources on the Internet in the last section, "A Vision for the Future of this Guide or Similar Efforts."

A GENERAL DESCRIPTION OF THE WABASH CENTER INTERNET GUIDE

Various types of guides to Internet resources in religion were already in existence when I began this project. The simplest and least useful kind of guide is just a list of links to religion related sites, without any annotations or subject organization. The next step up from there is to add subject divisions. The number of such divisions might range from two (Christianity and World Religions), up to something like one hundred. Generally speaking, the larger the number, the easier it is to find what you are looking for. Another important step forward in usefulness is the addition of annotations for the links. Some kind of rating system to indicate the better sites is also helpful. An internal search engine is sometimes valuable. Lastly, making the URL of the link visible rather than invisible provides the user with another piece of information about the site linked to.

The Wabash Center Internet Guide is now one of the largest and most comprehensive guides to religious resources on the Internet. It contains approximately 45 different subject area pages, and more than 20 other pages for material types, reference and teaching resources, etc. The subject heading pages are further divided into six subsections: syllabi, electronic texts, electronic journals, websites, bibliographies, and listserv discussion groups. Multiplying 45 × 6 equals 270, which indicates a very high level of "granularity" in the organization of materials. The total number of links is in the vicinity of 2,500. If all of the pages in the Wabash Center Guide were to be printed out on 8.5″ × 11″ paper, it would add up to about 400 pages. It offers a simple rating system, annotations, and visible URLs. The particular strengths of the Wabash Center Internet Guide are links to syllabi, electronic texts, and free electronic journals in religion.

HOW THE INTERNET CAN BE USED FOR ACADEMIC RESEARCH IN RELIGION

The following list indicates some of the ways materials currently on the Internet can be of assistance to those studying religion.

Syllabi. Professors can consult online syllabi to see how others approach the teaching of a certain subject. The number of syllabi now on the Internet is probably one percent of the total number of syllabi currently given to students in printed form. Nevertheless, the number of syllabi on the Internet is already significant, and it covers most of the basic course areas in religious studies. I am confident that in the future the number of syllabi on the Internet will continue to increase, and many such syllabi will begin to incorporate links to materials which are relevant to the course. The process of converting a word processor file to an HTML file is really quite simple with the right software, which can be obtained at reasonable cost or for free. Further, most institutions of higher education now have websites, so there is no major obstacle to a dramatic expansion in the number of online syllabi.

Electronic texts. Electronic texts can be used to supplement printed reading materials; in some cases, there is enough material on a given subject already available on the Internet that a student wouldn't need to purchase most of the books for a particular course. When I say this, I don't mean to imply that this possibility is preferable to the traditional pattern; I am simply describing the situation. Personally, I would much rather buy a copy of·Augustine's *Confessions* as a book than print it out on 8 1/2 by 11 inch paper and read it in that form; reading it on the computer screen is even less desirable as an option. Nevertheless, the existence of electronic texts opens up new options that are often valuable. The photocopied course packet, for example, is often an expensive, ungainly monstrosity that students are required to purchase. The Internet makes possible the creation of electronic course packets which are much more user friendly from the students' point of view. The scarcity of library resources can also be overcome through electronic reserves. If 30 (or 200) students need to read a chapter in a book of which the library only owns 2 copies, an electronic copy of that chapter can be made, thus avoiding the logjam at the reserve desk. This solution requires, of course, the appropriate technological infrastructure to be in place, in terms of student access to computers. (The copyright issues involved with reserves and course packets are being debated currently.) The existence of texts in electronic form also allows for texts to be searched for particular words or concepts. This feature is very popular in the field of biblical studies. Electronic texts also allow a passage to be clipped and pasted as a quotation in a paper. This avoids the need for retyping and the possibility of typos.

As of early 2000, when these words are being written, the total body of electronic texts in religious studies on the Internet is very substantial. The basic core of canonical scriptures in the major world religions is available online, often in several different English and non-English translations. Also, a very large number of theological and philosophical texts can be found on the Internet. In some cases, sophisticated searching and lexicographical analysis of these scriptures and texts is also available online. A considerable amount of secondary scholarship is present on the Internet, both in terms of introductory materials and more advanced essays. For the primary materials, it needs to be noted that the quality of the texts varies widely. It is often the case that older (out of date?) translations and scholarship have been placed on the Internet simply because they were in the public domain. Thus the Internet is often a strange combination of the latest technology with scholarship from past generations.

Electronic journals. There are a large number of electronic journals currently on the Internet, though the total number of print-only journals is still much larger. The Wabash Center Guide has focused on gathering links to free journals, rather than those that restrict access. I have included links to approximately 200 electronic publications in this guide. The quality of these publications varies widely, however, from well-established academic journals to ephemeral publications of little academic value. In my opinion, electronic journals will eventually completely replace print journals as a form of scholarly communication. This process is likely to take several decades to complete, however, and we are only in its infancy.

Websites. Websites, understood as a separate genre from texts and journals, have some value to academic scholarship in religion, in that they can provide both more "objective" scholarly introductions to a particular religion or topic and also more "subjective" or "committed" introductions by members of that religion. They often provide a combination of texts, images, and perhaps sound files that will be useful to students who are seeking to gain a broad exposure to a particular tradition. As with the other genres, however, they can vary greatly in their quality, depending on the intellectual abilities, aesthetic sensibilities, and institutional resources of the site's creators.

Bibliographies. There are a significant number of bibliographies in religious studies already on the Internet, and that number is likely to rise in the future. Since bibliographies are relatively easy to find in traditional print sources in most libraries today, this aspect of the situation does not involve any dramatic changes. It will simply be easier for researchers to obtain the information they are seeking without having to physically go to the library.

Listserv discussion groups. This is a new form of communication which has been brought into existence by the Internet. The novelty is found in the ease with which people who are geographically separated from each other can communicate very easily and inexpensively. Discussion groups serve as a form of daily informal conversation between members of a particular academic guild, or between people in different fields who are interested in a certain topic. The Wabash Center Guide typically provides a link to the homepage of a listserv, which offers a description of the group and provides instructions for subscribing.

Another variation on the listserv concept is seen in temporary groups formed to facilitate discussion within a particular course. Students can post responses to readings, react to what others have written, pose questions, etc. The professor can monitor all of this activity, make assignments and announcements, bring print or Internet resources to the attention of the class, etc.

THE CURRENT LIMITATIONS OF THE INTERNET

As stated above, one key limitation of the resources available on the Internet is seen in their often dated nature. A professor may want to assign as reading a text which is on the Internet, but be deterred by the fact that the only available translation is from the 19th century. If a more recent translation is available, particularly as an inexpensive paperback, this will most likely be seen as a superior alternative. A more substantial limitation is seen in the nonexistence of many modern texts in electronic form. If one is seeking texts by authors such as Schleiermacher, Kierkegaard, Buber, Barth, and the Niebuhrs, one will find next to nothing on the Internet currently. This situation is likely to change in the future as more texts are made available online, but I don't expect the change to be dramatic or rapid. The works of these authors are for the most part still within the publishing domain, not the public domain, and the need for publishers to earn income militates against the free dispersal of these texts in electronic form. There is also a large body of high quality secondary material that currently exists in printed form but not in electronic form. This situation is likely to continue for the foreseeable future, unless there is a large movement among the authors of such books to make their works available electronically. As noted above, the total number of print-only journals exceeds the number that are available electronically. This situation is likely to change more quickly, however, than the book publishing industry, because the overwhelming strain which expensive serials place on the budgets of academic libraries will break the back of the current system. The many advantages of electronic journals as a form of scholarly communication, along with their relatively inexpensive cost structure, spells doom for the traditional print journal system. It is likely that this breakdown of the traditional system will take the form of the academic community taking complete control of the journal publishing process, removing publishers and information brokers from the situation completely.

A VISION FOR THE FUTURE OF THIS GUIDE
OR SIMILAR EFFORTS

In my opinion, while the total number of high quality Internet resources in the field of religious studies is finite, this entire body of material is too large and too complicated for one person to organize effectively on an ongoing basis. If several different people try to manage this large task separately from each other, their efforts will be redundant as well as being insufficient. It is clear that the most rational plan is for different parts of an Internet guide in religious studies to be delegated to various persons. One person could be responsible for the page on ethics, another for the page on Hinduism, etc. A team of such persons could be recruited from the ranks of professors, advanced graduate students, or librarians with subject area expertise. Each could be paid a small amount, such as three to five thousand dollars per year, to spend a small number of hours per week maintaining and improving their page. This money could either come from a central source that sponsors the project, or from the budgets of the various institutions with which the page maintainers are affiliated. The overall guidance for the project could come from an organization such as the American Theological Library Association or the American Academy of Religion. The resulting guide would constitute the primary resource which students and professors would turn to when they are seeking to locate Internet resources in religion. In my view, the knowledgeable individuals and modest financial resources that are necessary to make this plan a reality are available within the North American academic community. All that is required is coordination of efforts in this direction by individuals in leadership positions in the American Theological Library Association or the American Academy of Religion.

Homiletics and Liturgics on the Internet

Robert R. Howard

SUMMARY. Electronic processing of information is radically transforming the way we do scholarly study, and the sibling fields of homiletics (the study of preaching) and liturgics (the study of worship) provide no exception to this axiom. This article will explore the many ways
in which the Internet has changed (mostly for good) this territory that is
in many ways very important to the training and practice of the clergy.
*[Article copies available for a fee from The Haworth Document Delivery Service:
1-800-342-9678. E-mail address: <getinfo@haworthpressinc.com> Website:
<http://www.HaworthPress.com> © 2001 by The Haworth Press, Inc. All rights
reserved.]*

KEYWORDS. Homiletics, liturgy, Internet

HOMILETICS AND THE WEB

First of all, let's dispense with the "preacher-helps" sorts of Web
sites, more of which are spilling forth even as you read these words.
Amid the cacophony, there are sites which are fine and helpful, and
then there are the others. Many others. One can download pre-cooked,
full-manuscript sermons, allied with the Lectionary or not. The
preacher may then just print them on *his own printer,* to give that

---

Robert R. Howard is Bibliographer in Homiletics and Liturgics, Vanderbilt Divinity Library, Vanderbilt Divinity School, 2201 West End Avenue, Nashville, TN
37235 (E-mail: Howard@library.vanderbilt.edu).

[Haworth co-indexing entry note]: "Homiletics and Liturgics on the Internet." Howard, Robert R.
Co-published simultaneously in *Journal of Religious & Theological Information* (The Haworth Information
Press, an imprint of The Haworth Press, Inc.) Vol. 3, No. 3/4, 2001, pp. 97-104; and: *Theological Librarians
and the Internet: Implications for Practice* (ed: Mark Stover) The Haworth Information Press, an imprint of
The Haworth Press, Inc., 2001, pp. 97-104. Single or multiple copies of this article are available for a fee
from The Haworth Document Delivery Service [1-800-342-9678, 9:00 a.m. - 5:00 p.m. (EST). E-mail
address: getinfo@haworthpressinc.com].

authentic feel. Needless to say, we shan't dally long here. The percep-
tive reader will notice that I have provided no Web addresses–and for
good reason.

More helpful are those "mega-sites" which contain categorized
collections of links, such as Richard Fairchild's "Sermon & Sermon-
Lectionary Resources" site (URL: <http://www.rockies.net/~spirit/
sermon.html>). Included in this site are links to full sermons, lectionary
helps (explanation and exegesis of assigned passages), online Bibles
(searchable in any number of ways), prayers, prayer books, children's
sermons, liturgical material, hymns, and that all-time favorite, "il-
lustrations-you-can-use!" In addition, buttons link the visitor to sea-
sonal and special/occasional resources. All in all, this is a comprehensive and generally helpful site. Other similarly helpful Web sites
include the "Desperate Preacher's Site" (URL: <http://desperatepreacher.
com/>–do they know their audience or what?!?), "Deacon Sil's Homiletic Resources Web site" (URL: <http://www.deaconsil.com/index.
html#resources>) and John Mark Ockerbloom's "Catholic Homily and
Preaching Material" site (URL: <http://www.cs.cmu.edu/People/spok/
catholic/homily.html>–maintained but no longer updated). Lectionary
preachers may want to explore these sites devoted to thoughtful commentary upon the assigned readings: Chris Haslam's "Commentaries on the
Revised Common Lectionary" (URL: <http://www.montreal.
anglican.org/comment/>), Jenee Woodard's "The Text This Week"
(URL: <http://www.textweek.com/>), and Bill Loader's "Lectionary
Resources" (URL: <http://wwwstaff.murdoch.edu.au/~loader/lectionary
index.html>). The Revised Common Lectionary readings themselves
(plus beautiful images) can be found at <http://divinity.library.vander
bilt.edu/lectionary/>. These Web sites provide practical aids for those
who wish to produce their *own* sermons.

For those interested in scholarly study of the various elements of
preaching, the Internet offers a breathtaking panoply of resources.
First, a few sites provide a categorized collection of links. The Wabash
Center for Teaching and Learning in Theology and Religion offers an
astonishing Webpage assemblage of links to syllabi and teaching resources, electronic texts, electronic journals, Web sites, bibliographies,
and listserv discussion groups, all related to the study of preaching. For
those pursuing historical or theoretical investigation of preaching, this site
is invaluable (URL: <http://www.wabashcenter.wabash.edu/Internet/
preach.htm>). Similarly, Religion Online has gathered a collection of

articles on various aspects of preaching (URL: http://www.religion-online.org/cgi-bin/relsearchd.dll?action=indexbycat&catid=20>). David Jacobsen has inaugurated a Web site focusing on homiletics, including helps for preaching apocalyptic texts, reviews of recent books in the field, social justice and preaching, and links to other sites of interest (URL: <http://www.wlu.ca/~wwwsem/dsj/dsjhome.html>).

On a more general note, the "HUMBUL Gateway" offers an entry into humanities-oriented Web sites and collections of links. The search page URL is: <http://users.ox.ac.uk/~humbul/search.html>. And the Wabash Center offers a page of links to resources in Religion and Theology, helpfully organized by topic and type of material. The URL is: <http://www.wabashcenter.wabash.edu/Internet/front.htm>.

A couple of online bibliographies list recent or significant books and periodicals: the Vanderbilt Divinity Library's Homiletics bibliography (URL: <http://divinity.library.vanderbilt.edu/bibs/homiletics.htm>) and Candler's Pitts Library's list of relevant periodicals (URL: <http://sys1.pitts.emory.edu/preach.html>). The "Religious Studies Web Guide" offers an astounding collection of links to online bibliographies, maintained by Saundra Lipton, treating a vast array of religious topics (URL: <http://www.acs.ucalgary.ca/~lipton/biblio.html>).

There is any number of other sorts of resources on the Web, related to homiletic theory: biblical, theological, historical, psychological, rhetorical, sociological, and hermeneutical Web sites. So-called "gateways" are usually the best places to start, and lest I overwhelm readers or typesetters, I'll restrain myself from piling on the URLs. A handful will suffice:

The "Resource Pages for Biblical Studies" (compiled by Torrey Seland, Volda College, Norway) lives up to its name, comprising translations and texts, electronically-published biblical studies, studies of the Mediterranean social world, and other related texts and studies which would inform the biblical student (Philo, Josephus, etc.). The URL is: <http://www.hivolda.no/asf/kkf/rel-stud.html>.

The "Resources for the Study of Christian Origins" page (maintained by Justin Meggitt, Fellow, College Lecturer and Director of Studies in Theology and Religious Studies at Corpus Christi College) is an astonishingly comprehensive collection of links related to anthropological, archaeological, historical, and theological links related to the first Christian centuries. The URL is: <http://homepages.camnews.net/jjm1000>.

Related to the previous site in many ways is the online, searchable version of the Patrologia Latina. For those interested in delving into original documents related to homiletical roots, here is an invaluable resource. The URL is: <http://pld.chadwyck.com/>.

For more contemporary concerns, a recent arrival called "Belief-net" offers links, articles, and discussion regarding world religions and spirituality, and issues concerning the interactions of religion and society. The URL is: <http://www.beliefnet.com/>.

A rapidly increasing number of print scholarly journals are putting their tables of contents online, and others have arisen which are entirely online. A helpful list with links to the journals can be found at this URL: <http://info.lib.uh.edu/wj/Webjour.html>.

Another fruitful avenue is called search engines–and what an astonishing world they open. For those who may not know, search engines will search one or more databases for instances of whatever word or word combinations are entered, and list the results, whether they be Web pages, bibliographical citations, e-mail discussion-group entries, or links to texts. Thus the earnest student can discover relevant portions of texts, listserv discussion-group exchanges by subject, and articles and essays by keyword, from around the globe. Here is a brief list of some of the more promising search engines I've discovered:

"All-in-One Biblical Resources Search" (maintained by Dr. Mark Goodacre of the University of Birmingham). Searches a host of other Web collections of resources–Biblical and beyond. One can search by biblical book, verse, topic, version, and so on. Also searches E-mail discussion list archives and other sites related to the ancient world. URL is: <http://www.bham.ac.uk/theology/goodacre/multibib.htm>.

"THEOLDI: Documentation of Theological and Interdisciplinary Literature" (School of Theology at University of Innsbruck). Searchable by author, title, subject, etc., displaying European article and essay bibliographical references. URL is: <http://starwww.uibk.ac.at/CGI/forms.cgi>.

For the more philosophically oriented, "Noesis: Philosophical Research Online" searches online Web sites, e-journals, encyclopedias, and other texts, by keyword. URL is: <http://noesis.evansville.edu/bin/index.cgi>.

"What Do You Want to Know Today?" searches a host of databases related to the ancient world, including historical texts, cultural practices, journal articles and essays, modern and ancient languages, and listserv discussions. URL is: <http://www.uky.edu/ArtsSciences/Classics/lexindex.html>.

"TOCS-IN" searches tables of contents of journals (both print and electronic) by keyword. URL is: <http://www.chass.utoronto.ca/cgi-bin/amphoras/tocfind>.

"Tile.net" searches E-mail discussion groups, Usenet newsgroups, and FTP sites by name, topic, or keyword. URL is: <http://tile.net/>. A similar search engine is "Fast FTP Search." URL is: <http://ftpsearch.lycos.com/>.

"The World Lecture Hall" is an incredible resource, containing links to pages created by faculty worldwide who are using the Web to deliver university-level academic courses in a host of fields, and has the added benefit of being searchable. The URL for the search page is: <http://www.utexas.edu/world/lecture/>. The American Academy of Religion has undertaken a project to collect syllabi, and assembled a database of said beasts which is searchable by keyword. The URL for the search page is: <http://www.wlu.ca/~wwwaar/home.html>.

University Microfilms International offers a searchable database of dissertations on a wide variety of topics, called "ProQuest Digital Dissertations." This database requires an institutional subscription, but makes available the abstracts, and indeed the full text of recent dissertations. The URL is: <http://wwwlib.umi.com/dissertations/main>. "Academic Dissertation Publishers" offers a growing number of dissertations online. The database is small so far, but searchable. URL is: <http://www.dissertation.com/>.

Finally, of course, one could search the entire Web to uncover other or more recent Web sites, collections of links, texts, etc. An ever-increasing number of search engines exist, of varying sophistication and coverage. One helpful assemblage of several major search engines can be found at this URL: <http://www.vanderbilt.edu/Internet.html>.

These, then, are but a sampling of the search engines, which promise to the homiletician rich fare. The scholar interested in researching topics related to the study of preaching can find information in the fields of theology, rhetoric, sociology, psychology, hermeneutics, biblical studies, church history, feminism, gender studies, preaching in other world religions, and much more.

A few discussion groups exist on the Internet which treat preaching. Most of them directly concern exegesis of upcoming lectionary passages, offer recent sermons for comment, or swap illustrations. The Rev. Dr. Douglas K. Showalter offers a "Forum on the Art of Preaching," which includes discussion of various homiletic issues. The URL is: <http://www.vsg.cape.com/~dougshow/second-site/wwwboard/board5/wwwboard.html>. Another may be found at the "Resource Publications, Inc." site (URL: <http://www.rpinet.com/wwwboard/forum4/>). And a recently inagurated one, "Homiletics," may be found at the URL: <http://www.egroups.com/messages/homiletics>. It must be said, though, that most of the exchanges in these discussions seem oriented more toward practical issues for the working pastor than scholarly consideration of homiletic problematics.

LITURGICS AND THE WEB

The situation is blessedly similar in this field. Although Homiletics and Liturgics are distinct, there is of course much overlap. So the aforementioned search engines and "mega sites" will prove helpful to liturgical inquirers as well. Similar to Homiletics, a vast number of Web sites exist, with varying degrees of quality and depth. I will again omit those sites that are pitched toward those who wish their liturgies handed to them ready-made.

Many of the aforementioned lectionary-oriented sites include liturgical material as well. Other, more specific, sites include "The Catholic Liturgical Library," including information and links related to the Latin liturgical traditions (URL: <http://www.catholicliturgy.com/>); "Lift Up Your Hearts," a "worship and spirituality site of the Evangelical Lutheran Church in Canada" (URL: <http://www.worship.on.ca/>); a collection of links related to Catholic worship (URL: <http://www. cs.cmu.edu/People/spok/catholic/worship.html>); the Catholic Online Community page of links related to liturgical matters (and search engine) (URL: <http://community.catholic.org/liturgy/liturgy.htm>); a collection of links for liturgical studies from Saint John's University's Alcuin and Clemens Libraries (URL: <http://www.csbsju.edu/library/Internet/theoltgy.html#LTGY>); an Order of Saint Benedict collection of links related to Eastern and Western liturgical topics (URL: <http://www.osb.org/liturgy/>); and the Wabash Center Liturgical Resources page, which includes links to other liturgical sites (URL: <http://www.wabashcenter.wabash.edu/Internet/liturgy.htm>).

A couple of immense bibliographies, including a host of topics related to liturgics, may be found at the Notre Dame Center for Pastoral Liturgy (URL: <http://www.nd.edu/~ndcpl/Bibliography/>); and the Spring Hill College site (compiled by William Harmless, S.J.) (URL: <http://camellia.shc.edu/theology/Liturgy.htm>). Another, somewhat less comprehensive, bibliography can be found at the Vanderbilt Divinity Library site (URL: <http://divinity.library.vanderbilt.edu/bibs/liturgics.htm>).

With regard to search engines, those mentioned previously serve the liturgical scholar equally well. And there do exist a number of listserv discussion groups concerning various liturgical issues, approaches, and confessional traditions. A search of the "E-Groups" Web site (URL: <http://www.egroups.com/>), or "The Directory of Scholarly and Professional E-Conferences" (URL: <http://www.n2h2.com/KOVACS/>), will produce a short list of such discussion groups.

CONCLUSIONS

Now that we've thoroughly scrambled the typesetter's equanimity with this tedious list of Weblink addresses, what may we say about the Web and homiletics and liturgics? First, there is no lack of opportunity. Resources, texts (historical and theological), discussions, and other sorts of material and interaction exist, in growing numbers. The problem seems to be one of discernment. At this point, scholarly efforts in these fields are random, with little interaction. Discussions of the finer points of homiletics are rare–though not entirely absent.

Reference librarians, then, may want to discover what *sort* of material the inquirers are seeking, in order best to direct them. Professors would probably want to explore the aforementioned sites (and others), to discover what best suits their particular research interests. Students would best be served by first sitting down and thinking through precisely what sort of information they want, then visiting a promising site or initiating a search. A final insight: with the advent of e-mail, homiletical and liturgical scholars are now easily accessible for conversation. Although this can sometimes become burdensome to the recipient of a flurry of trivialities, most professors welcome cogent inquiries.

At this point, the Internet has not profoundly affected *how* preaching and worship are done, although technological advances will surely not leave them untouched. Even though worship services may be accessed from one's home computer, and sermons enjoyed at one's leisure from the same, the acts seem consigned to face-to-face contact. Incarnation is hard to beat.

Scholarly study of these fields, though, is indeed undergoing a radical shift, as documentary material, both static and moving, becomes available. Further, the growing number of e-journals and the ease of contact provided by e-mail promises speedier discussion of various topics by more participants. Quality of the discussions will continue to be a challenge, but no more so, I suspect, than during the height of pamphleteering.

Of course, ten years from now some of what I've just declared will be proven unsound–but that is the nature of this new electronic beast!

Accessing Digital Images:
Sources for Christian Art on the Internet

Elizabeth Davis Deahl

SUMMARY. This article discusses sources for and issues related to digital Christian art images available on the Internet. An annotated list of relevant Web sites is listed, along with advice on how to locate specific images. Also included in the article are discussions of vocabulary, fact verification, and copyright issues. *[Article copies available for a fee from The Haworth Document Delivery Service: 1-800-342-9678. E-mail address: <getinfo@haworthpressinc.com> Website: <http://www.HaworthPress.com> © 2001 by The Haworth Press, Inc. All rights reserved.]*

KEYWORDS. Digital images, art history, Christian iconography, copyright, Internet

Images are unique sources of information. They can illustrate an idea or a concept, tell a story, or inspire devotion and creativity. Visual information is powerful communication, engendering silent but intimate dialogue between experience and imagination.

For the scholar, pictures of original works of art and photographic images of buildings and other spaces are merely substitutes for the original, but for practical purposes they allow an ease of access to objects that might exist at impossible distances. For artists and art

Elizabeth Davis Deahl, BA, MS, is Monograph Cataloger, Getty Research Institute for the History of Art and the Humanities, 1200 Getty Center Drive, Los Angeles, CA 90049 (E-mail: edeahl@getty.edu).

[Haworth co-indexing entry note]: "Accessing Digital Images: Sources for Christian Art on the Internet." Deahl, Elizabeth Davis. Co-published simultaneously in *Journal of Religious & Theological Information* (The Haworth Information Press, an imprint of The Haworth Press, Inc.) Vol. 3, No. 3/4, 2001, pp. 105-125; and: *Theological Librarians and the Internet: Implications for Practice* (ed: Mark Stover) The Haworth Information Press, an imprint of The Haworth Press, Inc., 2001, pp. 105-125. Single or multiple copies of this article are available for a fee from The Haworth Document Delivery Service [1-800-342-9678, 9:00 a.m. - 5:00 p.m. (EST). E-mail address: getinfo@haworthpressinc.com].

historians, and others who seek access to art in all its forms, these surrogate images serve a vital function. Since the camera became a important tool for documenting and distributing information in the nineteenth century, the process of organizing, indexing, storing, and retrieving images in museums and libraries has been a challenge to our profession. This challenge remains in the digital environment we work in today.

Finding the exact picture you have in mind can be like finding a needle in a haystack if you have to sift through the visually stimulating milieu of the World Wide Web (Dodds 1996). Knowledge of a few basic tools can make it easier to find original artwork as well as masterpieces from all over the world. The goal of this paper is to increase awareness of some of the types of images that can be found on the Internet, and some of the best ways to find them.

WHO NEEDS PICTURES AND WHY

"I need a reproduction of Andrei Rublev's 'Transfiguration.' I know it is in Moscow, but I also need to know exactly which church it is in."

"Can you help me find some religious images I can use to send e-mail Christmas cards?"

"I am an artist commissioned to do a painting of angels. Can you help me find some examples I can use for ideas?"

"Is there any digital clipart available on the Web that I can use in my church Web site?"

"Where can I find a detailed guide to the iconography of the Sistine Chapel ceiling?"

These questions exemplify the range of needs for visual information that librarians may encounter. The Internet can be used to satisfy all these requests, but as in any reference query, it is important to evaluate exactly what the need is and determine which tool is the most effective.

FACT-FINDING/VERIFICATION

Descriptive elements of works of art include: the artist's name and dates; date and proper title of the work; location and/or ownership of the work; provenance and other history; medium, dimensions and other physical characteristics. Many of the Web sites listed in this article provide part, if not all, of this kind of information. If you know the name of the work, the artist's name, or the institution where the work is held, you can use these facts to start your search.

If seeing a reproduction of the work isn't really necessary, or if you are having trouble with search terms, you can refer to one of the Getty Research Institute's controlled vocabularies: the Union List of Artist Names (ULAN) for biographical and bibliographical information on artists and architects; the Getty Thesaurus of Geographic Names (TGN) for information on places, including vernacular or historic names; or the Art and Architecture Thesaurus (AAT) for descriptive terminology. Knowing the proper term to use can often improve the results of your search (Bower 1996; Roberts 2000).

DESIGN INSPIRATION

Web sites that organize pictures thematically can be good places to browse for artists looking for design inspiration. Artists often use photographs of nature for pattern, composition, and color ideas. Architectural details, patterns found on fabric, details of material objects from the past and different cultures, and contemporary photographs of the people and places we see everyday, can all be used for creative stimulus. Browsing digital image collections with a wide variety of sources can be a very valuable method for expanding an artist's visual repertoire.

WEB DESIGN

Churches and other organizations that are designing their own Web pages can find several sources for original digital clipart on the Web. A few are listed below. It is possible to find animations, wallpaper designs, and images with religious themes that are offered at no charge. In addition, there are several commercial picture sources listed below where professional photographs and images of masterpieces of art may be obtained for reasonable fees.

ART APPRECIATION

For the virtual traveler, many of the world's premier museums give extensive visual access to their collections. In addition to information on exhibitions, events and programs, many museum Web sites now have virtual tours of their collections. For the *real* traveler, these sites can be invaluable in preparing for a visit. One can locate a specific museum using any of the major search engines, or use one of the Web guides that cross-index museums and other historic sites by location.

IMAGES FOR PUBLICATION

The researcher or scholar who has a need for a reproduction of a work of art for publication may find several commercial image brokers doing business on the Web. Millions of images are available through these companies, who have streamlined the process for licensing images for commercial use.

ART HISTORICAL EDUCATION AND RESEARCH

Many colleges and universities provide access to their visual collections and other art historical resources via the Internet. Occasionally, access is restricted to affiliated faculty, staff, and students. Some resources, such as the "Index to Christian Art" and the AMICO Library, are available to educational institutions by subscription. The Research Libraries Group (RLG) Museum Resources service is but one other example of current initiatives to "integrate discovery and delivery of visual and descriptive information" for educational purposes.

COPYRIGHT

In the United States, copyright law prevents the unlimited use and distribution of protected material without permission, except as defined under "fair use." How these laws translate into the digital environment is a topic of continuing intense debate. Some fear that the ease with which digital materials can be copied, manipulated, and distributed will lead to uncontrolled loss of rights for the copyright holder.

The release of the "Final Report to the Commissioner on the Conclusion of the Conference on Fair Use" (CONFU), in November 1998, and the related "White Paper Report," "Intellectual Property and the National Information Infrastructure: The Report of the Working Group on Intellectual Property," did little to resolve the issue (Lehman 1995; Lehman 1998). These documents, while not having the force of law, have not had much support from the educational and library communities, who feel that the guidelines remain ambiguous and incomplete (Green 1997; Sundt 1999).

There are several ways that digital artwork can be technologically protected from violation of copyright. Digital watermarking involves embedding an invisible mark of identification on the image that can be used to trace illegal manipulation or distribution. Some institutions control access to their collections using IP address restrictions or by requiring a password. A few Web sites are overlaying a copyright "stamp" directly on the image. And other sites permit unlimited use of small, thumbnail size images with low or poor resolution, and either restrict access to, or require payment for, larger, high quality images.

Under the Berne Convention (the International Convention for the Protection of Literary and Artistic Works), to which the United States became a signatory in 1989, art copyright falls into two categories: copyrighted works and public domain works. Artwork produced by an artist who is alive, or who has been dead less than 70 years, is copyright protected. The artist, or his estate, in most cases retains intellectual rights to the original work. The clear intent of copyright law was that the artist retains the copyright unless he specifically signed it away in a written agreement.

If an artist has been dead for more than seventy years, their work belongs in the public domain. However, a photograph of the work belongs to the photographer or the publisher of the photograph. In addition, although the sale or conveyance of a work of art does not itself constitute a transfer of copyright, museums and other owners of art works, often hold reproduction rights.

Copyrighted artists whose works are used for educational uses are provided for in the Fair Use Provision of the Copyright Act. Educational purposes include teaching, scholarship and research. For any publication, commercial use, or wide distribution that does not fall under the definition of "fair use," copyright permission needs to be obtained from the copyright holder.

Sources for copyright information on the Web can be found in the bibliography.

CONCLUSION

The Internet, with its explosive growth, has become an integral part of our lives. Digital technology has enabled just about anyone to upload an image on the Web. And although computerized access to information has greatly increased the speed and flexibility of most kinds of searching, in our experience we know that the hunt for the needle in the haystack requires not only patience and persistence, but also special knowledge and selective use of relevant tools. The following list of sources is a select group of sites that I feel meet a broad range of visual resources needs. And, as with everything else on the Internet, the numbers of good tools are increasing, as surely as they are also changing.

SOURCES

Classification and Indexing

The Getty Vocabulary Program

http://www.getty.edu/gri/vocabularies/

The Getty Vocabulary Program "builds, maintains, and disseminates vocabulary tools for the visual arts and architecture." The vocabularies produced by the Getty and available on the Web are:

The Art & Architecture Thesaurus (AAT)

http://shiva.pub.getty.edu/aat_browser/

The AAT is a structured vocabulary of over 125,000 terms used to describe art, architecture, decorative arts, material culture, and archival materials from antiquity to the present. The terminology "includes the materials and techniques relating to their construction and conservation (such as deacidification), their physical attributes (such as shape and color), terminology associated with their production and study (such as the roles of persons), vocabulary indicating their style or period, and concepts relating to their history, theory, criticism, and purpose."

The Union List of Artists Names (ULAN)

http://shiva.pub.getty.edu/ulan_browser/

ULAN contains around 220,000 names and other information about artists, from antiquity to the present, and is global in scope. "Linked to each record are names, relationships (including student-teacher relationships), locations (for birth, death, and activity), important dates (such as for birth and death), notes, and sources for the data. Names for any artist can include the vernacular, English, other languages, natural order, inverted order, nicknames, and pseudonyms. Among these names, one is flagged as the preferred name, or 'descriptor.' "

The Getty Thesaurus of Geographic Names (TGN)

http://shiva.pub.getty.edu/tgn_browser/

TGN contains approximately 1,000,000 names and other information about places. It "includes all continents and nations of the modern political world, as well as historical places. It includes physical features and administrative entities, such as cities and nations. The emphasis in TGN is on places important for art and architecture."

COMMERCIAL IMAGE BROKERS/STOCK PHOTOGRAPHY

Art Resource, Inc.

http://www.artres.com/

Art Resource is a large commercial photo archive of fine art, providing access to over 3 million images (photographs, paintings, sculpture, architecture, and the minor arts) by over 10,000 artists. As a stock agency for images mostly for commercial applications (publishing, advertising, television, Web sites, films, etc.), Art Resource represents major European agencies, as well as museums, archives, and individual artists. The Web site provides access (by artist, subject, museum and period) to only a small percentage of the images that are available through their service. This site has some useful information on copyright.

The Bridgeman Art Library

http://www.bridgeman.co.uk/

The Bridgeman Art Library represents over 800 museums, galleries and contemporary artists and is a source for over 100,000 fine art images for reproduction. The site allows browsing by broad topic, medium, nationality, century, artist, and location or searching by keyword, title, and artist. In addition, the user can link to images in the Library from Grove's Dictionary of Art Online. To view an image larger than thumbnail size, or to purchase publication rights, requires online registration (no charge).

CGFA (Carol Gerten's Fine Art)

http://sunsite.auc.dk/cgfa/

This private, non-profit "virtual museum" is supported in part by banner ads and by an online art print and poster store (Barewalls.com). It may be searched by artist's name or nationality, time period, or by keyword on the mirror site search engines. The scanned images may be viewed as thumbnails, and as full screen, but lose resolution at the larger size.

Corbis

http://www.corbis.com/

Corbis has become a leading player in making photographic and fine art images available commercially on the Internet. With over 2.1 million images available online from its collection of over 65 million images, the collection "represents a variety of perspectives, eras, geographical regions, and content categories–news, historical, contemporary, celebrity, and fine art." Corbis has accumulated some of the most significant collections of photographs in the world, including the famous Bettman Archive, and has made collaborations with other image providers as a rights managed service. Product lines include digital pictures, limited edition prints, photographic prints, Ansel Adams prints, e-mail greeting cards, and screensavers. The collection can be searched by keyword, or by broad category from this Web site, or from Alta Vista. Most images are available for downloading with a private use "Consumer Image License" for $3. Professional licensing is also available.

Saskia, Ltd.

http://www.saskia.com/

Saskia, which has been providing slide sets to educational institutions for over 30 years, now does business online. Their catalog may be browsed by artist, title, museum, site, catalog number or slide set number. Available products still include camera original art and architecture slides. Digital images are also now available for educational and research network use by signing a site license agreement; license fees are a reasonable $4 per image for a five-year term. Other license terms are available. Although the Web site does not show the works, Saskia remains an important source for high quality images.

Westock

http://www.weststock.com/

Westock is a commercial stock photography company of mostly contemporary scenes. Fees vary according to file size of the image (higher resolution, larger images cost more) and start at $10 per image for personal/home use. Images can be searched by keyword or browsed by topic.

CONTEMPORARY CHRISTIAN ART

Christianity & the Arts

http://www.christianarts.net/

This is the online edition of *Christianity & the Arts*, a magazine that covers the art scene for fine artists, writers, poets, performance artists, filmmakers, and musicians. The Web site maintains an online art gallery of contemporary Christian art and an artists directory. Artists are encouraged to submit works for consideration. Each work in the gallery is captioned with a physical description and contact information for the artist.

CrossSearch

http://www.crosssearch.com/Art/

The CrossSearch Online Christian Resource Directory, a service of the Gospel Communications Network, maintains (like its name implies) a directory of Christian resources on the Internet, including a list of resources in art. Web sites for individual artists, musicians, and performers can be found, as well as sources for posters, digital clipart, and original paintings, sculpture and crafts.

Crystal Cloud Graphics

http://www.fortunecity.com/roswell/avebury/18/index.html

This gallery of Web based original graphics includes icons and buttons, backgrounds, and animated images on religious, spiritual and esoteric themes. The artist allows free downloading of all of the art, but requests credit be given. Included are theme images for major world religions, religious holidays, angels, and astrology.

Religious Resources on the Net

http://www.aphids.com/relres/

In addition to providing Web design and hosting services for religious organizations, Aphids Communications maintains this searchable database of religious and Christian Web sites, including art and images sites. These include sources for contemporary Christian art, photography, clipart, denominational and organizational graphics, Judeo-Christian iconography as well as graphics tools and utilities.

COPYRIGHT CLEARINGHOUSES

The Artists Rights Society

http://www.arsny.com/

The Artists Rights Society, through reciprocal agreements with more than 20 other artists rights organizations worldwide, represents the intellectual property interests of more than 40,000 living artists and artists' estates. It "provides liaison services to those who wish to secure permission to reproduce art works in printed and electronic media, as well as in products based on an artist's work. Thus, ARS protects members' rights against piracy, illicit use, and copyright infringement by monitoring the use of the works, while providing reputable publishers and producers of commercial goods with a one-step clearing house for the rights and permissions interests of most prominent twentieth century artists." Their Web site is a good source of information on copyright law.

EDUCATIONAL/NON-PROFIT SITES

Art Index for College Teaching (AICT)

http://www.mcad.edu/AICT/index.html

Maintained and distributed by the Minneapolis College of Art & Design, this non-profit, non-commercial site is "dedicated to the principle of free exchange of image resources for and among members of the educational community." Authorization is specifically granted to educational institutions to make derivative copies; slides of images may be purchased as well. Images are grouped by period and shown as thumbnail sketches with brief descriptions. One of the most valuable features of this site is the textbook concordance: thirteen art history reference books (including the popular *Gardner's Art Through the Ages*, both 9th and 10th editions) are indexed by chapter and in text order to the images. Each image has tags providing a full "reverse concordance."

The Artchive

http://www.artchive.com/

The Artchive is a privately maintained site (i.e., a banner ad runs across the top) of approximately 2,000 scanned images from 200 different artists. Mark Harden, its developer, permits free "use up to five or six images from the site for any personal non-profit, educational purpose," and asks to be credited as the source for each image. The collection contains both public domain and copyrighted works of art and the site includes some basic information about copyright protection. The works are indexed by artist and a few period/style terms ("Rococo," "Cave paintings," "Women Artists," etc.). Some biographical data is included, with physical description, and a choice of image size from thumbnail to full screen.

Artcyclopedia

http://www.artcyclopedia.com/index.html

Artcylcopedia is an index of 7,000 different artists from museum sites, image archives and other online resources (700 sources at the time of this writing), with direct links to the image–an incredible 80,000 works in all. Indexed by artist's name, with limited indexing available by artistic movement, nation, timeline and medium. Excellent quality digital reproductions. Easy to use search interface.

Artserve (ANU)

http://rubens.anu.edu.au/index2.html

This cost-recovery service, from the Department of Art History & Visual Studies at the Australian National University, offers access to around 120,000 images, mostly original slides of European and Australian art and architecture. The thumbnail images are available for free, but higher resolution images are not; fees are based on file size in megabytes. The site contains lots of text information; a simple query searches the whole site. Images are grouped in hierarchical categories (e.g., Prints/Survey by artist; Painting/Sculpture/Architecture/Survey by place), with a unique collection of "Landscape, Fauna, Flora" of Australia. It is easy enough to navigate, but you have to know what you are looking for.

Christus Rex

http://www.christusrex.org/

Christus Rex, Inc. is a private, non-profit organization "dedicated to the dissemination of information on works of art preserved in churches, cathedrals and monasteries all over the world." In addition to over 10,000 images, this site contains ecclesiastical information, news, and history related to the Catholic church, and virtual tours of dozens of places. It contains detailed, well-indexed, and well-documented images and information on Jerusalem, the Vatican, and other sites. The site can also be searched by keyword.

Digital Imaging Project

http://www.bluffton.edu/~sullivanm/index/index2.html

This site indexes the personal collection of transparencies taken by the art historian, Mary Ann Sullivan, of Cliffton College, Ohio, who has granted permission for downloading any of the images for educational or personal use. The collection is indexed by artist, architect, site, and chronology. Each slide is captioned with brief descriptions and lots of historical background.

LUCi

http://vrc.ucr.edu/luci/luci.html

The Library of UC Images (LUCi) is a joint campus project uniting resources from several University of California visual collections. The current database incorporates images from the classical Greek and Roman periods only, from the slide libraries at UC Berkeley, UC Irvine, and UC Riverside. Anyone can access the thumbnail images, but the higher resolution images are password protected. The images were taken by UC faculty and staff at sites where photography was permitted; therefore copyright belongs to the individual photographers.

INTERNET SEARCH ENGINES

AltaVista

http://www.altavista.com/

AltaVista has a special tab for searching images using keywords. The "Show Me" feature can be set to limit searches to photos, graphics, buttons/banners, or images in color or black and white. "Sources" can limit searching to the whole Web, or to one of AltaVista's commercial partners: CDNOW (a music and video e-commerce site), the Corbis Collection or Getty Images.

Ditto.com

http://ditto.com/

This commercial site searches only for images on the Web. The search engine indexes millions of pictures, and returns thumbnail images. ditto.com claims that "high-quality, useful, non-objectionable picture-based results" are achieved because real people preview every picture it shows. Searchers can use the browse categories or latest favorites, or perform a keyword search.

Infoseek

http://www.go.com/Gallery/

Infoseek's "Image Gallery" uses a directory format to organize picture sites by broad topic. Subcategories are more detailed than Yahoo's and search results were larger. The site also allows keyword searching.

Lycos

http://www.lycos.com/

Lycos offers a multimedia advanced search function. Searches can be limited to All (media), Pictures, Movies, Streams, or Sounds. Results are displayed as thumbnail images with information on file size, date and brief descriptions.

World Wide Arts Resources

http://wwar.com/

World Wide Arts Resources maintains a database of arts information that covers a wide range of resources, from arts news, and sources for artists' materials, to galleries, agencies, and museums. The "Online exhibitions" and "Galleries" links can be good sources for images.

> *http://wwar.com/museums.html*
>
> Museum links on this site are listed by country or broad topic. The results screen with scope notes and descriptive paragraphs is a nice value-added feature of this site.

Yahoo! Picture gallery

http://gallery.yahoo.com/

Yahoo uses its traditional directory format to organize source sites for pictures into "Picture categories." One can also search this category for images using keywords.

Yahoo! Museums

> *http://dir.yahoo.com/Arts/Museums__Galleries__and_Centers/*
>
> Yahoo! lists museums under the category "Home > Arts > Museums, Galleries, and Centers."
>
> *http://dir.yahoo.com/Regional/Countries/*
>
> Museums are also organized geographically, either by country (e.g., "Home > Regional > Countries > Italy > Arts and Humanities > Museums, Galleries, and Centers") or by city (e.g., "Home > Regional > Countries > Israel > Districts and Regions > Jerusalem > Cities > Jerusalem > Entertainment and Arts > Museums, Galleries, and Centers").

SUBSCRIPTION COLLECTIONS

AMICO

http://www.rlg.org/amico/index.html

AMICO is a not-for-profit consortium of arts institutions who have created a digital library of images from their collections for educational use. Full access is by subscription only, but the Web site allows access to previously done searches saved as thumbnail sketches in the "Archives." Subscription cost is based on size of the subscribing institution. One nice feature is that the site provides a direct link from the image to the Web site of the copyright holder (member institution).

Index of Christian Art

http://www.princeton.edu/~ica/indexca.html

Princeton University's Index of Christian Art has been in existence for over 80 years, and is now a searchable database on the Internet. With full-text records for over 18,000 works of art dating from early apostolic times to A.D. 1400, the database is available for subscription to institutions for $1,500 annually. The 26,822 subject term index developed for the database is also available at the Web site.

WEB GUIDES

Exploring Image Collections on the Internet

http://libraries.mit.edu/rvc/imgcolls/imgcoll.html

This exceptionally well organized and thorough page of "resources at MIT and beyond" has links to dozens of image sites. Also included are resources on digital imaging technical issues, copyright, and animation, live action and video.

Image Collections and Digital Imaging Information

http://www.bc.edu/bc_org/avp/cas/fnart/links/imagecolls.html

A list of links to online image collections, maintained by Jeffrey Howe of Boston College, this site also includes links to information on copyright. His iconography links page <http://www.bc.edu/bc_org/avp/cas/fnart/links/iconography.html> is another very good source.

Stockphoto

http://www.stockphoto.net/AgencyList/AgencyPQR.html

The Stockphoto Network has compiled a list of worldwide stock photography agencies, complete with contact information and Web addresses for those doing business on the Internet. In addition, the net-work will distribute specific photography requests for large orders to as many as 300 professional photographers and photographic libraries worldwide free of charge.

Image Finders

http://witcombe.sbc.edu/ARTHLinks4.html#imagefinders

Chris Witcomb, professor of art history at Sweetbriar College, main-tains an extensive art history Web resource guide, which includes this image finders list.

WebSEEk

http://disney.ctr.columbia.edu/WebSEEK/

WebSEEk at Columbia University is a "content-based image and video search engine and catalog for the Web." To date, the site claims to have indexed over 665,000 images and videos on the web.

WWW Virtual Library

http://vlib.org/Home.html

The WWW Virtual Library maintains two lists of sites useful for finding images:

> The Virtual Library Museums Pages
>
> *http://www.icom.org/vlmp/*
>
> Links to Internet museum sites, searchable by keyword or brows-able by country
>
> The History of Art Virtual Library
>
> *http://www.hart.bbk.ac.uk/VirtualLibrary.html#images*
>
> List of large image collections on the web

BIBLIOGRAPHY

Aisbett, Janet, and Greg Gibbon. "A User-Dependent Definition of the Information in Images and Its Use in Information Retrieval." *Journal of Visual Communica-tion and Image Representation,* 8 (1997): 97-106.

Andrews, James, and Werner Schwiebenz. *The Kress Study Collection Virtual Mu-seum Project: a New Medium for Old Masters.* Vers. 96.12.3 [cited 23 Apr. 2000]. <http://www.arlisna.org/publications/werner.html>.

Archives and Museum Informatics [cited 23 Apr. 2000]. <http://www.archimuse.com/>.

Bakewell, Elizabeth, William O. Beeman, and Carol McMichael Reese. *Object, Image, Inquiry: the Art Historian at Work.* Santa Monica, CA: The Getty Art History Information Program, 1988.

Beaucamp, Carrie. *Museums in Cyberspace: Serving a Virtual Public on the Technocratic Frontier.* Vers. 98.10.2 U of Denver [cited 23 Apr. 2000]. <http://www.du.edu/~cbeaucha/cybermuseums.html>.

Blaze, Ron. *The Humanities: a Selective Guide to Information Resources.* Littleton, CO: Libraries Unlimited, 1994.

Bower, Jim, and Andrew Roberts, eds. *Museum and Cultural Heritage Information Standards Resource Guide.* The J. Paul Getty Trust and the International Committee for Documentation of the International Council of Museums/Comité international pour la documentation du Conseil international des musées (ICOM-CIDOC). 1996 [cited 23 Apr. 2000]. <http://www.icom.org/stand2.htm>.

Chen, Hsin-Lian, and Edie M. Rasmussen. "Intellectual Access to Images." *Library Trends*, 48 (1999): 291-302.

Cobbledick, Susie. "The Information-Seeking Behavior of Artists: Exploratory Interviews." *The Library Quarterly*, 66 (1996): 343-72.

Cohen, Harvey A. "Retrieval and Browsing of Images Using Image Thumbnails." *Journal of Visual Communication and Image Representation*, 8 (1997): 226-34.

Computers and the History of Art. CHArt [cited 23 Apr. 2000]. <http://www.chart.ac.uk/>.

Copy Law Online Resources. Law Offices of Lloyd J. Jassin [cited 23 Apr. 2000]. <http://copylaw.com/res.html>.

Delahunt, Michael. *ArtLex on Copyright* [cited 23 Apr. 2000]. <http://www.artlex.com/ArtLex/c/copyright.html>.

Dodds, Douglas. *Finding Needles in Virtual Haystacks.* ARLIS/UK & Ireland Conference paper, 1996 [cited 23 Apr. 2000]. <http://nile.dmu.ac.uk/elise/e12_dels/haystack.htm>.

———— "Integrating Access to Distributed Images: the Electronic Library Image Service for Europe (ELISE) Project." *Art Libraries Journal*, Vol. 24. 1999 40-43.

Esworthy, Cynthia. "From Monty Python to Leona Hemsley: A Guide to the Visual Artists Rights Act." *National Endowment for the Arts Art Forms.* 1997 [cited 23 Apr. 2000]. <http://arts.endow.gov/artforms/Manage/VARA.html>.

Exploring Image Collections on the Internet: Resources at MIT and Beyond. MIT Rotch Visual Collections [cited 23 Apr. 2000]. <http://libraries.mit.edu/rvc/imgcolls/imgco11.html>.

Fox, Edward A. "Digital Libraries Initiative (DLI) Projects 1994-1999." *Bulletin of the American Society for Information Science*, 26 (1999): 7-11.

Gill, Tony, and Catherine Grout. "Finding and Preserving Visual Arts Resources on the Internet." *Art Libraries Journal*, 22 (1997): 19-25.

Green, David. "CONFU Continues? Is It Time to Re-Group?" *NINCH News Brief.* 1997 [cited 23 Apr. 2000]. <http://www.ninch.org/News/CONFU_Report.html>.

Idris, F., and S. Panchanathan. "Review of Image and Video Indexing Techniques." *Journal of Visual Communication and Image Representation*, 8 (1997): 146-66.

Jones, Lois Swan. *Art Research Methods and Resources: A Guide to Finding Art Information*. Dubuque, Iowa: Kendall/Hunt, 1978.

Lehman, Bruce A. *The Conference on Fair Use: Final Report to the Commissioner on the Conclusion of the Conference on Fair Use (CONFU)*. Nov. 1998. Washington, DC [cited 23 Apr. 2000]. <http://www.uspto.gov/web/offices/dcom/olia/confu/confurep.htm>.

_____ *Intellectual Property and the National Information Infrastructure: The Report of the Working Group on Intellectual Property Rights*. Sept. 1995. Washington, D.C. <http://www.uspto.gov/web/offices/com/doc/ipnii/index.html>.

Library of Congress. *U.S. Copyright Office Home Page* [cited 23 Apr. 2000]. <http://lcweb.loc.gov/copyright/>.

McLaughlin, Margaret L. "The Art Site on the World Wide Web." *Journal of Communication*. 46 (1996) [cited 23 Apr. 2000]. <http://www.ascusc.org/jcmc/vol1/issue4/mclaugh.html>.

OSLA Arts & Law Home Page. Ocean State Lawyers for the Arts (OSLA) [cited 23 Apr. 2000]. <http://www.artslaw.org/>.

PACA Web Site Home Page. The Picture Agency Council of America [cited 23 Apr. 2000]. <http://www.pacaoffice.org/>.

Reed, Marcia. "Navigator, Mapmaker, Stargazer: Charting the New Electronic Sources in Art History." *Library Trends*, 40 (1992): 733-55.

Roberts, Andrew, and Leonard Will. *Recent Museum Documentation Initiatives: Standards and Guidelines*. The International Committee for Documentation of the International Council of Museums/Comité international pour la documentation du Conseil international des musées (ICOM-CIDOC). Vers. 99.10.5 [cited 23 Apr. 2000]. <http://www.cidoc.icom.org/stand3st.htm>.

Smith, John R., and Shih-Fu Chang. "Searching for Images and Videos on the World Wide Web." 96.8.16 [cited 23 Apr. 2000]. <http://www.ctr.columbia.edu/webseek/paper/>.

Sklar, Hinda F. "Why Make Images Available Online: User Perspectives." *Collection Management*, 22 (1998): 113-22.

Stapleton, Mike. "Aquarelle: A Resource Directory System for the European Cultural Heritage." *Art Libraries Journal,* 24 (1999): 43-47.

Stephenson, Christie. "Recent Developments in Cultural Heritage Image Databases: Directions for User-Centered Design." *Library Trends*, 48 (1999): 410-37.

Sundt, Christine L. "Testing the Limits: the CONFU Digital-Images and Multimedia Guidelines and Their Consequences for Libraries and Educators." *Journal of the American Society for Information Science*, 50 (1999): 1328-36.

Tennant, Roy. "Everything You Wanted to Know About Digital Imaging But Were Afraid to Ask." *Library Journal*, 123 (1998): 33, 35.

_____ "The Purpose of Digital Capture: Artifact of Intellectual Content?" *Library Journal*, 124 (1999): 28.

Van Camp, Anne. "Providing Access to International Primary Research Resources in the Humanities." *Art Libraries Journal*, 24 (1999): 22-24.

Vicars-Harris, Oliver. "COLLAGE: 'The Corporation of London Library & Art Gallery Electronic.'" *Art Libraries Journal*, 24 (1999): 48-51.

ALPHABETICAL SOURCE LIST

AltaVista
http://www.altavista.com/

AMICO Library
http://www.rlg.org/amico/index.html

Art & Architecture Thesaurus
http://shiva.pub.getty.edu/aat_browser/

Art Images for College Teaching (AICT)
http://www.mcad.edu/AICT/index.html

Art Resource, Inc.
http://www.artres.com/

The Artchive
http://www.artchive.com/

Artcyclopedia
http://www.artcyclopedia.com/

The Artists Rights Society
http://www.arsny.com/

Artserve (ANU)
http://rubens.anu.edu.au/index2.html

The Bridgeman Art Library
http://www.bridgeman.co.uk/

CGFA (Carol Gerten's Fine Art)
http://sunsite.auc.dk/cgfa/

Christianity & the Arts
http://www.christianarts.net/

Christus Rex
http://rubens.anu.edu.au/index2.html

Corbis
http://www.corbis.com/

CrossSearch
http://www.crosssearch.com/Art/

Crystal Cloud Graphics
http://www.fortunecity.com/roswell/avebury/18/index.html

Digital Imaging Project (Mary Ann Sullivan)
http://www.bluffton.edu/~sullivanm/index/index2.html

Ditto.com
http://ditto.com

Exploring Image Collections on the Internet (MIT)
http://libraries.mit.edu/rvc/imgcolls/imgco11.html

Getty Thesaurus of Geographic Names
http://shiva.pub.getty.edu/tgn_browser/

The Getty Vocabularies Program
http://www.getty.edu/gri/vocabularies/

The History of Art Virtual Library
http://www.hart.bbk.ac.uk/VirtualLibrary.html#images

Image Collections and Digital Imaging Information (Boston College)
http://www.bc.edu/bc_org/avp/cas/fnart/links/imagecolls.html

Image Finders (Sweetbriar College)
http://witcombe.sbc.edu/ARTHLinks4.html#imagefinders

Index of Christian Art
http://www.princeton.edu/~ica/indexca.html

Infoseek
http://www.go.com/Gallery/

LUCi
http://vrc.ucr.edu/luci/luci.html

Lycos
http://www.lycos.com/

Religious Resources on the Net
http://www.aphids.com/relres/

Saskia, Ltd.
http://www.saskia.com/

Stockphoto
http://www.stockphoto.net/

Union List of Artist Names
http://shiva.pub.getty.edu/ulan_browser/

The Virtual Library Museums Page
http://www.icom.org/vlmp/

WebSEEk
http://disney.ctr.columbia.edu/WebSEEK/

Westock
http://www.westock.com/

World Wide Arts Resources
http://wwar.com/

Yahoo! Museums
http://dir.yahoo.com/Arts/Museums__Galleries__and_Centers/

Yahoo! Museums (geographic)
http://dir.yahoo.com/Regional/Countries/

Yahoo! Picture gallery
http://gallery.yahoo.com/

Opening the Front Door:
Designing a Usable Library Web Site

Andrew J. Keck

SUMMARY. The library Web site is a significant access point to a library's collections, resources, and services. A Web site can and should provide information about the library in a way that can be efficiently navigated and used by all library patrons. The usability of a library Web site can be improved through changes in organization and design informed by the experiences of real users. User expectations should be primary in determining the content, purpose, organization, and design of the site. *[Article copies available for a fee from The Haworth Document Delivery Service: 1-800-342-9678. E-mail address: <getinfo@haworthpress inc.com> Website: <http://www.HaworthPress.com> © 2001 by The Haworth Press, Inc. All rights reserved.]*

KEYWORDS. Web site, Web pages, library, design, usability

A favorite "Far Side" comic strip shows a boy pushing on the door to get into the "Midvale School for the Gifted" but the door is clearly labeled "pull." The virtual front door to our libraries is the library Web page. Even with the best design, some users will misunderstand, misinterpret, and be misguided by the library Web site. This difficulty is due to the challenge of rendering within a single Web site the complex

Andrew J. Keck, BA, MTS, MSLS, is Electronic Services Librarian, Divinity School Library, Duke University, 103 Gray Building, Box 90972, Durham, NC 27708-0972 (E-mail: andy.keck@duke.edu).

[Haworth co-indexing entry note]: "Opening the Front Door: Designing a Usable Library Web Site." Keck, Andrew J. Co-published simultaneously in *Journal of Religious & Theological Information* (The Haworth Information Press, an imprint of The Haworth Press, Inc.) Vol. 3, No. 3/4, 2001, pp. 127-137; and: *Theological Librarians and the Internet: Implications for Practice* (ed: Mark Stover) The Haworth Information Press, an imprint of The Haworth Press, Inc., 2001, pp. 127-137. Single or multiple copies of this article are available for a fee from The Haworth Document Delivery Service [1-800-342-9678, 9:00 a.m. - 5:00 p.m. (EST). E-mail address: getinfo@haworthpressinc.com].

set of resources and services that are found within a library. Despite this challenge, a user's ability to efficiently use a library Web site can be improved through making changes based upon the experiences of real users. User preferences and expectations should inform the purpose, content, organization, and design of a library Web site.

PURPOSE AND IMPORTANCE

The purpose of the library Web site is to be an access point to the library's collections, resources, and services. Libraries that have both a Web site and a Web-enabled online catalog tend to view the online catalog as being a part of the Web site. The catalogs (both card and online) allow patrons to see what resources are available within the library but tend to be much more limited in their ability to offer information about library services, library staff, basic research advice, and resources available beyond the library collections. For this reason, the library Web site is perhaps the most all-inclusive access point to the library. The library's Web site derives its importance in ways both internal and external to the institution that it serves.

Internally, the importance of the library Web site is directly related to the library's significance within an institution. The primary users and patrons of an academic library tend to be internal: faculty, staff, and students. At a basic level, the library provides access to resources that help faculty and students grow in knowledge, understanding, and (in theological libraries especially) faith. Patrons further distribute the impact of the library through their papers, sermons, and dialogues. Therefore, the library and library Web site have a very significant and critical role in the intellectual life of a seminary or theological school. Library Web pages can serve primary internal users through providing efficient access to library services and collections.

The library Web site is a point of outreach for the institution, as well as the library, as it is widely available to people from outside of the institution and indeed around the world. A Web site can and should provide information about the library and its collections in a way that is understandable to outside patrons. Of course, there are some Web pages that are useful for all users such as lists of recommended Web sites, online catalogs, and interactive reference forms. Alumni, local pastors, genealogical researchers, laity, and others that make use of library resources enhance the library and institution's reputation in the community and beyond.

On the one hand, the importance and purpose of a library's Web site comes from its users and their purposes. But on the other hand, part of its importance and purpose is generated from the information, tools, and services that are made available online. There is much competition for a user's time and attention on the web. In a World Wide Web of 10 million Web sites, Web sites of libraries with the largest collections are on equal footing with the Web sites of new theological libraries with no books at all! A library can still have an important Web presence even if a library doesn't have a great physical collection. The difference is in the information and resources that are placed on that Web site.

INFORMATION AND RESOURCES

The library Web page has given librarians the ability to integrate digital and physical resources into a single information center. A library Web site brings together the physical resources housed within a library, the physical resources available in other libraries and research centers, and the virtual resources that are found, created, bought, or leased. Given the hypertext reality of the Web, libraries are able to link to freely available resources around the world. In this way, the library's Web pages are not only a potential provider of information resources but also a gateway to many other resources.

One of the roles of the library Web site is to deliver information about the library. Library pages sometimes forget the basic questions of patrons. In the excitement of incorporating virtual and physical collections, things like library hours, directions, maps, and borrowing privileges may be forgotten. They seem rather mundane issues but can be critically important to all users. Libraries must develop a Web page that assumes that the user may not know anything about the library. Timely announcements about weather-related closings (or other changes in service) are as important on the Web page as on the front entrance.

An important role of the library Web pages is to allow access to the library's physical and digital collections to the greatest degree that it is possible. For libraries where this technology is enabled, bibliographical databases and online catalogs can be linked to and/or searched from the library's Web pages. The library Web page can allow some libraries to integrate bibliographic tools and digital resources into one place so that the digital materials can be found and delivered electronically. Even more exciting are developing technologies that allow users to search several bibliographic and full-text resources simultaneously. Vendors of bibliographic tools and databases are allowing more and more customization to their interfaces so libraries can effectively manage and integrate these tools into the library Web page.

Digital resources may not be available to all Web site users because they are often bought or leased to the library with certain licensing restrictions. Unauthorized users of the Web site need to know which databases and tools require authorization. Authorized users must know how to be authenticated in order to use much of this information. This usually means that they must be on the campus network or be able to configure their home computers in a way that makes this work. It is a challenge to ensure that the authorized users know how to be authenticated and all visitors know which databases and tools require authentication.

Along with incorporating content and tools from other sources, librarians have a responsibility to use the Web site to teach, help, and inform. A library website can be a good place for tutorials and help screens to assist people in using collections and associated online catalogs, databases, and electronic journals. Research guides can help users through the exploration process and give guidance in investigating specific areas of knowledge. Also, the library Web page can highlight new acquisitions, new digital resources, and other events of interest to the library community. The challenge of adding features to a library Web site is organizing them in a way that is helpful.

ORGANIZATION

Web pages notwithstanding; libraries are complex organizations. The exponential increase in the amount of information has corresponded with an increase in the information tools, which in turn has corresponded with increased user confusion. In the modern library, even the physical library can be complex and confusing. Journals are a great example. Libraries have some journals in electronic format, some bound, some filmed, some unbound, some off-site, some on the current periodical shelves, some at the bindery, some available through other affiliated libraries, and some that can be obtained through interlibrary loan. Part of the challenge of creating a usable Web site is just the challenge of trying to simplify and organize information. The more important challenge, from the user's perspective, is for a Web site to communicate effectively about the library and its resources without the benefit of direct personal contact with a librarian.

The library makes a considerable investment of time and money into organizing print resources in order to provide access to them. This work is completed in order to simplify as much as possible the ability of a patron to find resources that fit his/her research need. No less is needed within the library Web site. The importance of the library Web site and the varieties of information and services that can be included on its Web pages make the organization of the homepage and Web site as a whole an especially arduous challenge. Like print resources, the Web site must be organized in a manner friendly to the user so that user needs are most important.

One of the mistakes made by library webmasters is to make the library Web site too library-centered. In other words, librarians like to design library Web sites that are most useful and understandable to librarians. It's too easy to add library jargon, categories, and preferences to the Web interface instead of considering how the average patron might approach the Web site. As much as librarians would like to create Web sites for themselves, library Web pages should be user-centered. The average person hitting the library Web page may not necessarily understand what "research guide" even means, much less intuitively know that he/she should be able to get information about researching the Bible in that category.

Librarians have used the Web for making lists ever since it began: lists of Web sites, lists of electronic journals, lists of databases, etc. Small lists can be navigated easily. Librarians have a compelling need to organize longer lists–to give them subject headings or classifications. This indeed can be very helpful to the user but in many cases creates confusion with a multiplicity of lists and the standard problems of subject classification.

In addition to the problems with lists, librarians must face the "let's put it on the Web page" syndrome. This syndrome arises from the ability of the Web to make documents widely and electronically available. Almost any document can become a Web page since at least somebody, somewhere, might be interested in it. Since Web pages are cheap, it is easy to develop a large Web site filled with all sorts of arcane internal documents that are of little or no interest to the average user. It can be difficult for a single Web site to be both an Internet for library users and Intranet for library staff and may be necessary for these two functions to be separated within the Web site or separated into different Web sites.

However one deals with internal documents, there are two problems that arise as one increases the size of the library Web site: one is navigational and the other political. The navigational problem is that the number of Web pages increases the complexity of the Web site and thus the layers of Web pages that must be created. At a certain point, one can no longer have a link on the front page to all of the other pages on the library Web site. Consequently, the library webmaster must "bury" some pages into pages perhaps several layers (and several clicks for the user) beneath the "home page." This can become the political problem. When someone requests that a page be placed on the library Web site, they not only want it to be available but also easily accessible to users.

Although the problems of proper organization can never be completely solved, there are a few basic principles that should mitigate their impact. First, have a method of keyword searching all and/or part of your Web site. Although librarians have developed a healthy mistrust of keyword searching, when patrons are confused about the subject categories they head straight for the search mechanism. Second, patrons don't really care as much as librarians about issues such as format, origin, and cost. It is far simpler for the patron to find one page on Biblical studies that includes databases, e-journals, and Web sites than to search separate lists for each. Third, create a site map that users can refer to concerning the site's structure and organization.

DESIGN

There is often a thin line between organization and design. Organizational challenges lead to design challenges and designs often lead to organizational problems. There are many ways to design a library Web page–there is no standard template and indeed many different models. A major part of the design goal should be usability for the patron. One of the limits and liabilities of the Web is that not all users will see and use a Web page in the same way. Part of the way a Web page is seen and interpreted will be personal–patrons will bring with them their experience of navigating other library and non-library Web pages. Another determining factor regarding how a Web page will be viewed is practical: Web browser brand, Web browser version and settings, operating system, and monitor resolution all change the way that a Web site is viewed. Perhaps most importantly, the type of connection to the Internet will determine the speed at which they can use and navigate your Web site.

The first thing that a Website design should do is to adhere to Web standards. This can be difficult given the different implementations and interpretations of those standards by the major Web browsers. The focus should be on designing for the majority's lowest common denominator. For example, the majority of people will be using a graphical browser but probably not the latest release since most people do not instantly upgrade their software. Even then, it is possible to include features found on new browsers as long as those features have no essential impact on the older browsers. New features that generate errors or gibberish on older browsers should be avoided.

Bandwidth is an essential issue that is often overlooked but makes a large difference to users connecting to the library's Web site over a modem connection. The bandwidth issue isn't always noticeable to library webmasters due to the fact that library Web pages are developed on a campus network instead of over a modem line. According to Jakob Nielson, page sizes need to be kept below 34 kilobytes for modem users to achieve a 10-second response time.[1] That doesn't mean that you can't have high-bandwidth pages with graphics or compressed video of your latest renovations or booktalk. However, it is helpful to warn users about high-bandwidth pages on your site since users tend to be impatient unless they are forewarned and expecting a longer wait.

The impatience of users also needs to inform the way in which the library Web site is designed. Simplicity is one of the hardest things to achieve on a library Web site yet it is the most essential. What is simple for the user may not always correspond to what is simplest for the library webmaster to achieve. Web users have learned to scan and click. Therefore, it is important to attend to distractions, white space, short texts, descriptive and simple language.

The library webmaster should remove all unnecessary distractions. Distractions include anything that unnecessarily blinks, rotates, or moves upon the page. While these animations are fun to use, they do not belong on a library's home page. The use of frames is also a distraction. One of the most frustrating experiences on the Web involves being caught in some "frame purgatory" that one cannot escape.

Just as in printed publications, white space and margins add to the readability of a document. One of the limitations of computer monitors is that it is difficult to read across the screen. Therefore, it is helpful visually to set up your pages in several columns or in one column with generous margins. Because of differences in monitors and their resolutions, what appears to be sufficient white space on one monitor may not be sufficient on another. Be sure to test the Web page at different resolutions.

Since users tend to scan quickly, short texts are more likely to be read than longer texts. Sentences, paragraphs, and words need to be short. Be generous in your use of categories, subcategories, and bullets. Instead of putting a lot of text on one page, begin with a summary or enticing first paragraph and then link to its continuation on another page.

Keep titles simple yet descriptive from the title of the Web page itself to the title of each subheading. This doesn't necessarily have anything to do with a user's vocabulary skills but rather the method by which users scan and pick out keywords and phrases. One of the new features incorporated in the HTML standard is the ability to add "titles" to links so that a user with mouse over a particular link can view a popup box that adds more description. If users aren't sure about what the ATLA Database is, perhaps the popup box could indicate that it indexes multi-authored books, journals and Doctor of Ministry projects.

USABILITY TESTING

The library's Web site can be organized, simplified, and redesigned, but how does one determine if the web pages are really more usable? The way to test usability is to watch actual users accomplish common tasks utilizing the library Web site. There are several steps to a usability study: define the parameters, determine the tasks, develop the process, recruit the participants, complete the study, and evaluate the data.

The parameters of the usability study define which parts of the site to study. In most cases, one will want to primarily study things over which one has control. If the online catalog is bought from a vendor and the library has little influence regarding its redesign, there may be no use in studying the catalog. Some parts of a library Web site also may not be useful or of interest to most patrons. Most usability tests begin at the home page and investigate top-level navigation as well as the navigation within significant sections of the Web site.

The tasks for the user to perform must be actual tasks or questions that users would normally face. It is natural to pick tasks that highlight already recognized problems or tasks that require the user to find information buried deep within your Web site. It is usually good to have several questions of this nature, as you will be able to observe what users try to do in order to solve the task, which will be quite informative. In addition to several "tough" questions, be sure to include common (and potentially easy) tasks. This will help the self-esteem of the participant as well as perhaps highlight changes that could be made in the Web site to make the completing of these common tasks more efficient.

Although one could simply observe users completing the tasks, there can be some use in employing other kinds of observational measurement. Timing participants and/or counting mouse clicks as they complete each task can help determine whether a particular person's difficulty with a task is representative of a larger group. These measures may also provide a baseline by which to compare future studies on the redesigned Web site. Be sure to document which Web pages a participant uses for each task. Testing sessions can be audio and/or videotaped to capture screen images and verbal feedback. Instructing the participant to think aloud while completing the tasks will assist in analyzing the thought processes of each participant.

The next step is recruiting the participants. Jakob Nielson recently suggested that a usability study could be done with just five persons.[2] Whether you do five or more it is important to have a group representative of most, if not all, of your primary patrons. Ideally, the usability study is done before the Web pages go "live" so that the participants have no prior experience in using the site and so that you can make the necessary usability changes before it goes "live." As an incentive, it is often helpful to offer some small token of appreciation for their time and effort. Although the study is really about the Web site, your participants are ultimately considered "research subjects" and should be informed ahead of time about the purpose and time commitments of the study. Some institutions may need to have participants complete consent forms, especially if you use video or audio recording.

The study should be completed, if possible, in a room with minimal distractions. The participant should usually be given a list of the tasks/questions in writing so that they can refer back to it easily to make sure that all of the items have been completed. If you are timing the tasks, you will need to determine some arbitrary time to start and stop the test–perhaps when the participant begins reading the question until the participant indicates that he/she is done. If you are trying to record numerous behaviors like clicks, pages clicked to, etc., you may want to consider having another person available to help you record the desired information.

Although the measurements are important, they should not get in the way of the observations. This is not a strictly scientific study and the difference of a few seconds or mouse clicks should not make any difference to the your overall analysis of the Web site. The analysis of the usability testing data will be critical to determining the redesign of the library Web site. The problem and its solution in some cases will be quite self-evident. However, some problems will be difficult to define and even more difficult to solve without a major redesign of the Web site. It is important to continue testing and retesting the design especially in these difficult cases.

REDESIGN

Once the data has been analyzed one can begin work on redesign. Some changes will be minor such as adding a more prominent link or changing the terminology used in titles or headings. Other changes may arrive at the very heart of how a Web site is organized and may entail a more complete redesign. The trick, of course, is to solve the problems discovered by usability testing so that the Web site usability is actually improved. To find solutions to some of the more vexing problems, it can be very useful to visit other library Web sites to see how they handle a particular task. This is a good practice not only for finding solutions to specific problems learned through usability testing but also to learn strategies that other libraries use to teach or inform their patrons.

For example, suppose usability testing showed that the library's Web page containing annotated links to recommended Web pages was difficult to find and use. One might consider putting the link in a more prominent location and adding a searching feature. But upon visiting several library Web sites, there may be other solutions in place that involve integrating the Web pages in a "research guide" or highlighting a specific Web site each week, etc.

Ongoing and continual usability testing can be very useful in order to ensure improvement, especially as a Web site matures and grows. As the library changes, so must its Web site and one should periodically refresh one's Web design. As technology and access to technology continues to change, the library Web site must continue to change. One may need to change the scale and design as monitors with better resolution become more common or add more multimedia elements to the design as faster connections become more common. If patrons prefer to obtain library information from other Web sites, it suggests something about the need for improvement in the design.

CONCLUSION

A library's Web site can be, and often is, a patron's first experience and impression of a library. If the library's Web site is judged difficult to use, then there can be an assumption that the library itself may be difficult to use (which may be true!). Since libraries are in the service business, it is critical that the library Web site be as service oriented as the library staff. In order to accomplish this goal, user's experiences and expectations need to inform the organization and design process of the entire library including the library Web site.

In the future, libraries and the World Wide Web will continue to change and grow. Libraries will continue to manage and intcgrate physical and virtual resources. The World Wide Web will continue to spread to new places and new users. Patrons may view the library Web site (or the future equivalent) in their cars, on their phones, on their televisions, and perhaps on their living rooms walls. Users will continue to expand around the world with the Internet becoming more heterogeneous in terms of language, class, and ethnicity. The browser and the Web page will continue to incorporate new technologies that will add new opportunities to serve library patrons. At the same time, these same technologies will likely pose challenges to creating a usable library Web site that can facilitate the transfer of information between library and patron. By keeping the focus of design on the user, library Web sites can continue to be developed that will be useful, usable and used.

NOTES

1. Jakob Nielsen, *Designing Web Usability* (Indianapolis: New Riders Publishing, 2000), 48.

2. Jakob Nielsen, "Why You Only Need to Test With 5 Users," *Jakob Nielsen's Alertbox* (March 19, 2000); available from http://www.useit.com/alertbox/20000319.html; accessed 10 April 2000.

Using the Web in Religious Studies Courses

Rebecca Moore

SUMMARY. This article describes various in-class assignments and experiments using Web-based assignments conducted in religious studies courses over the past three years. The author notes both the advantages and disadvantages of using the Internet with students. While a number of advantages accrue to teachers, some concerns remain: lack of Web literacy, cost and access for students, copyright considerations, beta-testing course assignments, and grading final results. Nevertheless, students gain practical experience using the Internet, evaluating sources, reading primary source texts, and conducting research for projects. For these reasons the author plans to continue to integrate Web assignments into courses. *[Article copies available for a fee from The Haworth Document Delivery Service: 1-800-342-9678. E-mail address: <getinfo@haworth pressinc.com> Website: <http://www.HaworthPress.com> © 2001 by The Haworth Press, Inc. All rights reserved.]*

KEYWORDS. Internet, religious studies, Web, students

It was the first day of Religious Studies 101: World Religions. We were talking about the world's religions and I said that Christianity still had more adherents than any other religion. A student piped up and said that Islam had more. I replied, not yet, but that in this century Islam probably would overtake Christianity. The student insisted that

Rebecca Moore, PhD, teaches in the Department of Religious Studies, San Diego State University, 5500 Campanile Drive, San Diego, CA 92182-8143.

[Haworth co-indexing entry note]: "Using the Web in Religious Studies Courses." Moore, Rebecca. Co-published simultaneously in *Journal of Religious & Theological Information* (The Haworth Information Press, an imprint of The Haworth Press, Inc.) Vol. 3, No. 3/4, 2001, pp. 139-150; and: *Theological Librarians and the Internet: Implications for Practice* (ed: Mark Stover) The Haworth Information Press, an imprint of The Haworth Press, Inc., 2001, pp. 139-150. Single or multiple copies of this article are available for a fee from The Haworth Document Delivery Service [1-800-342-9678, 9:00 a.m. - 5:00 p.m. (EST). E-mail address: getinfo@haworthpressinc.com].

Islam was currently larger. The next class period I was able to report back that Christianity is still the largest, with 2 billion believers, as compared with Islam, with 1.2 billion. And I gave students the source: <http://www.adherents.com>.

Just as the Religious Studies students I teach rely on the Internet more and more for finding information and for conducting research, I find that I too am using it more frequently. I have immediate access to the Web from my office computer through the university server. I don't have to use a modem, my access is quick, and except for certain hours of the day, the service is rapid. I can print out e-mail messages and information I find on the department's printer. I can make changes rapidly on my homepage (<http://www-rohan.sdsu.edu/~remoore>). I can toggle instantly between word-processing, Net surfing, and e-mailing, and find that I do. In fact, I probably am using Web resources more than my students are.

I have become committed to integrating Web-based resources into my syllabus, into my instruction, and into course materials. At the same time, however, I have become aware of a growing disjunction between the Web's convenience for me, and its lack of convenience for students. What I take for granted–ready access and no cost–does not exist for students. Some students pay the going rate of $20 a month for access to a server, which is slowed down greatly by using a modem. Some students use the free computer access on campus, but this means they have to *be* on campus, they have to wait to get a terminal, and they have to pay $.10 a copy when they print out material off the Web.

This article, therefore, reports anecdotally on two aspects of Web use in religious studies courses. First, it describes my findings as a teacher who uses the Web a great deal in a variety of instructional ways. I discuss how I integrated readings directly into a syllabus on the history of Christianity, as well as experiments in having students evaluate Web sources. Then, it describes my findings regarding student use and the disadvantages as well as advantages the Web presents for students.

USING READINGS DIRECTLY FROM THE WEB

Because I have found the Web useful, cheap, and convenient, I assumed that students would have the same experience. I decided to incorporate readings in the history of Christianity taken from the Web into *Religious Studies 325: Christianity.* This upper division course attracts about 60 students wanting to fulfill their general education requirement in the humanities. Students who enroll also tend to have an interest in Christianity, either because of a deep religious commitment or a profound questioning of the tradition in which they were raised. I used Internet readings in primary sources to supplement Mary Jo Weaver's textbook *Introduction to Christianity.*[1] I thought that I would save the students money and time by letting them download the material at their convenience, rather than purchase a course packet and face the potential costs of copyright fees. I also thought that they would prefer Internet readings to making photocopies of readings placed on reserve in the Library. In theory, they could get the readings from any computer with Web access.

An academic searching for primary sources soon discovers a great number of *good* resources in religious studies on the Internet. Several articles in this volume call attention to these sources in greater detail than I will.[2] A look at the Web site for the Christianity class (<http://www-rohan.sdsu.edu/~remoore/christianity.html>) shows how I incorporated links directly to the readings from the syllabus, and also shows the type of primary sources one can find on Christianity. An obvious starting point is the Christian Classics Ethereal Library, sponsored by Wheaton College, which presents the classic, and copyright-free, *Ante-Nicene, Nicene,* and *Post-Nicene Fathers* translations (<http://ccel.wheaton.edu/fathers2>).[3] Because CCEL used to take a long time to access I looked for alternatives to the same sources, and identified <http://www.stmichael.org/search.html>, sponsored by St. Michael the Archangel Orthodox Church as another site that has similar material from the early church. The Internet Medieval Sourcebook from Fordham University also provides material from the early church into the middle ages, at <http://www.fordham.edu/halsall/sbook. html>, as does New Advent, which identifies itself only as a "Catholic Web site" (<http://www.newadvent.org/fathers>). Also at New Advent is *The Catholic Encyclopedia,* an older version of the hardcopy update, *The New Catholic Encyclopedia.*[4] Some items in *The Catholic Encyclopedia,* which dates from the early twentieth century (<http://www.newadvent.org/cathen/>), must be used with caution. The words of the Nicene Creed, or the Canons of Trent, do not change. But the interpretation of these primary texts seems incredibly archaic at times. An entry under "Canon of the New Testament," for example, seems light years behind contemporary biblical scholarship.

In addition to locating primary source texts from Martin Luther to Ellen Gould White, and from Mary Baker Eddy to J. Gresham Machen, one can also find journal articles that students may find more interesting than other types of primary sources. Articles from *Maryknoll Magazine*, for example (<http://www.maryknoll.org/MEDIA/MAGAZINE/mfc.htm>), introduced students to the modern world of missions, an interesting and provocative switch from the role missions played historically. They read about liberation theology and the contemporary church in Africa in the journal *CrossCurrents*, which posts the articles from past issues on-line (see <http://www.crosscurrents.org/articlelist.htm>).

In short, using primary source texts from the Internet allowed me to develop a course packet for students quickly and inexpensively. I was able to bring together classic texts and contemporary issues. I could custom design readings which related to the main text students were reading. I could avoid some copyright problems, although not all of them (see below). A drawback, of course, is that URLs do not exist in perpetuity, and as I checked them in the writing of this article I found at least one that was defunct. But I was pleased with the breadth and depth I was able to achieve in using Internet readings.

EVALUATING WEB SITES

Some teachers prohibit their students from using the Internet as an information source. By fiat, they say, "No Internet References." There are some sound reasons for making this prohibition. The information on the Web has not undergone the scrutiny that academic publications require. No peer review process exists which could limit what is published on the Web. Moreover, most sites are commercial, and are designed to sell a product. Organizational sites are also designed to sell ideas, rather than products: they advocate a point of view. If a student went to <http://www.mlking.org> expecting to find impartial information about Dr. Martin Luther King, Jr., the student would eventually discover–we hope!–that this is a hate site intended to defame the civil rights leader. Academically, therefore, it might seem to make sense to keep students away from the Internet, and to direct them toward scholarly resources that have gone through an extensive evaluation process.

Plenty of good sites–scholarly, peer-reviewed, well maintained, and organized–exist on the Internet as well, and excluding the use of the Internet may be a case of throwing the baby out with the bath water. Rather than exclude Web-based resources from the pool of available information, therefore, I have decided to try to educate students in the evaluation of sources. This is not an easy task. The projects I have used to help build student awareness of information quality have had mixed results.

What I have tried to do is to provide some rudimentary instruction on search engines, the search process, and URLs and domain names. While the domain name for educational institutions, the suffix "edu," is no guarantee of quality, it nevertheless indicates mission or motive: that is, education. A case in point is when librarians at the Love Library at San Diego State University were asked to obtain a copy of the Nuremberg Trials transcripts on medical experimentation. They learned that the library's hard copy of the documents was missing. They turned to the Web for transcripts and found three sites:

<http://www.ushmm.org/research/doctors/Nuremberg_Code.htm>
<http://ecco.bsee.swin.edu/au/studes/ethics/Nuremberg.html> and
<http://www.aches-mc.org/nurm.htm>.

The librarians had to evaluate the three sites themselves to determine issues of authority, currency, accuracy, and bias. While the U.S. Holocaust Museum is probably fairly credible, and the Advocacy Committee for Human Experimentation Survivors & Mind Control might be credible, the librarians felt that the site sponsored by the University of Swinburn in Australia probably provided the best transcript for students in its medical school program. This was a case of "edu" actually indicating scholarly merit.

My earliest experiment was to have an Honors class in "Religion and Society" at the University of North Dakota develop a list of criteria for using the Internet. They came up with an excellent list which included issues of sponsorship (who sponsors the site? is it an official or authorized site, e.g., the *official* Oprah Winfrey fan club? is it a primary or secondary source?); credibility (authorship noted? credentials? editorial board?); access (is the site frequently updated? is the e-mail address working?); and the purpose of the site. One of the more helpful observations included: "Some clues that an Internet site is not credible are vague references, connections to sources that are known not to be credible, and any use of Elvis and aliens in the same sentence used as scientific proof." While the criteria the class came up with was great, the students themselves failed to follow their own instructions when asked to find a "credible" site and an "incredible" site concerning UFOs. Incredible was easy; credible was more difficult to find and to assess.

More successful projects have consisted of short Web exploration exercises, conducted after in-class instruction on evaluation. An upper-division class on the millennium which was comprised primarily of Religious Studies majors completed an open-ended assignment which required students to find one "good" Web site and one "bad" site on the millennium or the apocalypse. We discussed what we meant by "good" and "bad." The former implied credible or accurate information about Y2K preparedness, historical facts, or some kind of academic or scientific information (for example, the Federation of American Scientists' *Millennia Monitor* at <http://www.fas.org/2000/about.htm.>). Students considered a site "bad" if it was alarmist, sought to sell something, spelled "millennium" incorrectly, was too sectarian, or was over the top (for example, numerology proves that Al Gore *is* the Beast in Revelation, <http://www.yk.rim.or.jp/~elieshoh/666.htm>). I did point out that a sectarian site might indeed be the best site if one wanted to study sectarianism, just as the Church of Scientology homepage (<http://www.scientology.org/scn_home.htm>) is a good place to examine what Scientologists say about themselves. But for some students, sectarian sites were good because they supported the confessional commitment the student already had. It was hard to argue with a student who found the site by *Left Behind* authors Tim LeHaye and Jerry Jenkins good because it corresponded with her beliefs in the Rapture (<http://www.leftbehind.com>). These problems may not occur in science courses or even social science courses, but in religious studies students' beliefs and commitments always come into the equation.

The students in the millennium class had difficulty completing a Web site Evaluation Guide that I had received and reproduced from librarians at the Rod Library at the University of Northern Iowa. How were they to evaluate accuracy? What if they could not locate the authority who wrote the site? It became clear that students needed more instruction in finding information on the Web site itself, such as who the sponsoring organization might be, or in locating and assessing credentials. One student wrote that "This was a time consuming exercise for negligible gain. It was extremely frustrating and irritating."

I simplified the Web site evaluation guide and re-wrote the assignment for a large general education class in World Religions. The first part of the assignment was closed: I asked students to identify the "best" one of three sites on Sikhism. They received instruction in how to do Web searches from Mark Stover, a librarian at San Diego State University, and got the criteria for determining what was "good" in advance. The second part was open: I asked students to find five sites on a particular world religion that they would actually be studying and which they would use in their research. Students were to identify the top two sites and explain their value in terms of the criteria Mark and I had given them.

The results were both encouraging and discouraging. On the encouraging side, most students were able to identify a personal home-page on Sikhism as being inadequate. They noted spelling errors, grammatical problems, and the fact that the site had not been recently updated. Unfortunately, they dismissed the information provided by the Ontario Consultants for Religious Tolerance (<http://www.reli gioustolerance.org>) because this small non-profit group had advertising on the page to support its massive educational program. Some students were able to go beyond the bells and whistles of the more polished sites to correctly identify sites that had valuable, and credible, information. Others rated sites on their design rather than their content. Some failed to see that some sites contained bias, or had least had the potential for bias. Others found scholarly sites that I could add to my personal list of useful educational Web tools.

Perhaps I am being overly critical. How often do we ask undergraduates to actually *evaluate* the sources they use? Usually we ask for a bibliography, and may ultimately criticize the bibliography, without providing instruction on judging the worth of sources. An assignment for the same World Religion course, related to the Web site evaluation, asked students to use the San Diego State University Love Library's on-line databases to locate bibliographic information from three periodicals. Once students found three potentially useful sources, they had to actually go to the stacks to photocopy an article from a magazine and a journal, and then print out a full-text article from the database. This assignment asked students to write an abstract of the articles, and to explain why they thought the articles would be useful. While students were able to write the abstracts, few actually discussed the value of the articles. Thus, a student who found an article on psychedelic drugs and Buddhism seemed unaware that the article actually contained virtually no information about Buddhism. Nevertheless, I think that the more that teachers ask students to make evaluative judgments, the better they will get at it, and using the Internet is a good way to give students immediate practice.

Experimentation with longer evaluation projects has produced better results. In some of my classes students may opt for an independent research project, the sole purpose of which is to find and evaluate Web sites. Some of the topics researched have included Women and Religion, Christian Reconstructionism, and Web sites on other world religions, such as Judaism, or Wicca. Part of the motivation was selfish: I was looking for Web sites on different topics and had students doing some of the legwork. In these longer projects I gave students little or no instruction on making evaluations. They were to develop and write down their own criteria for evaluating quality. One student wrote as criteria: "large content, good and useful information, good links, and good documentation." Students came up with a mixed bag of sites: some extremely scholarly and academic, such as Labyrinth (<http://www.georgetown.edu/labyrinth/labyrinth.home.html> or Diotima (http://www.uky.edu/ArtsSciences/Classics/gender.html); others something less, such as the Religion Depot (<http://www.edepot.com/religion.shtml>). They did not seem able to differentiate between a site produced by a university or a scholar and one produced by an individual or a company with a point of view or product to sell. And yet, one student noted that "[a]lthough this site isn't a scholarly site, it does have articles from Marianne Williamson on the Meaning of Life and J. Richards['] translation of *Dhammapada–Sayings of the Buddha.*" She was able to recognize both the lack of scholarship and the usefulness of the site at the same time.

THE DOWN SIDE OF USING THE INTERNET

Aside from the fact that students routinely cut and paste information they find on the Internet into their research papers, other considerations and problems exist with using the Internet as a teaching tool. These include Web literacy, access and cost, copyright considerations, beta-testing one's own assignments, and the amount of time spent grading Internet projects.

At some institutions teachers may assume that students had computer instruction in high school, that they used computers at home, and that they already know how to use e-mail and to search the Web. That is not the case at San Diego State University. Some students come in as freshmen entirely Web literate, and comfortable with accessing study guides posted on my homepage. Other students either missed out on computer instruction because they come from a foreign country, are older, or have a school background where computer access was limited. This raises the question of how much time a teacher is willing to devote to instructing students in the basic skills needed just to access course materials, let alone benefiting from completing Web exercises. Because class time is limited, it may be necessary to put course materials on reserve in the library to help those students who just aren't ready to jump into Internet use.

Access and cost also make using the Internet less convenient for students. I have not yet surveyed any classes as to the number of students who own computers, and who have Internet access at home. This information would vary from campus to campus: at the University of North Dakota, all of the dorms were wired into the University server. If a student lived in a dorm, access was free and easy. But not all students live in dorms, as at San Diego State University, where the majority of students live off campus and commute to school. Access through a modem can be time-consuming. Students in the Christianity course, where they were required to download Internet readings, made a variety of comments. One student complained about the cost of printing out the readings. Another said that students would have come to class better prepared, and having done the readings, if they already had the readings available in a course packet. To verify this, I surveyed the students in the Christianity class to see if they preferred a course packet or Internet readings. A slight majority favored readings from the Internet to paying $25 or $30 for a packet (3/5 to 2/5, from 40 respondents). If using the Internet saves students money by eliminating the need for course packets and copyright fees, then it can be a boon. And yet, the words of the young woman who said students didn't have the readings for class continues to haunt me.

Another issue involves copyright claims and fair use. I asked the sponsors of the sources I'd used in the Christianity syllabus what copyright fees, if any, were charged. Most replied that they were copyright-free, since they had long since fallen into the public domain.

The exceptions were two magazines, both of which were nevertheless willing to waive copyright fees for student use as long as we provided the appropriate copyright information at the bottom of the articles. Clearly copyright needs to be addressed on a case by case basis. A rule of thumb, however, was provided by the manager of CCEL, who said, "Most of the items are public domain–those that are not, have explicit copyright notices."

Beta-testing one's own assignments takes time, but is crucial for the success of any Internet assignment. Even testing up to the last minute is no guarantee that URLs or links will still work. Obviously one cannot plan for every contingency or disaster, but it does pay to check the URLs on the day an assignment is made to see if they still work. It is easy enough to announce a new URL, or to write it on the board, and it saves the heartache and hassle of students returning the following week without an assignment because it wasn't available. This relates to accessibility as well: if a site takes forever to load, it probably isn't going to be very useful. I found this out in a New Testament course, where I learned that the excellent Bible search engine <http://www.bham.ac.uk/theology/goodacre/multibib.htm> from the University of Birmingham in England was virtually inaccessible (although I was able to load it quickly while writing this article). In addition to listing "Multibible," then, I also gave students the URL for Bible Gateway, <http://bible.gospelcom.net/bible>, which is always accessible, but more limited in its sources.[5]

Does using the Internet actually save time? Certainly up-loading assignments and maintaining an accurate homepage take some time, although it doesn't seem much more than if one were to type up an assignment and have it photocopied for distribution. The ease of looking things up at a terminal in one's office, as opposed to running to the library to find various resources, is tremendous. In terms of grading assignments, however, I'm not convinced that the Internet necessarily saves time. In closed assignments, like the Sikhism one described above, the strengths and weaknesses of the sites are given, and evaluative papers are easy to correct. But in open assignments, the teacher should definitely check at least one or two URLs to assess their value, and to see if the student is on the right track. Having graded fifty Web assignments, with a minimum of two sites per assignment to view, I can say that this can be time-consuming and tedious, especially if one wants to make at least one constructive comment on the assignment sheet. On the other hand, with students doing the same religions, I quickly became familiar with particular sites (such as <http://www. lds.org>, the homepage of the Church of Jesus Christ, Latter Day Saints, or <http://www.iskcon.org>, and the homepage of the Hare Krishnas). The more evaluative work that is assigned, the more thoughtful grading is needed. So using the Web may not always save time.

CONCLUSIONS

In spite of these caveats and concerns–especially those involving access and cost to students–I plan to continue to use Web-based resources in my courses. I am heartened by the possibilities of using the Internet to help students gain critical thinking skills. If students can learn to judge the value of a Web site, they may be able to evaluate other print resources. If students have access to a variety of primary sources, they may be able to learn how to read difficult texts without having to buy collections of abridged readings. If students can learn that the Internet is a good tool for research, but that actually reading something takes time and effort, they may be able to transfer the skills they learn to other tasks and problems.

I have no doubt that using the Internet in courses is a two-edged sword. We may give students the impression that the quick way is the best way. Or that appearance means more than substance. Yet I would rather try to tame the beast–the Internet–than let it carry students away, which is what will happen if I step out of the picture.

ENDNOTES

1. Mary Jo Weaver, with David Brakke and Jason Bivins, *Introduction to Christianity*, 3d edition (Belmont, CA: Wadsworth Publishing, 1998).
2. A few hardcopy resources include the following: Jason D. Baker, *Christian cyberspace companion: A guide to the Internet and Christian online resources*, 2d. ed. (Grand Rapids MI: Baker Books, 1997); Patrick Durusau, *High places in cyberspace: A guide to Biblical and religious studies, classics, and archaeological resources on the Internet*, 2d. ed. (Atlanta GA: Scholars Press, 1998); Irving Green, *Judaism on the Web* (New York: MIS Press, 1997); and John Raymond, *Catholics on the Internet* (Rocklin CA: Prima, 1997).
3. Alexander Roberts and James Donaldson, eds., *The Ante-Nicene Fathers: Translations of the writings of the Fathers down to A.D. 325* (Grand Rapids, MI: W.B. Eerdmans, 1969-1973); Philip Schaff, *A Select library of the Nicene and post-*

Nicene fathers of the Christian church, First series (Grand Rapids, MI: W.R. Eerd-mans Pub. Co., 1956); Philip Schaff and Henry Wace, eds., *A Select library of Nicene and post-Nicene fathers of the Christian church*, Second series (Grand Rapids, MI: W. B. Eerdmans Pub. Co., 1952-57).

4. Charles G. Herbermann et al., eds., *The Catholic encyclopedia: An internation-al work of reference on the constitution, doctrine, discipline, and history of the Cath-olic Church* (New York: Encyclopedia Press, 1913-1914); *New Catholic encyclope-dia* (New York: McGraw-Hill [1967-79]).

5. I would like to note that Bible Gateway is attempting to make the site more user-friendly to vision-impaired readers by providing key-stroke access in addition to mouse-based searching.

Some Selected Internet Resources
for Novice Researchers of Christian History

Michael Strickland

SUMMARY. This article attempts to assist novice researchers of Christian history explore the Internet. It contains a helpful starting point and key Web resources for the study of Christian history, with a primary focus on English language and Protestant information. *[Article copies available for a fee from The Haworth Document Delivery Service: 1-800-342-9678. E-mail address: <getinfo@haworthpressinc.com> Website: <http://www.Haworth Press.com>* © 2001 by The Haworth Press, Inc. All rights reserved.]

KEYWORDS. History of Christianity, Internet research

The Internet is filled with sites containing a wide range of resources for researchers in Christian history, and they continue to grow at a staggering rate. It is astounding when one considers how much has become available to the average researcher during the past ten years. With such a daunting amount of information available, where does a novice researcher begin his or her Internet research? What sites are the most useful? Instead of attempting to provide a comprehensive guide, this paper will focus on some of the resources available to novice researchers in their study of the history of Christianity. The Internet resources selected for this paper will be limited to English language

---

Michael Strickland, MDiv, MA, MLIS, is Library Director, Memphis Theological Seminary, Memphis, TN 38104.

[Haworth co-indexing entry note]: "Some Selected Internet Resources for Novice Researchers of Christian History." Strickland, Michael. Co-published simultaneously in *Journal of Religious & Theological Information* (The Haworth Information Press, an imprint of The Haworth Press, Inc.) Vol. 3, No. 3/4, 2001, pp. 151-160; and: *Theological Librarians and the Internet: Implications for Practice* (ed: Mark Stover) The Haworth Information Press, an imprint of The Haworth Press, Inc., 2001, pp. 151-160. Single or multiple copies of this article are available for a fee from The Haworth Document Delivery Service [1-800-342-9678, 9:00 a.m. - 5:00 p.m. (EST). E-mail address: getinfo@haworthpressinc.com].

ones. Although I have tried to be inclusive, I must confess that as a Protestant many of these selected resources are weighted toward American Protestant Christianity. I will also be writing from the standpoint of a theological librarian.

It is important to note that as the number of Christian history resources continue to grow the need for librarians, especially theological librarians, to examine, choose and organize the best and most useful sites will also continue to grow. As a result, it is very important that theological librarians help cull through the prolific maze of Web sites and help select the best and most useful sites for students, faculty and general researchers of Christian History.

In order to help organize the information available, I will break these Internet resources down into four main areas: theological libraries, multi-resource Web sites, Christian History Web sites, and ready reference Web sites. I have made no attempt to be exhaustive. I have selected some of the Internet resources that I believe can be good starting points for a novice researcher of Christian History.

THEOLOGICAL LIBRARIES

More and more theological librarians are sifting though theological and religious information found on the Web and selecting some of the more useful Web sites for their patrons. We are fortunate that through the World Wide Web most of this information is available to us as well. I increasingly find theological library Web sites to be more and more valuable in helping to find and organize the massive amount of theological and religious information on the Web. Several theological libraries have taken it upon themselves to organize their Web sites thematically. For instance, I personally found Vanderbilt Divinity Library's Web page *Church History and History of Christian Thought* (*http://divinity.library.vanderbilt.edu/chsub.htm*) with its links to bibliographic and electronic resources very helpful. Another extremely helpful and useful resource is Yale University Divinity Library's *Research Guide, Christianity: Church History* (*http://www.library.yale. edu/div/history.htm*). The site contains links to information about theological and religious indexes, abstracts, reference tools, bibliographies, selected journals and Internet resources along with sites with electronic texts and primary sources. Other theological libraries that provide excellent links to resources in Christian History include: Princeton, Duke, Emory, and Graduate Theological Union.

If you want to start with the best place to research Christian History on the Web, I suggest that you start with the online catalog of your nearest theological library. This may sound like a silly proposition but most theological libraries holdings are now available online. Today one can generally search the holdings of such places as Harvard, Princeton, Yale, Duke, Vanderbilt, and Graduate Theological Union just to name a few with relative ease. There are several excellent resources available to help Christian history researchers explore various theological library catalogues online. The first resource is the *Wabash Center's Individual Library Links* located at *http://www.wabash center.wabash.edu/Internet/library.htm#Libraries*. This resource contains links to several theological libraries listed in alphabetical order. Another resource that provides links to theological libraries is Saundra Lipton's *Religious Studies Web Guide* (*http://www.acs.ucalgary. ca/~lipton/catalogues.html*). Lipton's guide also includes links to Religious Archives and Special Collections, which also could prove highly useful for Christian History researchers. The third resource, *The Association of Theological Schools Membership Directory* (http://www.ats.edu/sets/membfst.htm) contains alphabetical, denominational and geographical indexes of member schools. Most of these member schools contain links to their theological libraries.

MULTI-RESOURCE WEB SITES

Increasing numbers of theological libraries are providing users with access to databases such as OCLC's New FirstSearch and Gale Publishing Groups InfoTrac. In fact, within the New FirstSearch itself, some libraries provide access to the American Theological Library Association's Religion Database, which is highly recommended to consult, if available online. New FirstSearch (*http://newfirstsearch.oclc.org*) also provides access to WorldCat, a database that contains the holdings of most libraries throughout the world, Electronic Collections Online, Net-First, and ArticleFirst. It also provides access to a wide range of general and specific databases. Gale Publishing Group's InfoTrac (*http://www. galegroup.com/library/resrcs/catalog/infoWeb.htm*) also provides access to full-text, reference and custom databases. It is amazing the amount of information that can be found on Christian history simply by consulting these two resources if they are available to users via the Internet. A word of warning: many theological libraries have restrictions on the availability and usage of these resources, so check with your nearest library.

There are also several general Web sites that I believe researchers of Christian History will find useful and productive in their research. The first religious Web sites that I would recommend include the *Wabash Center for Teaching and Learning Theology and Religion*, (*http://www.wabashcenter.wabash.edu/*), Saundra Lipton's *Religious Studies Web Guide*, (*http://www.acs.ucalgary.ca/~lipton/*), and John Gresham's *Finding God in Cyberspace.*

Wabash Center Guide to Internet Resources for Teaching and Learning Theology and Religion (*http://www.wabashcenter.wabash. edu/Internet/front.htm*) is a selective, annotated guide to a wide variety of electronic resources designed specifically for those who are teaching or studying religion and theology. The material is divided into various types: syllabi, electronic texts, electronic journals, Web sites, bibliographies, listserv discussion groups, and even some liturgical resources. In particular, researchers may find the syllabi and bibliographies of Christian History valuable and helpful in their research.

Religious Studies Web Guide (*http://www.acs.ucalgary.ca/~lipton/ index.html*) focuses on resources available to researchers involved in the academic study of religion. Maintained by Saundra Lipton at the University of Calgary and Cheryl Adams at the Library of Congress, *Religious Studies Web Guide* also includes pointers to journals in religious studies. *Religious. Studies Web Guide's* resources are arranged by format, religious group and selected topics. This site contains a number of links to other Web sites useful for the academic study of religion.

John L. Gresham's *Finding God in Cyberspace: A Guide to Religious Studies Resources on the Internet* (*http://www.fontbonne.edu/ libserv/fgic/fgic.htm*) provides a selective listing of the best Internet resources of interest to religious studies scholars and students of religion. Rather than attempt a comprehensive listing of religious information on the Internet, this guide selectively points to the best gateways to specific types of religious information.

Other Internet resources that researchers of Christian History may find valuable include Internet Search Engines such as *Yahoo, Alta-Vista, Lycos, Excite, About.Com* and *GoTo.Com* along with meta-search engines such as *Webcrawler.* For example, *Yahoo*'s Religion and Society section contains links to a variety of religious resources. There are also specifically Christian search engines such as *Cross Daily.Com* (*http://www.crossdaily.com*) and *Goshen.Net* (*http://www. gosearch.net*) that also contain Christian History links. *CrossSearch: Online Christian Resource Directory* (*http://www.crosssearch.com*) contains an extensive list of links with a search engine. *Christianity. Net/SEARCH* (*http://www.christianity.net/search/*) is another searchable database of nearly 10,000 links to Christian Web sites. They can be searched by main category as well as through a built-in search engine.

Metasearch engines, *Metacrawler* (*http://www.metacrawler.com*), *Monstercrawler* (*http://www.monstercrawler.com*) or *Searchpower. Com* (*http://www.Searchpower.com*), which claims to be the world's largest search engine directory, can search the databases of multiple search engines. Metasearch engines may also prove to be a valuable resource and time-saver for novice researchers.

Search engines and theological libraries, however, are not the only resources one can find on the World Wide Web pertaining to Christian History. There are several excellent Christian History multi-resource Web sites that contain invaluable links to materials or information. Below are some the best multi-resource Christian History Web sites.

APS Research Guide to Resources in Theology (*http://www.utoronto. ca/stmikes/theobook.htm*) is an extremely valuable resource that many historical researchers will find useful. It contains an extensive Catholic section as well as a strong Orthodox section. It also includes links to Anglican, Ecumenical, Evangelical and Protestant resources, as well as links to manuscripts, texts and miscellaneous materials.

Computer-Assisted Theology: Internet Resources (*http://info. ox.ac.uk/ctitext/theology/*) contains listings covering the history of theology. It also contains links to numerous religious and denominational resources including religious studies institutions, departments and digital libraries.

The Academic Info: Religion Gateway (*http://www.academicinfo. net/religindex.html*) is a site compiled by Mike Madin, formerly a University of Washington graduate student. The site provides a gateway to several quality educational resources in the area of the history of Christianity.

Religious Resources on the Net (*http://www.aphids.com/relres/*) is a comprehensive, searchable database of religious and Christian Web sites on the Internet. *Religious Resources* is part of the religion mega-site from Aphids Communications. Visitors to the Web site can browse through selected topics or use the search engine to search for Christian history resources.

Religion Religions Religious Studies (*http://www.clas.ufl.edu/users/ gthursby/rel/*) located at the University of Florida includes information and links for study and interpretation of religions. I believe it to be one of the best resources on Religious Studies and religious traditions on the Internet. Researchers of Christian History will also find this resource useful.

Another excellent Internet resource for novice Christian history researchers is the *Virtual Religion Index: Links to Research in Religion* (*http://religion.rutgers.edu/vri/index.html*). The Christian Tradition Index is an extremely valuable and useful tool.

American Religious Experience (*http://www.wvu.edu/col103/relst/ www/are.htm*), a project of the University of West Virginia, encourages the development and publication of American religion manuscripts and other information on the Internet. This site contains several potentially useful links to a novice Christian history researcher including links to American Religious History, Ancient History of Religion, American Frontier History, Religious Movements, Religion in the United States, and Women and Religion. One will also find links to book reviews on American Religious History, recently featured articles and a link to the *Journal of Southern Religion.*

Religion, Society and Culture in Newfoundland and Labrador, created by Dr. Hans Rollmann (*http://www.ucs.mun.cal/~hrollman/*), is without doubt one of the best Christian history sites on the Web. Although designed primarily for users in Canada, all researchers benefit from Rollmann's site, which links users with a variety of Christian groups. The groups range from Anglicans, Catholics, Congregationalists and the Salvation Army along with links to Native Religions. I highly recommend his Restoration Movement page (*http://www.mun. ca/rels/restmov/index.htm*). This is one of the best sites on the Web for information about the Restoration Movement, which spawned the birth of the Christian Church (Disciples of Christ) and United Church of Christ (UCC).

Some of the best Catholic multi-resource Web sites include: *Theology Library* (*http://www.mcgill.pvt.k12.al.us/jerryd/cm/history.htm*), an extensive Catholic collection of Internet resources in the spirit of the Second Vatican Council, and *Catholic Resources on the Net* (*http://www.cs.cmu.edu/People/spok/catholic.html*), an excellent collection of links related to the Roman Catholic church. These sites include Catholic and early church documents, liturgical information, people, and organizations.

Institute for the Study of American Evangelicals or ISAE (*http://www.wheaton.edu/isae/wwwsite.htm#AmRelHistory*) Web site located at Wheaton College is another excellent resource. The ISAE promotes research and support of evangelical Christianity in the United States and Canada. This site contains links to other related sites such as the *H-AmRel* Web site, Religion in America, Religion in the South and Religion in United States Syllabus. Besides containing information about itself, the site contains links to other Web addresses that Christian history researchers might find useful. One of the more interesting links is to the *Billy Graham Center Archives,* also located at Wheaton College (*http://www.wheaton.edu/bgc/archives/archhp1.html*). This site provides finding aids and unpublished documents on the history of North American nondenominational Protestant efforts to spread the Christian message, as well as missionary efforts throughout the world.

The University of Virginia's *Religious Movements Homepage* (*http://www.religiousmovements.org*) is another excellent site. It is dedicated to the study of religious movements on the Web and around the world. A novice researcher might find it a treasure trove of information on various religious movements throughout history.

World Lecture Hall: Religious Studies (*http://www.utexas.edu/world/lecture/rel/*) contains links to several history of religion course syllabi, discussions, and pointers to Internet resources.

Christian history researchers will also find *The Electronically Linked Academy* or TELA from Scholars Press (*http://scholar.cc.emory.edu*) very useful. The site includes pointers to five religious studies organizations (AAR, APA, ASOR, ASP, and SBL) and provides information about religious teaching and publishing. For example, *Religious and Theological Journals* (*http://scholar.cc.emory.edu/scripts/publications/pub-online.html*), a page within the TELA site, points to several electronic journals in religion.

CHRISTIAN HISTORY WEB SITES

Christian Classics Ethereal Library (*http://ccel.wheaton.edu/*) is undoubtedly one of the best resources for classic Christian texts on the

Internet. For those interested in early church history this site is a must. Another excellent textual resource for early church documents is the Institute for Christian Leadership's *Guide to Early Church Documents* (*http://www.iclnet.org/pub/resources/christian-history.html*) which includes links to creeds and canons as well as several early Christian documents. Among those historical documents are those of the *Project Wittenberg* (*http://www.iclnet.org/pub/resources/text/wittenberg/wittenberg-home.html*), which contain documents by Martin Luther and other Lutheran theologians.

Church History (*http://www.Churchhistory.net*) is another resource for the early church documents. This site created by David Russell focuses primarily on the first three centuries of the church's history; it also links to Russell's Reformation Resources Web site. Another good resource is the University of Pennsylvania's Religious Texts and Resources (*http://ccat.sas.upenn.edu/rs/texts.html*) which contains texts of the church fathers and other religions. *Early Church Writings* (*http://www.cs.cmu.edu/People/spok/catholic/writings.html*), a page within the "Catholic Resources on the Net" site, also includes an excellent collection of links to early church documents on the Internet.

Some other general Christian History sites include *Christian History* magazine's Web site (*http://www.christianity.net*) which includes pointers to several potentially useful sites for researchers. Among them are links to General Christian History, General History, Early Church, Dead Sea Scrolls, Celtic Christianity, Middle Ages, Reformation, Victorian Britain, American Christianity, Catholicism, Denominational History, Evangelicalism and Fundamentalism and [Christian] Personalities. *ChristianHistory.net* is *Christian History*'s weekly online magazine. It too contains links to articles and other resources related to Christian history.

Hall of Church History (*http://www.gty.org/~phil/hall.htm*) is one of the Internet's better Christian history pages. The Web site offers "Theology From A Bunch of Dead Guys" which include Church Fathers, Medieval Churchmen, Heretics, Eastern Orthodox, Catholics, Reformers, Puritans, Anabaptists, Arminians, Cultists, Unorthodox, Baptists, and "Recent Stalwarts." Many of the links will be especially useful for researching personalities or documents.

An excellent Catholic Christian History site is the Clemens and Alcuin Joint Libraries' *Internet Theology Resources: Church History and Historical Theology* (*http://www.csbsju.edu/library/internet/*

theochht.html). Created by St. Benedict and St. John's Universities in Minnesota, this site offers extensive research guides and links to several major online directories. Meanwhile, *The Holy See Vatican Web Site (http://www.vatican.va/)*, the official home page of the Vatican, is also a good source for Catholic historical information. For instance, it includes papal documents that can be read in seven different languages.

CHRISTIAN HISTORY READY REFERENCE WEB SITES

There are several excellent sites that provide novice researchers with quick reference to facts and figures pertaining to Christian History. The number of these "ready" reference sites also continues to grow. I have selected just a few of these important resources now available on the World Wide Web.

One of the most important ready reference sites is the Lilly Foundation's *American Religion Data Archive (http://www.arda.tm)*, housed at Purdue University. The archive collects quantitative data sets for the study of American religion. Its goal is to preserve data, improve data, increase the use of data, and allow comparisons across data files. Researchers will increasingly find this an important resource on the evolution of American Christianity.

Britannica.Com (http://www.britannica.com), the Web site of the *Encyclopedia Britannica*, contains some excellent refereed links to resources in Christian History. *Britannica's* editorial staff rates the Web sites they include on their list. The *Britannica* list is not just a mere collection of Web sites relating to the topic of Christian history. The editors strive to choose what they consider the best sites. It is a great resource and will become increasingly valuable in the years to come.

An excellent religious encyclopedia available on the Web is *The Ecole Initiative (http://www2.evansville.edu/ecoleWeb/)* an interactive hypertext encyclopedia on early church history that will be of value to researchers of early Christian history. Another religious encyclopedia that may also prove valuable to Christian History researchers, *The Catholic Encyclopedia (http://www.newadvent.org/cathen/)* is an online version of the 1913 edition.

Some important ready reference Web sites for researchers of Christian History during the Medieval period include *The Online Reference Book for Medieval Studies, Catholic Online Saints Index* and *Medi-*

eval Feminist Index. The Online Reference Book for Medieval Studies (*http://orb.rhodes.edu*), or the ORB, is an academic site, written and maintained by medieval scholars primarily for instructors and serious students of the Middle Ages. The *Catholic Online Saints Index* (*http://www.catholic.org/saints/stsindex.html*), is a searchable index of patron saints. The *Medieval Feminist Index* (*http://www.haverford. edu/library/reference/mschaus/mfi/mfi.html*), or MFI, is an Internet database that can be searched for citations to journal articles and essays on topics dealing with medieval women. The MFI focuses primarily on geographical areas where Europeans traveled during the medieval period.

CONCLUSION

In light of the massive amounts of information relating to the history of Christianity available on the Internet, this paper had to be broad in scope. Rather than provide a comprehensive listing, I have instead attempted to provide samples of resources available in Christian History that I found useful in my own research. It is my hope that this collection of selected resources will provide novice researchers in Christian history with a few starting points from which to begin their own research.

Theoretical and Conceptual Foundations for Web Site Design in Religious and Theological Academic Libraries

Mark Stover

SUMMARY. This article develops a theoretical and conceptual basis for Web site design in academic theological libraries. The article discusses the locus of librarians in the organization of information, the mission of higher education and of the academic library, the purpose of the theological library, the changing role of libraries, the function of libraries as represented on the Web, the nature of hypermedia documents, and criteria for the design and content of Web pages. *[Article copies available for a fee from The Haworth Document Delivery Service: 1-800-342-9678. E-mail address: <getinfo@haworthpressinc.com> Website: <http://www.Haworth Press.com> © 2001 by The Haworth Press, Inc. All rights reserved.]*

KEYWORDS. Web site design, theological libraries, mission of higher education, role of libraries

INTRODUCTION

Religious and theological academic libraries (comprised primarily of seminary libraries and religious college libraries) have specific needs in terms of Web site design. They must take into consideration

Mark Stover, MAR, MLS, PhD, is Psychological and Behavioral Sciences Librarian, San Diego State University, 5500 Campanile Drive, San Diego, CA 92182-8050 (E-mail: mstover@mail.sdsu.edu).

[Haworth co-indexing entry note]: "Theoretical and Conceptual Foundations for Web Site Design in Religious and Theological Academic Libraries." Stover, Mark. Co-published simultaneously in *Journal of Religious & Theological Information* (The Haworth Information Press, an imprint of The Haworth Press, Inc.) Vol. 3, No. 3/4, 2001, pp. 161-201; and: *Theological Librarians and the Internet: Implications for Practice* (ed: Mark Stover) The Haworth Information Press, an imprint of The Haworth Press, Inc., 2001, pp. 161-201. Single or multiple copies of this article are available for a fee from The Haworth Document Delivery Service [1-800-342-9678, 9:00 a.m. - 5:00 p.m. (EST). E-mail address: getinfo@haworthpressinc. com].

not only the needs of their students, but also the mission of the theological seminary, principles of good Web page design, and the role of library Web sites. This article will seek to develop theoretical and conceptual foundations for religious and theological academic library Web sites. It will be inclusive of the following fields of study: higher education, academic libraries, library and information science, human-computer interaction, hypermedia, and Web page design.

The topics to be discussed include the locus of librarians in the organization of information, the mission of higher education and of the academic library, the purpose of the theological library, the changing role of libraries, the function of libraries as represented on the Web, the nature of hypermedia documents, and criteria for the design and content of Web pages. For the purposes of this article, theological academic libraries will be defined as those libraries that focus on theological studies in colleges and seminaries. Thus, church and synagogue libraries, as well as libraries serving religious schools for children, will be excluded from the scope of this paper.

THE PLACE OF LIBRARIANS
IN THE ORGANIZATION OF INFORMATION

Many authors express the belief that librarians possess special skills in the management and organization of information (Mason 1990; Davidson and Rusk 1996; Rowland 1994), and that the emergence of the Web has provided librarians with a special opportunity to showcase these talents as a profession. As Kruger writes, "The discipline of the librarian will have to be introduced onto the Net." He goes on to say that, "It is the craft of the librarian that is required to engineer change on the Web" (Kruger 1995, 493). Rosenfeld and Morville (1998, 17) add that, "Librarianship is an important discipline to turn to for information architecture expertise."

Davidson and Rusk (1996), in an article on Web design within an academic environment, imply that librarians are experts in knowledge organization and thus need to be utilized in the Web design process. Rowland (1994, 144), in a journal article written for non-librarians, describes librarians as "professional information managers whose role is to guide students and researchers through the confusing maze of products and services that have proliferated in a very few years." These comments and similar expressions (Powell 1994; Stern 1995) abound in the library literature. Clearly, librarians are perceived, at least in their own communities, as having information organizing skills which can be applied to the Web.

Along with their perceived expertise in organizing knowledge, librarians (especially academic librarians) are also viewed by some as potential authenticators of the authority of information on the Web. According to Anderson (1992), the library plays a role in creating or ascribing authority to a book or document. By placing a work within the collection, the library is making a statement about the work: that it has at least some measure of credibility, that the author and publisher are who they say they are, and that the work may be beneficial to at least some in the research community. Anderson believes that the library in its electronic form should continue this tradition. He states, "By preserving and making these linkages in hypermedia, the library represents to readers the official publication" (Anderson 1992, 115-116).

Along the same lines, Noam (1996, 9) writes that, "In the validation of information, the university will become more important than ever. With the explosive growth in the production of knowledge, society requires credible gatekeepers of information, and has entrusted some of that function to universities and its resident experts, not to information networks." Given that the above quotation appeared in a journal whose readership consists primarily of librarians and information professionals, it is clear that the author views librarians as comprising at least one contingency of the "resident experts" that colleges and universities use as knowledge gatekeepers. While the role of librarians in the authentication of information may be a debatable topic, its very acknowledgment is relevant given the many concerns voiced today about the difficulty of locating authoritative information on the Web (Brandt 1996; Tillman 1995).

THE MISSION OF HIGHER EDUCATION

The late Bart Giamatti, president of Yale University, wrote that colleges and universities, "must know what they are about, [must] know why they exist and [must know] where they are going" (1988, 37-38). Over the past century, this knowledge (of the past, present, and future) has largely been interpreted by American colleges and universities as the three-fold mission of research, teaching, and public service (Blackburn and Lawrence 1995; Campbell 1995; Centra 1993).

As Keohane (1993) has written, another way to frame the purpose of higher education would be to divide it up into the discovery of knowledge (research), the sharing of knowledge (teaching), and the application of knowledge in improving the human condition (public service).

Even today, in the face of changing technologies, methodologies, and constituencies (Fairweather 1996; Koepplin and Wilson 1985), this long-accepted mission of the academy is embraced. Teaching methods can change, research tools can change, and public service can find new forms of delivery, but the mission remains the same (McClure and Lopata 1996). Indeed, many authors (Campbell 1995; Blackburn and Lawrence 1995) have demonstrated the continuing relevance for teaching, research, and public service across the spectrum of small colleges and large universities, including state-supported, private, and religious-oriented institutions, as well as historically black colleges. While there is some perception that the research facet of the educational mission is the sole domain of the large university, most commentators do not support this notion. Schuman writes that even the historical importance of teaching in the small college "does not, of course, mean that research, publication, [and] community service will be excluded" from the mission of the college (1995, 22).

The tripartite mission of the academy in the United States is rooted in the land-grant model developed in the nineteenth century (Cardozier 1987; Campbell 1995). The British model of undergraduate instruction combined with the uniquely American land-grant ideal of public service to form the higher education model of the late nineteenth century (Keohane 1993). While research almost always played a role in the American university experience, the German standard of pure research at the graduate level heavily influenced American higher education so much so that in some universities today the domain of research stands above teaching and service in the minds of faculty and administrators (Bavaro 1995). While this last point has long been debated (Baker 1986; Sandmann and Gillespie 1991), the consensus is that most higher education administrators encourage a balanced approach (Park 1996; Ehrlich and Frey 1995; DeNeef and Goodwin 1995; Atkinson and Tuzin 1992). As Campbell (1995, 102) writes, "To ask which of the three is the most important is to miss their obvious interrelatedness. Indeed, they are equally important."

Perhaps the most misunderstood facet of the college and university mission is service. Blackburn and Lawrence write that service seems to encompass "everything that is neither teaching, research, nor scholarship" (1995, 222). The authors further distinguish between internal and external service. Internal service routinely includes campus committee activities, speaking to alumni, or sponsoring student organizations. External service includes consulting (either for a fee or pro bono) and working within a professional association. Centra (1993) delineates various kinds of public service, including: (1) "national missions," which uses the original model of the land-grant college where faculty consult with local (or sometimes national) industry; (2) assistance to community groups; (3) continuing education; and (4) professional activities.

Fear and Sandmann (1995) and Martin (1977) see public service as the least-favored, but perhaps most important, part of the trilateral mission of higher education. Service can be viewed from various perspectives, including faculty-based (where teaching and research are a form of service); consultant-based (where faculty serve as consultants to government, industry, and non-profit organizations); and student-based (where students are encouraged to serve the community in various ways).

THE MISSION OF THEOLOGICAL SCHOOLS AND SEMINARIES

Theological schools and seminaries are "special-purpose institutions," operating primarily at the post-baccalaureate level of higher education, that offer academic and professional theological degrees in preparation for "positions of religious leadership" (Association of Theological Schools 2000). Graduates of these schools may serve as ordained clergy, teachers at various levels of the educational process, non-ordained religious professionals, or in a variety of lay positions in the religious community.

The mission of these schools is similar to the mission of other institutions of higher learning, encompassing teaching, research, and service. According to the accreditation standards of the primary accreditation body for theological higher education, "these schools have, at their center, the work of learning, teaching, and research that together comprise theological scholarship. These activities are ordered to educational goals through the structure and purposes of the theological curriculum" (Association of Theological Schools 2000).

While there are many analogies between secular universities and theological seminaries, it is clear that "the theological character of [these] schools is central to their identity" (Association of Theological Schools 2000). Thus, the mission of theological seminaries will be equally driven by the generic mission of the academy (research, teaching, and service) as well as by their religious identity. In addition, various theological distinctives and denominational affiliations will also serve to inform the purpose and mission of these theological schools.

THE MISSION OF THE ACADEMIC LIBRARY

Why do academic libraries exist? The question of mission is at the heart of modern academic librarianship, and thus is highly relevant to those who work and teach in the higher education library community. By analogy it is also relevant to the question of library Web page design, since the purpose and goal of the library Web site should be grounded in the mission of the library.

The literature of librarianship espouses two distinct approaches to the purpose of the academic library (B. Lynch 1995; C. Lynch 1995). Some library commentators speak of the "mission" or "purpose" of the academic library. This approach emphasizes the theoretical intent of the library. Other writers speak of the "function" or "role" of the higher education library. This perspective approaches the question of the existence of the college or university library in terms of a practical consequence of its theoretical orientation. These perspectives are not mutually exclusive; indeed, they are each valid and important in their own way, and complement each other.

Many authors who write about the mission of the academic library recognize that it must be subordinate to the mission of its parent institution (Euster 1995; Wolff 1995; Josey 1975). Atkins (1991, 1) asserts: "Throughout the history of American higher education, the academic library has supported the university in its educational mission." McConnell (1993, 35) quotes the strategic plan of the Arizona State University Libraries when he writes that the "mission of the University Libraries is to enhance and participate in the current and anticipated instructional, research, service and other strategic goals of Arizona State University." This discussion is sometimes framed within the context of the three-fold mission of the academy, as is the case with the above reference, but more often than not it is left as a generalized notion. Regardless of the degree of specificity, this paper terms the latter perspective as the "subordinate" view of the mission of the academic library.

Most authors who discuss the role or function of higher education libraries advocate the idea of collection, organization, and dissemination (or access) (Euster 1995; C. Lynch 1995). That is, the library should be in the business of collecting, organizing, and disseminating information. (This idea is equivalent to the traditional division of labor in libraries among the three areas of collection development, cataloging, and reference). In fact, this nearly universal ideal of librarianship is not limited to college and university libraries. This perspective is referred to in this study as the "universal" view of the role or function of academic libraries.

Lynch can be said to embrace the subordinate view of the academic library mission in that she believes that the academic library has traditionally "supported the teaching, research, and service missions of the university" (B. Lynch 1995, 3-4). Even so, the library has been able to remain relatively autonomous in the campus environment due to the stability of the academic mission. Lynch also notes, however, that as the academy "changes and information technologies continue to develop rapidly, library services and operations will be determined collaboratively in the context of the university's goals and mission."

Euster (1995, 12-13) makes another case for the subordinate perspective. She believes that the academic library must fit into the three-fold mission (teaching, research, and service) of higher education, but she also subscribes to the universal view when she states that even in the midst of technological change, the "underlying role of the library remains the acquisition, organization, and dissemination of recorded knowledge and information for students, faculty, and community users."

C. Lynch (1995, 93-94) argues for both perspectives (subordinate and universal) when he writes about the mission and role of academic libraries. He describes the changing role of the academic library in light of both information technology as well as the broader purposes of the higher education. He seems to view the mission of the academy as being summarized by "teaching, learning, research, and scholarly communication," which is a modified version of the three-fold academic mission. On the other hand he also expresses his belief that the basic role of academic libraries is "to select and acquire, organize, provide access to, and preserve, information of all types," which is the universal perspective on the academic library. Finally, he asserts that changes in academic libraries "must and increasingly will be guided by the priorities of their host higher educational institutions," which again echoes the subordinate view of the mission of higher education libraries.

Another advocate of both perspectives is Buckland (1989; 1992) who clearly distinguishes between role and mission. His view of the role of libraries is that they should "facilitate access to documents." His view of the mission of libraries is that they should "support the mission of the institution or the interests of the population served" (1992, 3). Along much the same lines, Churchwell (1975, 21) states, "As a primary supporter of academic programs, the library is not free to set its own goals and immediate objectives; it must wait for the colleges and universities it serves to establish their goals, objectives, and educational policies."

Atkinson advances the universal perspective on the function of higher education libraries (collection, organization, and access to information). He writes:

> Academic libraries exist for only one purpose: to provide local users–scholars and students–with access to the information they need for their education and research. The library achieves that purpose by ensuring that needed sources of information remain accessible and reliable (that is, authentic, unaltered) over time, and by establishing conventionalized relationships among published sources so that users can make decisions about which sources to consult and interpret in which order. Collection building is one of the primary means used by the library to ensure access and establish source relationships. (1995, 43)

Atkinson's reference to "education and research" is an allusion to two-thirds of the tripartite mission of the academy. Thus, while universalizing library mission, he also provides a reference to the subordinate view as well.

Berring (1995, 97) echoes the universal perspective when he writes, "throughout history, librarians have carried out three basic functions. First, they have gathered and protected data; second, they have organized and stored that data according to some system; third, they have distributed that data to users." In a similar fashion, Martin (1996, 291) maintains that "to best serve the research and scholarly community in its need for information resources, libraries must continue to serve the role that they have traditionally served–of identifying, locating, and organizing information." Finally, Schnell (1995, 440) writes that "traditionally, the role of libraries has been to acquire, organize, and make accessible information in a wide variety of formats."

Both collection development and the provision of access to information imply the necessity of preservation of information (Berring 1995; Stover 1999). Thus, preservation can perhaps be thought of as the fourth facet of the function of academic libraries.

Despite the tendency of some in the literature to focus on role or function to the detriment of mission, there is a consensus among academic librarians that the mission of the college or university library is inextricably connected with the tripartite mission of higher education. This is demonstrated by literature that focuses on traditional librarianship (McGowan and Dow 1995; Slattery 1994; Black and Leysen 1994) as well as by literature that emphasizes information technology (Chiang and Elkington 1994; Wilkins and Nantz 1995; McConnell 1993). The *mission* of the academic library is to support research, teaching, and service within the parameters of its parent institution. The *role* of the academic library is to collect, preserve, organize, and provide access to information in support of the broader library and institutional mission.

THE MISSION OF THE THEOLOGICAL LIBRARY

The Association of Theological Schools (ATS) publishes guidelines on their Web site for theological libraries (Association of Theological Schools 2000). These guidelines include parameters for the library collection, the library's contribution to the theological education process, and necessary resources in the work of theological librarianship.

The ATS accreditation guidelines assert that the theological "library is a central resource for theological scholarship and the theological curriculum. It is integral to the purpose of the school through its contribution to teaching, learning, and research, and it functions as a partner in curriculum development and implementation" (Association of Theological Schools 2000). The document goes on to state that "to accomplish its task, the library requires appropriate collections, effective information technology, and sufficient human and physical resources."

While the theological library's mission is analogous in many ways to its secular counterpart, it also has several additional facets that make it unique among academic libraries. The textual tradition is given prominence in most religious communities. Thus, "theological study requires extensive encounter with historical and contemporary texts" (Association of Theological Schools 2000). In addition, most theological libraries support the goals and aims of a particular religious tradition, and thus will often seek to preserve archival collections associated with a denomination or spiritual community. While print materials are highly valued among theological librarians, ATS also encourages these libraries to collect and preserve "other media and electronic resources as appropriate to the curriculum, and ensure access to relevant remote databases."

The theological library can fulfill its teaching, learning, and research responsibilities through a variety of means, including reference service, collection development, assistance in utilizing computing technology, teaching of theological bibliography, and service to the broader religious community. The library should also seek to collaborate with the teaching faculty and other parts of the campus community in the curriculum development process. Finally, library staff should plan for and anticipate "future intellectual and technological developments that might affect the library" (Association of Theological Schools 2000).

The theological academic library, like its cousin in the secular university, must integrate the mission of its parent institution into its own existential purpose. Thus, theological libraries must support the teaching, research, and service goals of the seminary community. These goals, while analogous to the threefold mission of the university, are sometimes quite different in their application.

Likewise, the role of the theological library is similar to the role of all libraries: to select, preserve, organize, and provide access to information resources. Given the prominence that the textual tradition has in religious communities, and given the fact that most theological seminaries are firmly grounded almost exclusively in the humanities, it is not surprising that the book and other print formats are strongly emphasized in most theological libraries. Nevertheless, the emergence of the Internet and the added value of electronic information has persuaded many theological librarians to focus more and more attention on electronic databases, digital publishing, and Web based religious and theological resources. Thus, the role of the theological library is expanding to include electronic data in its mandate to collect, organize, and provide access to the world's storehouses of information.

THE CHANGING ROLE OF THE ACADEMIC LIBRARY

Change in Higher Education

Certain themes clearly resonate from the literature regarding the future mission and role of the academic library. These include the following: (1) colleges and universities are changing; (2) academic libraries are changing; (3) many traditional aspects of the mission and function of the library will stay the same; (4) there will be new roles for the academic library; and (5) a transition to a future electronic library is occurring.

Johnson (1995) sees a variety of radical changes related to information technology that will affect the academy of the twenty-first century. These changes include how knowledge is delivered to students (the classroom model will migrate to a computer-based model); how faculty and staff are trained; and political ramifications related to accountability, funding, administration, and management.

Kling and Lamb (1996) write about a variety of factors that are transforming the higher education landscape vis-à-vis information technology (specifically electronic publishing). These include such issues as the changes (positive or negative) to scholarship and research, intellectual property rights, delivery of education, authenticity of knowledge, the quality of work life, and social equity.

Change in Academic Libraries

The higher education environment is clearly in a state of flux and change, and the academic library is also experiencing change, both as a result of broader institutional changes as well as a result of factors outside the academy (Dougherty and Hughes 1991). Information technology is clearly the focus of much change in the college and university library setting (see, for example, Bazillion and Braun 1995, and St. Lifer 1996).

Some writers (C. Lynch 1995; Kling and Lamb 1996) have commented on the rapid rate of change (specifically related to information technology) within American academic libraries. These changes have challenged the technological and intellectual capacities of librarians (Rowland 1994), and have forced libraries to seek out more collaborative relationships with other campus entities (B. Lynch 1995).

Some writers see the changes as more incremental. Schnell (1995, 440) believes that "by expanding the range of formats to include Internet information resources, [libraries] can support the growing demand among their clients for access to networked resources." This viewpoint builds on the traditional foundations of librarianship while incrementally preparing for future change.

Others frame this discussion within the context of the traditional library functions of selection, organization, and dissemination (McCabe and Person 1995). Okerson (1996, 181) focuses on collection building, stating that "the traditional mission of research libraries [was] to create and maintain large self-sufficient collections for their users," but that this is changing today. Zhou (1994) adds to this her views on collection development in the age of the Internet, and emphasizes the transition from ownership to access. Other writers, such as Kovacs, Schloman, and McDaniel (1994), discuss the impact of electronic media and resources on the very nature of reference librarianship.

Finally, some authors speak in almost apocalyptic tones about change in academic libraries. An article that best exemplifies this approach (Stoffle, Renaud, and Veldof 1996, 214) discusses why academic libraries must radically change or risk extinction. The authors assert that these changes must be made at a fundamental level, they must be irreversible, and they must be made quickly. This viewpoint criticizes the reliance on the traditional mission of supporting research and teaching, and instead posits a model that focuses on risk-taking, customer satisfaction, and collaboration. The authors state that "a basic rethinking of the mission, values, and assumptions under which library personnel work and plan is necessary." While this radical perspective certainly has many attractive attributes, it would seem to be lacking in a vital connection to the traditional mission of the academy and the universal functions of libraries.

Continuity in Academic Libraries

While much of the academic library literature emphasizes change, another equally large group focuses on continuity (Euster 1995; Riggs 1996). These writings do not deny the reality of change or the necessity for future adaptation, but they emphasize that change must be gradual and grounded in the foundational tenets of librarianship. As Martin (1996, 291) writes, "to best serve the research and scholarly community in its need for information resources, libraries must continue to serve the role that they have traditionally served–of identifying, locating, and organizing information."

Other authors describe continuity in terms of specific functions of the library. Anderson (1992) argues for a continuing role for collection development in the networked library, and Borgman (1996, 493) advocates continuity in terms of access to information when she writes that the task of libraries is "to provide primary information services for the networked world."

Finally, Levy and Marshall (1995) begin their discussion of digital libraries by stating that all libraries have three common properties: documents, technology, and work (or people). This definition enables the information professional to make the transition to the future electronic library without leaving behind the foundational roots of the profession.

New Roles for Libraries

Another theme that is dominant in the literature is that of new roles for libraries and librarians in the age of the Internet. Day and Armstrong (1996) write about the need for librarians to engage instructional faculty in discussions about the content of Web resources and links, to teach effective search strategies to faculty, and to keep up with changes in technology. Stover (1999) discusses the new role that librarians and libraries may play in the field of scholarly electronic publishing.

Some writers (Neal 1996; Hirshon 1993; St. Lifer 1996) temper an optimistic view of the future with caution. Academic librarians may potentially "provide the critical infrastructure for a rapidly changing information environment" (Neal 1996, 76), but this may also come with a radically different definition of the role of professional librarians. There will be higher expectations for librarians, who will be expected to work longer hours and become more technologically adept (St. Lifer 1996). The number of credentialed librarians may decrease, as more support staff with computer prowess take on roles that were previously reserved for librarians with graduate degrees (Neal 1996).

Rowland (1994, 150) provides perhaps the most grandiose scenario of the future role of the librarian. He states that "librarians and their clients are being challenged to understand, control, and use [the information] highway to bring the world to a new level of literacy and understanding." While this statement is optimistic in its portrayal of librarians, it may also prove to be prescient if the profession successfully meets the information needs of the global community.

The Library of the Future

A final theme that resonates throughout the academic library literature is that of the library of the future (Saunders and Mitchell 1996; Campbell 1994). This projected entity, called at various times an electronic library, a digital library, a virtual library, or a networked library, is thought by some to contain the solution to many of the problems facing academia today. These problems include the serials pricing crisis, the issue of scholarly communication overload, and campus politics.

However, while information technology may solve some higher education problems, newer challenges for campus information professionals will quickly rise up in their place. While technology will certainly drive the library of the future, it clearly is not a panacea to the multiplicity of issues that currently confront libraries in higher education (Dougherty and Hughes 1991; Price 1994).

THE NATURE OF LIBRARIES ON THE WEB

Four themes resound in the literature of academic libraries and the Web: the necessity of using the Internet to perform traditional library tasks, the requirement that librarians design library Web pages, the metaphor of the Web as a gateway to library resources, and the picture of the Web library as a surrogate for the physical library in its traditional mission and functions.

Several authors have discussed the imperative to perform traditional library tasks using the Web and other facets of the Internet (Bell 1995; Martin 1996). These tasks usually involve some aspect of traditional reference work (Baker 1995; Martin 1997; Jensen and Sih 1995), but other aspects of librarianship such as cataloging and collection development are also mentioned (Bell 1995; Martin 1997).

Some believe that librarians (as opposed to other members of the campus community) should be the primary force in the development of library Web. As one author states, "librarians are the best people to develop Web pages. We know what our patrons need, we know where the holes in our collections exist, and where they can be supplemented by additional resources, and we know how to organize those resources" (Bell 1995, 29).

Davidson and Rusk (1996) make a different kind of argument when they relate their experience in developing a Web site in an academic team setting. They note the importance of having a librarian presence on university Web teams, for political reasons as well as for reasons related to the abilities of librarians. This argument echoes perceptions discussed earlier in this literature review that present librarians as proficient knowledge navigators whose expertise, as Kruger (1995, 493) asserts, "will have to be introduced onto the Net" and whose craft will be "required to engineer change on the Web."

A distinction is needed between the first opinion (that librarians should be the primary impetus behind library Web sites because "they know the territory") and the second opinion (that librarians should impact the entire spectrum of college and university Web sites because of their extensive expertise in the organization of information). The first assertion would seem to have merit simply at face value. The second assertion is more open to debate, and will probably only be confirmed (or negated) after political and market forces have their way in the higher education environment.

A third theme discerned from the literature views the Web as a gateway to authenticated resources (Lester 1995; Mitchell and Mooney 1996; Ensor 1995), both traditional and digital (Balas 1996). As Stearns (1996, 55) notes, library Web pages are "doorways into virtual libraries."

The gateway metaphor is useful in some ways, but it tends to limit the library's potential resources and activities somewhat. Perhaps a better image comprises the fourth theme, that of the library Web site as a surrogate of the physical library (Davison and Rusk 1996; Tenopir 1996). This metaphor depicts the Web library as fulfilling the goals and functions of the traditional library. As Tenopir (1996, 128) states (in the context of making remarks pertaining to the WWW), "the librarian's task of selection, evaluation, and pointing to authoritative and high-quality content is more important than ever."

The surrogate model enables the Web library to function in a variety of roles. The Web site could support the three-fold mission of higher education in the following ways: providing access to research tools and resources for faculty and students (research), strengthening the curriculum by mounting full-text reserve materials on the Web (teaching), and maintaining a public access Web-based online catalog and providing links to other Internet sites (public service). Lowry, Soderdahl, and Dewey (1996, 640) echo this model when they describe the University of Iowa Libraries Web-based information system as a mechanism for "delivering information, communicating with clients, facilitating use of the Internet and other electronic resources, and as a teaching tool."

The traditional functions of the library (collecting, organizing, and providing access to information) could be continued under the surrogate model in the following ways. The traditional role of library collection development can be emulated through both digital full-text publications mounted on the Web site as well as links to other relevant Internet sites. The function of information organization can be recreated on the library Web site through proper classification of resources and links, collocation (placing similar resources together), cross-referencing, and indexing. The role of providing access to information can be fulfilled through the provision of search engines, Web-based online catalog search interfaces, and timely updates.

While the above illustrations exemplify the surrogate model of the library Web site, there are potentially many more ways that libraries can replicate the traditional academic library mission and function. Theological librarians should use a full measure of creativity and thoughtfulness in seeking to emulate (and indeed, in some ways to go beyond) the traditional library goal of supporting the parent institution and meeting the information needs of its users.

THE NATURE OF HYPERMEDIA DOCUMENTS

Nature of Hypermedia in General

Hypermedia and hypertext are at the core of the Web. Designing a Web site necessarily requires taking into consideration the nature of hypermedia (Van Brakel, Roeloffze, and Van Heerden 1995; Strain and Berry 1996).

Many writers have ably described the colorful history of hypermedia (Nielsen 1995a; Welsch 1992). It is sufficient to note here that while Ted Nelson and others played a foundational and ideological role in the creation and growth of the hypertext concept, the venue that popularized hypermedia for literally millions of users has been the enormous attraction of the Web.

The original definition of hypertext was simply "nonsequential writing" (Welsch 1992). The early days of computing did not allow for the inclusion of graphics and other multimedia formats. However, recent advances in computer technology have permitted the addition of sound, pictures, and video into the array of formats that once only included text. Today, many believe that the term "hypermedia" is becoming a more accurate and more accepted way to describe this phenomenon (Welsch 1992; Nanard and Nanard 1995).

Hypertext thus began as a text-oriented method of arranging non-linear information. As Langford (1993, 221) states, a "hyperdocument is an electronically stored text divided into discrete information nodes, which are linked in a way which is not necessarily linear." However, Welsch asserts that the recent "expansion of the scope of hypertext may lead to an expansion of our ideas on what constitutes 'reading and writing'–to include access to and use of graphics, sound, moving images, and other formats" (1992, 615-616), an entity that he prefers to call a "hypersystem." Isakowitz, Stohr, and Balasubramanian (1995, 4) provide an even broader definition when they state that hypermedia is a method of "managing relationships among information objects."

Hypermedia is viewed from two distinct perspectives in the literature. The first viewpoint is that hypermedia will create enormous changes in society and in recorded knowledge. Nelson and other hypertext pioneers (Welsch 1992; Nielsen 1995a) advocated this perspective early in its use, but others have more recently advanced this viewpoint. Barrett (1992, 1) writes that "sociomedia signifies that when we design computer media we are hardwiring a mechanism for the social construction of knowledge." He goes on to say that hypermedia forces the individual "to look outward from the machine into the complex interaction of human relationships which define 'university' and 'education,' human relationships that are the real content of all educational technology."

The second perspective on hypermedia is more subdued. This perspective characterizes hypermedia as simply a tool for information organization and retrieval that can be used, abused, or ignored (Agosti and Smeaton 1996). Hypermedia does not, in this position, completely ignore or discard the entire history of human thought that has utilized sequential thinking as the primary organizing feature of rational communication. As Atkinson (1993, 201) cautions, although hypermedia is primarily nonsequential, at least some structure and sequence is required for all types of communication.

Hypermedia Design

Some describe the hypermedia design process as "currently more of an art than a science" (Isakowitz et al. 1995, 34). Hypermedia applications cover a wide range of possibilities, so it is clear that "no single formal design technique is relevant for designing all of them" (Nanard and Nanard 1995, 50). However, it must also be said that the literature does contain some hypermedia design principles that can equally apply to a broad array of hypermedia information resources.

Users of hypermedia resources understand (or fail to understand) the meaning of the hypermedia document primarily through the way that it is designed (Thuring, Hannemann, and Haake 1995) and organized (Atkinson 1993). As one article states, "the major purpose of reading a document is comprehension, and reading a hyperdocument is no exception" (Thuring et al. 1995, 57).

Two important features of hypermedia design (related to comprehension) that are discussed at length in the literature are coherence and cognitive overhead (Thuring et al. 1995). Local coherence occurs when the author of the hyperdocument uses the same skills that linear text authors use to create a unified document. Words flow into clauses, which flow into sentences, which flow into paragraphs, which flow into documents, and all of these factors work together to produce a coherent entity. Global coherence goes beyond the individual document to create a coherent connection between the local document and all connected documents. The user sees and understands the connection between the document that he or she is viewing and all linked documents.

Cognitive overhead results from "the limited capacity of human information processing" (Thuring et al. 1995, 59). One of the consequences of too much cognitive overhead is information overload (Nielsen 1995a, 217-245). Two ways to reduce cognitive overhead are improving orientation (so that the user knows where he or she is located at any given time) and facilitating navigation (so that the user can easily get from one place to another). Disorientation and lack of ease in navigation are two common problems often cited by users of hyperdocuments (Thuring et al. 1995; Zhu 1995; Shneiderman 1992).

Hypertext researchers do not always view disorientation as negative. Some see it as related more to the complexity of the information than to the cognitive overhead of the hypertext technology, and others see it as an enjoyable and positive experience (Strain and Berry 1996, 228-229). Notwithstanding this dissenting opinion, most would still agree that the design of hypertext documents should strive to avoid user disorientation and excessive cognitive overhead (Thuring et al. 1995).

While increasing coherence and reducing cognitive overhead are perhaps the two most important design features of a hypermedia document, other important hypermedia criteria are also found in the literature. These include purpose and intention (Langford 1993), richness, ease of use, consistency, self-evidence, predictability, and readability (Garzotto, Mainetti, and Paolini 1995; Heckel 1991).

Positive Outcomes of Hypermedia Approaches to Information Retrieval

The role of hypermedia in information retrieval may also be significant. A small body of literature suggests that positive outcomes can be expected when a hypermedia approach to information retrieval is utilized. For example, Dimitroff and Wolfram (1995, 22) argue that "a hypertext-based approach to bibliographic retrieval could be appropriate for a variety of searcher experience levels."

In another study, Large, Beheshti, Breuleux, and Renaud (1995), suggest a direct correlation between multimedia and comprehension within a learning environment. Zhu (1995) found that users preferred the hypertext version of a sample book database rather than the print version, that users preferred browsing over querying, and that they generally chose content-based browsing over using an index.

Nielsen (1995a, 279-307) observes that while some studies show significant problems with hypertext systems, many others find that hypertext is superior in many ways to other modes of communication and that hypertext offers many advantages to traditional text. These studies include both quantitative benchmark research as well as qualitative observational research.

Marchionini (1995) points out that there are two primary methods through which information-seekers find information: formal or analytical searching, and browsing. While it is true that most users seem to prefer browsing over analytical searching (Zhu 1995), more and more studies are indicating that a formal approach to searching "hyperbases" may be in some ways more efficient and more useful (Agosti and Smeaton 1996; Frei and Stieger 1995). Formal searching is best performed in hypermedia applications that are intentionally designed to "guide readers through an information space, controlling their exploration along the lines of a predefined structure" (Thuring et al. 1995, 57), and is "more adequate for tasks requiring deep understanding and learning." On the other hand, "browsing is particularly effective for information problems that are ill-defined or interdisciplinary and when the goal of information seeking is to gather overview information about a topic or to keep abreast of developments in a field" (Marchionini 1995, 100). Given these factors, it would seem that the best hypermedia documents would allow for a combination of browsing and analytical searching (Nielsen 1995a, 224).

GENERAL DESIGN ISSUES

The design and content of a Web site present a tremendous challenge. On one hand, the designer must present information that is well-organized and easy to maneuver (Rosenfeld and Morville 1998; Tilton, Steadman, and Jones 1996; Nielsen 1995a). On the other hand, the Web site should also be visually attractive (Lynch and Horton 1999). As one author states, the model Web site should not "offend a well-developed aesthetic sense or stymie the efficient delivery of information" (Gardner 1996, 55).

An important principle of design, applicable to pre-computing designs as well as present day computer interfaces, is for the designer to take responsibility for his or her work. In other words, the designer should avoid blaming the end user (or the information itself) for any flaws in the design. As Tufte states, one should never "fault the data for an excess of complication" or "fault viewers for a lack of understanding" (Tufte 1990, 53).

Tufte goes on to say that confusing the user with "cluttered" information can be avoided by revealing detail and complexity in an elegant way. Information does not have to be simplistic to be communicated clearly. Richness and clarity can go hand in hand if the information interface is properly designed. Tufte writes that "among the most powerful devices for reducing noise and enriching the content of displays is the technique of layering and separation, visually stratifying various aspects of the data" (Tufte 1990, 53). This technique can be utilized in a variety of ways, but a good example is the simple act of dividing up a document into paragraphs.

The balance between practical and aesthetic issues has long been a major problem for designers. Norman (1988, 151) writes:

> If everyday design were ruled by aesthetics, life might be more pleasing to the eye but less comfortable; if ruled by usability, it might be more comfortable but uglier. If cost or ease of manufacture dominated, products might not be attractive, functional, or durable. Clearly, each consideration has its place. Trouble occurs when one dominates all the others.

Norman outlines why designers often fail. These reasons include (1) the propensity of putting aesthetics first, (2) the fact that designers are not typical users (they are experts and so do not realize that typical users might have problems), and (3) the fact that "designers must please their clients, and the clients may not be the users" (1988, 151). He closes his argument by summarizing the complex rules of design with two tenets: (1) Ensure that the user can figure out what to do next. (2) Ensure that the user can determine what is happening (1988, 188).

The world of software interface design and the field of human-computer interaction both echo the general design principles delineated here. Heckel (1991), in his modern classic, *The Elements of Friendly Software Design*, suggests that software designers observe the following rules when creating interfaces: know your audience; maintain the user's interest; communicate visually; communicate with metaphors; give the user control; help the user cope; orient the user in the world; serve both the novice and the experienced user; and make the design simple, but not too simple.

Perhaps the most influential writer in the human-computer interaction movement is Shneiderman (1992). In his *Designing the User Interface: Strategies for Effective Human-Computer Interaction*, Shneiderman writes about the need for proper functionality in the computer interface. This includes reliability, availability, security, and data integrity, as well as standardization, integration, consistency, and portability (Shneiderman 1992, 10-11). Moreover, he describes the necessity of a good data display, which includes consistency of display, efficient assimilation of information by the user, minimal human memory requirements for the user, and flexible user control of the data display. In addition, his book includes other important requisites for developing an effective user interface, such as keeping the needs of the user in mind, the importance of a fast response time, aesthetic considerations, and the need for testing, evaluation, and iteration.

Finally, other electronic page design considerations are often mentioned in the literature. These include physical presence, resolution and screen size, interactivity, and motion and sound (Boling 1994). A related factor is usability. Nielsen (1995a, 283-284) describes usability parameters for hypertext systems, including the following: easy to learn, efficient to use, easy to remember, few errors, and pleasant to use.

GENERAL WEB DESIGN ISSUES

Introduction

A growing body of literature sets forth various criteria for excellence in Web design (Boling and Kirkley 1996a; Lynch and Horton 1999; Snyder 1996; Waters 1996). An early article on library Web design (Stover and Zink 1996, 19-20) outlined a rubric for general Web site design. It provides several categories of suggestions when constructing a Web site, including planning, layout, organization, links, graphics, content, and reliability.

While general, accepted· principles for Web design exist, these guidelines are not absolute (Strain and Berry 1996). Good Web design will vary from site-to-site, depending on the goals of the site and the nature of the institution that is sponsoring the site (Paton 1995; Strain and Berry 1996; Metz and Junion-Metz 1996). For example, an academic library Web site will necessarily look quite different than an advertising agency Web site. These differences tend to be found in the areas of content, layout, and use of graphics. Since this study deals with academic library Web sites in theological schools, any debatable issues of Web design discussed here will naturally be resolved by deferring to the mission and role of the theological library.

Planning

Planning, which includes identifying the prospective audience and defining the goal and purpose of the site, is clearly a useful way to begin the Web design process (Rosenfeld and Morville 1998; Lynch and Horton 1999). McLeod and White (1995, 45) remark that "many university Web systems resemble strip malls in a state of perpetual remodeling instead of the well-organized academic institutions they represent," and this could well be due to a lack of planning.

Layout

Layout is another important consideration for Web designers (Nicotera 1999). One of the characteristics of good layout is consistency (Lynch and Horton 1999). "A common, consistent theme or 'look and feel' should be evident" (Stover and Zink 1996, 19), and the Web site should reflect consistency in design and colors. Tilton et al. (1996, 368) write that "consistency is what brings your site together so that it becomes a cohesive whole." According to these authors, consistency can be achieved through the common use of headers and footers, common graphic elements, and consistent style.

An artistic or aesthetic look is also a vital part of good layout (Waters 1996). Creativity and personality are two terms often used to define this facet of layout. Another author believes that the layout of Web sites should be interesting, attractive, and entertaining (Greengard 1996).

A third aspect of layout is using an everyday metaphor "to leverage users' familiar experiences" (Stover and Zink 1996, 19; Kupersmith 1998; Rosenfeld and Morville 1998). Some obvious metaphors are a book, a tree with branches, or a building. These images should assist the user in navigating the Web site and in organizing the information in their minds.

Another facet of good layout is to minimize scrolling by keeping pages as short as possible (Falcigno and Green 1995; McLeod and White 1995; Child 1996; Nielsen 1996). This is important for a variety of reasons, not the least of which is that scrolling through long Web pages is tedious. On the other hand, Levine (1996) notes that if the Web site presents "text that people will want to read at length, it's all right to use longer, scrolling pages." Others point out that too many short pages with more links increases cognitive overhead and thus may end up disorienting the user (Lynch and Horton 1999; Strain and Berry 1996).

Other important suggestions in the literature relating to layout include offering a text-only alternative (McLeod and White 1995), avoiding dark backgrounds, sending the appropriate message to the user through the "visual design" (Boling and Kirkley 1996b), gradual font size changes (Tilton et al. 1996) and, within reason, designing the Web site for the lowest common denominator Web browser (Child 1996).

Some common design errors that are related to layout include pages that are too short, pages that are too long, and too many short pages. Nielsen (1996) lists other layout errors, such as using frames when unnecessary, scrolling text, and constantly running animations. Caywood (1996) is more positive (though somewhat vague) when she states that a good Web design is intuitive, friendly, exciting, and interactive.

Organization

A good Web site should also be well-organized and have a "clear ordering of information" (Tilton et al. 1996). It should have a table of contents, generally on the home page, that gives the user a sense of direction (Snyder 1996; Paton 1995). The home page is critical to the success of the Web site. The page should provide an overview of the site (Snyder 1996) and should be viewed as a graphical guidepost to the rest of the site. A table of contents by itself does not necessarily solve all Web site organizational problems, since an undescriptive table of contents is mostly worthless.

Rosenfeld and Morville (1998) note that labeling systems (representations of larger portions of data) are crucial in organizing a Web site for successful information retrieval. While there are various kinds of labels that one can use when designing the site (textual and iconic, controlled vocabulary and user-based labels), it is important to remember that labels in Web sites should be consistent, professional, easily understood, and customer-oriented.

Boling and Kirkley (1996a) present another strategy related to Web site organization. They suggest that each page (not just the home page) have a table of contents at the top of the page, so that the user can select items anywhere in the document without having to scroll down. Related suggestions include organizing the Web site through outlining and indexing (Tilton et al. 1996), through directory pages (Paton 1995), or through a site map (Nielsen 1996).

Another facet of Web site organization is providing a sense of context so that the user knows where he or she is at any given time

(Strain and Berry 1996; Stover and Zink 1996). One way to do this is to "provide a clear, consistent navigation structure" (Tilton et al. 1996, 365-366). An early survey of Web users demonstrated that a frequent problem was the inability of the user to determine where he or she is at any given time (Pitkow and Kehoe 1996). More recent studies have corroborated this finding (Nielsen 2000).

Search engines, such as AltaVista and Infoseek, have become an extremely important tool in global and local Web organization. Proper HTML markup (including accurate metadata elements) and notification to facilitate global search engine indexing are crucial in Web design (Stover and Zink 1996). Local search engines are also necessary, especially if the site contains voluminous information (Snyder 1996; Nielsen 1996; Paton 1995; Rosenfeld and Morville 1998).

Another important way to create a viable organized structure is to include a "return to home page" button on each document in the site, something that Snyder (1996) calls an anchoring navigation tool. This would entail both the main library home page being linked back to the main institutional home page (Stover and Zink 1996; Paton 1995) and each library Web page being linked back to the main library home page (Tilton et al. 1996). This assures that the user will always have access back to a primary starting point from which to undertake further investigation of the Web site. Boling and Kirkley (1996b) call this "accessibility," and they emphasize the use of "landmarks" that can guide the user back to the home page through a consistently used picture or name (see also Strain and Berry 1996). These navigational aids are becoming more and more important today because of Web search engines that often bring the user in through the "backdoor" of a Web site. In these cases the user often does not have any knowledge of the nature or organization of the site (Snyder 1996, 27).

"Chunking" is an important concept mentioned in the literature (Boling and Kirkley 1996a). Chunking refers to the method of breaking up information into small pieces that are hyperlinked together, usually existing on separate pages. The proponents of chunking advocate "grouping limited bits of information into similar categories so that the user can more easily process the overall information" (Stover and Zink 1996, 10). A small amount of information tends to focus the attention of the user and incrementally builds his or her knowledge base (Van Brakel et al. 1995).

Chunking utilizes the hypertext structure of the Web and prevents pages from becoming overly long, but Web designers should use this strategy with caution. As Boling and Kirkley point out, it is possible to "chunk" information into such small pieces that the user must move constantly back and forth between pages. Instead, they suggest looking for "natural break points when the size of the document becomes difficult to edit or begins to take a long time to load when accessed through the Web" (Boling and Kirkley 1996a, 15).

Related to chunking is the problem of multiple levels in a Web site. Boling and Kirkley (1996a) remark that a balance is needed between having too many levels (which keeps the user from feeling like he will never reach any content) and not enough levels (which makes the home page unwieldy). DeMause (1995b) discusses the related idea that users should never be more than "three clicks from content" on the Web. In other words, there should be no more than three layers of menus between the first page that a user views and the actual content.

Links

Greengard (1996) writes about two types of Web users: hunters (they know exactly that for which they are looking), and gatherers (they just browse). The Web designer must try to satisfy both users. Marchionini (1995) concurs with this assessment in his book on information retrieval and browsing. Search engines satisfy the hunters, but gatherers must be given an information environment that is conducive to browsing. On the Web, links (also called hotlinks) are the key element to a good browsable structure.

Levine (1996) states that "the presence and placement of links affects the utility of your pages. Links provide connections to other content, organizational markers and a means to define terms and provide references. Links can support or detract from your presentation." An observation by Van Brakel et al. (1995, 385) adds that "links are the heartbeat of any hypertext document," and that "the total set of links effectively defines the structure of the document."

Links are clearly important, but many authors warn against providing too many links on a page (DeMause 1995a; Boling and Kirkley 1996a; Stover and Zink 1996). DeMause (1995b) notes that Bell Labs psychological research led to restricting telephone numbers to seven digits, and from this concludes that the ideal number of links on a page is seven (and no more than nine). Any more than this, he asserts, will lead to information overload.

Other problems related to links include meaningless linked text, out of context links, faulty links, unannotated links, and orphan pages that do not have originating links. Levine (1996) believes that there is a direct connection between the accuracy of links on a Web site and the perceived reliability of the content of the information.

Graphics

Multimedia asserts its place on the Web primarily through graphics (Ubois 1996). For this reason many Web page producers have become enamored with utilizing pictures and other graphical media on Web sites. Levine (1996) writes that "images can add a lot to the visual appeal and information content of a page. For some subjects and some readers, images may be the sole most effective means to communicate your message."

However, many have cautioned against overusing graphics, primarily because of bandwidth limitations (Waters 1996; Nielsen 1996; Greengard 1996) but also because of usability and layout problems (Lynch and Horton 1999) as well as issues related to access for the disabled (Balas 2000; Rouse 1999). Nielsen (2000, 42) writes that "every Web usability study I have conducted since 1994 has shown the same thing: Users beg us to speed up page downloads." This problem generally relates to large graphics or to too many small graphics in combination with a slow Internet dialup connection. Levine (1996) adds that if used poorly, "images can confuse your audience, distract from your message, and render mute a critical message." Nielsen (1995b) believes that the "unconstrained use of multimedia results in user interfaces that confuse users and make it harder for them to understand the information."

The appropriate purpose of graphics on the Web is an issue on which consensus is lacking. Some believe that graphics and art on a Web site are inappropriate if they are only decorative and do not serve a functional purpose, but this point is debatable especially in light of the "aesthetic" aspects of good Web design. In the final analysis, the purpose of images on a Web site should probably be closely related to the goal of the site.

Some suggestions for moderate use of graphics on Web sites include: limiting the size of graphics, using the ALT tag for users who have turned off image loading on their browsers, limiting the number of graphics, using thumbnail images linked to larger images, and warning the user in advance of the actual byte size if an image is large (Stover and Zink 1996; Vind 2000).

Naroyan (1996, 39) asserts that text-based pages are "not as graphically appealing" as pages with large graphics. On the other hand, Mellendorf (1996, 21) maintains that graphics have an addictive nature, that "their overuse impedes efficient Web processing," and that "often images are not necessary to a home page's primary function." Perhaps the best advice comes from Jurist (1996) when she suggests that graphics on Web sites be designed for the average user, that smaller is better, and that sometimes words are simply better than images.

Content

While graphics may have their place on the Web, the content of a Web site is clearly the most significant aspect (Nielsen 2000). As Snyder (1996, 28) states, "content is king." Content refers to the actual information offered on the Web site, but it also relates to the way that information is presented. Originality of content is important, but so is clear and concise writing (Stover and Zink 1996). Overly long paragraphs should be avoided (Nielsen 2000), and a combination of prose and menus generally creates a more readable atmosphere (Tilton et al. 1996).

Levine (1996) makes several suggestions regarding content, including placing content as high up in the Web hierarchy as possible, keeping text to a minimum when possible (avoiding verbosity), and providing "context" links so that users can educate themselves on complex topics that are mentioned in the text. Caywood (1996) advises that content should include a stated scope, clear and descriptive headings, and information organized by needs of user. Stover and Zink (1996, 20) write that the "purpose of the home page should be stated explicitly, concisely, and clearly," and Strain and Berry (1996) add that there should be a descriptive title on each page.

Credibility/Reliability

The credibility and reliability of the information contained on a Web site builds on the notion of content importance. The content of a Web site may be unique, interesting, and clearly communicated, but it will be largely useless if the information is not authoritative and credible.

Various authors have noted the value of content credibility on the Web (Tillman 1995; Caywood 1996; Lynch 1996). Content credibility can be established by various means, including identification of author (Tilton et al. 1996; Grassian 1996; Paton 1995), accuracy of information (Snyder 1996; Grassian 1996), date of last update (Greengard 1996; Tilton et al. 1996; Nielsen 1996a; Grassian 1996), and provision of contact person (Falcigno and Green 1995; Boling and Kirkley 1996a; Tilton et al. 1996; McLeod and White 1995; Greengard 1996; Grassian 1996).

The identification of the author (or authors) of a Web site is critical. It allows the user to judge the authority of the information through the author's reputation and affiliation. Accuracy of information adds the resonance of authority to a document. The existence of a "date of last update" lets the user know that the Web site is a fluid document that assigns importance to the current nature of information. The provision of a contact person allows the user to communicate with a designated administrator of the Web site, thus making the site interactive and open to the needs and desires of its users.

LIBRARY WEB DESIGN ISSUES

Introduction

Much of the literature on library Web design echoes the literature on general Web design. For example, several books and articles emphasize the importance of such design and organization issues as up-to-date information (Cole 1995), quality content (Vandergrift 1996), planning (Garlock and Piontek 1996), access speeds (Cox 1996), moderation in using graphics (Koopman and Hay 1996; Cole 1995), reasonable text length (Vandergrift 1996), and the necessity of an internal search engine (Koopman and Hay 1996). However, some of the library Web literature focuses on issues that are unique to libraries, and this section will concentrate on these concerns.

Some of the literature is primarily descriptive (rather than prescriptive) in presenting the nature of contemporary library Web sites. An early study (Koopman 1995) describes one academic library as using a metaphor of the digital office; using contextual pictures and redundant text to reinforce concepts; utilizing the academic mission statements and catalog descriptions to provide a familiar and consistent context; utilizing an internal search engine; using forms and e-mail functionality for communication; and following the rule of allowing no more than three menu layers before the user reaches actual content.

Later in the article Koopman compares and contrasts the above Web site with another academic library Web site. She describes the use of an image map on the home page, but also the availability of a text-only version. Moreover, she discusses the practice of limiting menus to a single screen, as well as the idea that the library Web site should contain "applications, administrative information about the site and its staff, links to external Internet resources, and bibliographic databases" (Koopman 1995, 18).

More recent studies describe various facets of academic library Web sites, including electronic serials on the Web site (Rich and Rabine 1999), comparisons between two year and four year college library Web sites (Cohen and Still 1999), link management in academic library Web sites (Quinn 1999; Dewey 1999), and home page layout comparisons among ARL library Web sites (King 1998).

Other literature contains normative guidelines for developing library Web sites (Vandergrift 1996; Guenther 1999; D'Angelo and Little 1998). The following section will survey this subset of the literature under the headings of selection of library Web information, organization of library Web information, and access to library Web information.

Selection of Information

Selection of information resources (or collection development) was historically performed through the purchase of books or other media for a local library collection. In the Web environment, selection is done primarily through the provision of links to other related Web sites (Koopman 1995; Powell 1994; Vandergrift 1996), although sometimes it occurs through links to local resources (Powell 1994). Indeed, a few library Web sites even have formal or informal guidelines for Web collection, and some librarians are becoming as serious about collecting high quality electronic information for their "collections" as their counterparts in the print environment (Hockey 1994). As Cole (1995, 49) writes, links to other Web sites should only "point to information resources of reasonably well-known quality and authority."

Organization of Information

Librarians have traditionally organized information through descriptive and subject cataloging and through subject bibliographies. In addition, outside vendors compiled indexes and abstracts of most periodical-based literature. The library made all of this organized information available through card catalogs (and later online catalogs) and through periodical indexes (first in print, and later available in electronic format). Much of the work of organization of information follows the rule of collocation, which states that similar resources should be presented together (regardless of whether the items physically existed or were merely surrogate pointers in the catalog).

Today, the role of libraries in organizing information is applied in the Web environment primarily through electronic databases (catalogs and indexes), but also through the way that the library Web site is organized. Pasicznyuk (1996) writes of the importance of bibliographic control for library Web sites, and Powell (1994, 62) asserts that every library Web site needs to have "a basic document classifying some diverse information resources by general subject classification." Paton (1995) describes "catalog pages" which are "used to provide access to a large number of online resources, often arranged by subject."

Access to Information

Traditional libraries have attempted to provide access to information through a variety of means, including physical access (open stacks, generous library hours of service) as well as intellectual access (reference assistance, bibliographic instruction, access to periodical indexes, and well-organized online catalogs). In the Web environment, access to information can be provided through the supplying of basic library information like hours, staff, and physical resources (Garlock and Piontek 1996), a connection to the library's online catalog (Garlock and Piontek 1996), and other databases (Koopman 1995; Powell 1994). These other databases may be a combination of bibliographic and full-text, and can be either locally based or remotely based.

In addition, access to information in the Web environment implies the existence of patron assistance, whether in the form of online reference (Koopman and Hay 1996), help screens (Koopman 1995), or information requests (Powell 1994). These presume the existence of feedback forms or other modes of communication between the patron and the library (Garlock and Piontek 1996).

The literature also includes other statements about library Web sites that do not fit neatly into the three-fold library function of collection, organization, and access. These include the consideration of the mission of the library (Garlock and Piontek 1996), developing new full text resources (Koopman and Hay 1996; Garlock and Piontek 1996; Stover 1999), and creating new services for both local and global users (Pasicznyuk 1996).

CONCLUSION

This article has established a theoretical and conceptual foundation for constructing Web sites for religious and theological academic libraries. It has demonstrated the necessity of including in these sites a variety of considerations, including the mission of the academy, the purpose of theological education, the role of libraries, the design and organization of hypermedia documents, and the design, organization, and content of Web pages.

The Web has undergone significant changes since its advent in the early 1990s. HTML coding has become more complex, and a plethora of design tools (including CSS, DHTML, Java, Active Server Pages, CGI scripts, and SSI) make Web design a demanding and rigorous exercise. Yet, most of the principles discussed in this article transcend incremental technological advances such as more sophisticated Web authoring tools, powerful programming languages, and new graphics formats. Good page design will always rely on centuries old enduring precepts of color, lines, balance, shape, and contrast. Usability will continue to be important, as well as sensitivity to the size of users' bandwidth. Well-organized Web sites will continue to be based on established principles of thesaurus construction, representational labeling, and information seeking behavior. Academic libraries will continue to find their identity in the mission of their parent institution and in the universal function of libraries. Theological librarians will continue to support teaching, research, and service within the context of theological education, and they will continue to select, organize, preserve, and provide access to theological information resources in a variety of formats.

What will religious and theological Web sites in higher education look like in the distant future? One can only speculate, but I am certain that the best theological library Web sites will be easy to use, well-organized, full of relevant information, attractively designed, and fully supportive of the goals and values of theological education.

REFERENCES

Abels, E. G. 1996. The e-mail reference interview. *RQ* 35(3):345-358.

Agosti, M., and A. F. Smeaton. 1996. *Information retrieval and hypertext*. Boston: Kluwer Academic Publishers.

American Theological Library Association. 2000. *Introduction to ATLA*. Available from World Wide Web: (http://www.atla.com/intro.html).

Anderson, G. T. 1992. Dimensions, context, and freedom: The library in the social creation of knowledge. In *Sociomedia: Multimedia, hypermedia, and the social construction of knowledge*, ed. E. Barrett, 107-124. Cambridge, MA: MIT Press.

Arms, C. 1990. *Campus strategies for libraries and electronic information*. Rockport, MA: Digital Press.

Association of Theological Schools 2000. *Accreditation*. Available from World Wide Web: (http://www.ats.edu/).

Atkins, S. E. 1991. *The academic library in the American university*. Chicago: American Library Association.

Atkinson, R. 1993. Networks, hypertext, and academic information services: Some longer-range implications. *College and Research Libraries* 54(3):199-215.

Atkinson, R. 1995. The academic library collection in an on-line environment. In *Information technology and the remaking of the university library*, ed. B. Lynch, 43-62. San Francisco: Jossey-Bass.

Atkinson, R. C., and D. Tuzin. 1992. Equilibrium in the research university. *Change* 24(3):20-27.

Baker, N. 1995. Virtual librarianship: Expanding adult services with the World Wide Web. *RQ* 35(2):169-173.

Baker, P. J. 1986. The helter-skelter relationship between teaching and research: A cluster of problems and small wins. *Teaching Sociology* 14(1):50-66.

Balas, J. 1996. Building virtual libraries. *Computers in Libraries* 16(2):48-50.

Balas, J. 1999. The 'don'ts' of Web page design. *Computers in Libraries* 19(8):46-49.

Balas, J. 2000. Doing it right: Web design for library types. *Computers in Libraries* 20(1):56-59.

Barrett, E. 1992. Sociomedia: An introduction. In *Sociomedia: Multimedia, hypermedia, and the social construction of knowledge*, ed. E. Barrett, 1-10. Cambridge, MA: MIT Press.

Bavaro, J. A. 1995. *A review of the construct of scholarship in the literature*. ERIC Document Reproduction Service No. ED 381064.

Bazillion, R., and C. Braun. 1995. *Academic libraries as high-tech gateways: A guide to design and space decisions*. Chicago: American Library Association.

Bell, C. 1995. Using the World Wide Web in libraries. *PNLA Quarterly* 60, 29-30.

Berring, R. 1995. Future librarians. In *Future libraries*, eds. R. H. Bloch and C. Hesse, 94-115. Berkeley, CA: University of California Press.

Black, W. K., and J. M Leysen. 1994. Scholarship and the academic librarian. *College and Research Libraries* 55(3):229-241.

Blackburn, R. T., and J. H. Lawrence. 1995. *Faculty at work: Motivation, expectation, satisfaction*. Baltimore: The Johns Hopkins University Press.

Boling, E. 1994. Meeting the challenge of the electronic page: Extending instructional design skills. *Educational Technology* 34(7):13-18.

Boling, E., and S. Kirkley. 1996a. Helping students design World Wide Web documents: Part I: Planning and designing the site. *Hypernexus: Journal of Hypermedia and Multimedia Studies* 6(4):13-18.

Boling, E., and S. Kirkley. 1996b. Helping students design World Wide Web documents: Part II: Designing and maintaining the pages. *Hypernexus: Journal of Hypermedia and Multimedia Studies* 7(1):12-18.

Borgman, C. L. 1996. Why are online catalogs still hard to use? *Journal of the American Society for Information Science* 47(7):493-503.

Boss, R. W., and H. S. White. 1998. Web page design. *Library Technology Reports* 34(5):609-613.

Brandt, D. S. 1996. Evaluating information on the Internet. *Computers in Libraries* 16(5):44-48.

Brandt, D. S. 2000. Web sites and Web authoring programs: Trade-off or terror? *Computers in Libraries* 20(1):60-63.

Buckland, M. K. 1989. Foundations of academic librarianship. *College and Research Libraries* 50(4):389-396.

Buckland, M. K. 1992. *Redesigning library services: A manifesto.* Chicago: American Library Association.

Butler, B. B. 1996. Electronic course reserves and digital libraries. *Journal of Academic Librarianship* 22(2):124-127.

Campbell, J. R. 1995. *Reclaiming a lost heritage: Land-grant and other higher education initiatives for the twenty-first century.* Ames, IA: Iowa State University Press.

Cardozier, V. R. 1987. *American higher education: An international perspective.* Brookfield, VT: Gower Publishing.

Carroll, J. W. 1997. *Being there: Culture and formation in two theological schools.* New York: Oxford University Press.

Caywood, C. 1996. Selection criteria for World Wide Web resources. *Public Libraries*, 35, 169.

Centra, J. A. 1980. *Determining faculty effectiveness: Assessing teaching, research, and service for personnel decisions and improvement.* San Francisco: Jossey-Bass.

Centra, J. A. 1993. *Reflective faculty evaluation: Enhancing teaching and determining faculty effectiveness.* San Francisco: Jossey-Bass.

Chiang, W. S., and N. E. Elkington. 1994. *Electronic access to information: A new service paradigm.* Mountain View, CA: Research Libraries Group.

Child, D. A. 1996. An introduction to World Wide Web page design. *T.H.E. Journal.* Available from World Wide Web: (http://www.thejournal.com/magazine/vault/a78.cfm).

Churchwell, C. D. 1975. The library in academia: An associate provost's view. In *New dimensions for library service*, ed. E. J. Josey, 21-33. Metuchen, NJ: Scarecrow Press.

Cohen, L. B., and J. M. Still. 1999. A comparison of research university and two-year college library Web sites: Content, functionality, and form. *College and Research Libraries* 60(3):275-289.

Cole, T. W. 1995. Mosaic on public-access PCs: Letting the World Wide Web into the library. *Internet Librarian* 15(1):44-50.

Cox, A. 1996. Hypermedia library guides for academic libraries on the World Wide Web. *Program* 30(1):39-50.

Coyne, R. 1995. *Designing information technology in the postmodern age.* Cambridge, MA: The MIT Press.

D'Angelo, J., and S. K. Little. 1998. Successful Web pages: What are they and do they exist? *Information Technology and Libraries* 17(2):71-81.

Davidson, J., and C. Rusk. 1996. Creating a university Web in a team environment. *The Journal of Academic Librarianship* 22(4):302-305.

Day, P. A., and K. L. Armstrong. 1996. Librarians, faculty, and the Internet: Developing a new information partnership. *Computers in Libraries* 16(5):56-59.

DeMause, N. 1995a. Sure sign of a neophyte: Overusing hyperlinks. *Web Week* 1(4):26.

DeMause, N. 1995b. The virtues of restraint. *Web Week* 1(5):27.

DeNeef, A. L., and C. D. Goodwin. 1995. *The academic's handbook.* 2nd ed. Durham, NC: Duke University Press.

Dewey, B. I. 1999. In search of services: Analyzing the findability of links on CIC university libraries' Web pages. *Information Technology and Libraries* 18(4):210-214.

Diamond, R. M. 1995. *Preparing for promotion and tenure review: A faculty guide.* Bolton, MA: Anker Publishing.

Dimitroff, A., and D. Wolfram. 1995. Searcher response in a hypertext-based bibliographic information retrieval system. *Journal of the American Society for Information Science* 46(1):22-29.

Dougherty, R. M., and C. Hughes. 1991. *Preferred futures for libraries: A summary of six workshops with university provosts and library directors.* Mountain View, CA: Research Libraries Group.

Duval, B. K., and L. Main. 1995. Building home pages. *Library Software Review* 14(4):218-227.

Ehrlich, T., and J. Frey. 1995. *The courage to inquire: Ideals and realities in higher education.* Bloomington, IN: Indiana University Press.

Ensor, P. 1995. The wonderful world of the Web in the library. *Technicalities* 15(3):6-7.

Euster, J. R. 1995. The academic library: Its place and role in the institution. In *Academic libraries: Their rationale and role in American education*, eds. G. B. McCabe and R. J. Person, 1-13. Westport, CT: Greenwood Press.

Fairweather, J. S. 1996. *Faculty work and public trust: Restoring the value of teaching and public service in American academic life.* Boston: Allyn and Bacon.

Falcigno, K., and T. Green. 1995. Home page, sweet home page. *Database* 18(2):20-28.

Fear, F. A., and L. Sandmann. 1995. Unpacking the service category: Reconceptualizing university outreach for the 21st century. *Continuing Higher Education Review* 59(3):110-122.

Frei, H. P., and D. Stieger. 1995. The use of semantic links in hypertext information retrieval. *Information Processing and Management* 31(1):1-13.

Gardner, E. 1996. Want a course in site design? Try this (if you dare). *Web Week* 2(18):55-56.

Garlock, K. L., and S. Piontek. 1996. *Building the service-based library Web site: A step-by-step guide to design and options.* Chicago: American Library Association.

Garzotto, F., L. Mainetti, and P. Paolini. 1995. Hypermedia design, analysis, and evaluation issues. *Communications of the ACM* 38(8):74-86.

Gates, J. K. 1983. *Guide to the use of libraries and information sources.* New York: McGraw-Hill.

Giamatti, A. B. 1988. *A free and ordered space: The real world of the university.* New York: Norton.

Glogoff, S. 1995. Library instruction in the electronic library: The University of Arizona's electronic library education centers. *Reference Services Review* 23(2):7-12.

Gorman, M. 1992. Foreword. In *Redesigning library services: A manifesto,* ed. M. Buckland, v-vii. Chicago: American Library Association.

Grassian, E. 1996. *Thinking critically about World Wide Web resources.* Available from World Wide Web: (http://www.library.ucla.edu/libraries/college/instruct/ web/critical.htm).

Greenberg, C. J. 1998. Beyond HTML. *Information Outlook* 2(11):26-30.

Greengard, S. 1996. Home, home on the Web. *Personnel Journal* 75(3):26-33.

Guenther, K. 1999. Publicity through better Web site design. *Computers in Libraries* 19(8):62-67.

Guenther, R. S. 1996. The challenges of electronic texts in the library: Bibliographic control and access. In *Scholarly publishing: The electronic frontier*, eds. R. P. Peek and G. B. Newby, 251-275. Cambridge, MA: MIT Press.

Heckel, P. 1991. *The elements of friendly software design.* 2nd ed. San Francisco: Sybex.

Hirshon, A. 1993. *After the electronic revolution, will you be the first to go?* Chicago: American Library Association.

Hockey, S. 1994. Evaluating electronic texts in the humanities. *Library Trends* 42(4):676-693.

Huang, S. 1993. *Modern library technology and reference services.* New York: The Haworth Press, Inc.

Internet Public Library. 1996. *About the ready reference collection.* Available from World Wide Web: (http://ipl.sils.umich.edu/ref/RR/Rabt.html).

Isakowitz, T., E. A. Stohr, and P. Balasubramanian. 1995. RMM: A methodology for structured hypermedia design. *Communications of the ACM* 38(8):34-44.

Jensen, A., and J. Sih. 1995. Using e-mail and the Internet to teach users at their desktops. *Online* 19(5):82-86.

Johnson, R. M. 1995. New technologies, old politics: Political dimensions in the management of academic support services. In *Information technology and the remaking of the university library,* ed. B. Lynch, 19-31. San Francisco: Jossey-Bass.

Josey, E. J. 1975. *New dimensions for library service*. Metuchen, NJ: Scarecrow Press.

Jurist, S. 1996. Top 10 rules for creating graphics for the Web. *College and Research Libraries News*, 57(7):418-421.

Kahn, P. 1995. Visual cues for local and global coherence in the WWW. *Communications of the ACM* 38(8):67-69.

Karp, R. S., and A. J. Keck. 1996. Theological librarianship: Toward a profile of a profession. *College and Research Libraries* 57(1):35-43.

Keohane, N. O. 1993. The mission of the research university. *Daedalus* 122(4):101-126.

King, D. L. 1998. Library home page design: A comparison of page layout for front-ends to ARL library Web sites. *College and Research Libraries* 59(5):458-465.

Kling, R., and R. Lamb. 1996. Analyzing alternate visions of electronic publishing and digital libraries. In *Scholarly publishing: The electronic frontier*, eds. R. P. Peek and G. B. Newby, 17-54. Cambridge, MA: MIT Press.

Koepplin, L. W., and D. A. Wilson. 1985. *The future of state universities: Issues in teaching, research, and public service*. New Brunswick, NJ: Rutgers University Press.

Koopman, A. 1995. Library Web implementation: A tale of two sites. *Cause/Effect* 18(4):15-21, 29.

Koopman, A., and S. Hay. 1996. Large-scale application of a Web browser. *College and Research Libraries News* 57(1):12-15.

Kovacs, D. K., B. F. Schloman, and J. A. McDaniel. 1994. A model for planning and providing reference services using Internet resources. *Library Trends* 42(4): 638-647.

Kruger, P. 1995. Links in a tangled Web. *The Electronic Library* 13(5):492-493.

Kupersmith, J. 1998. You are here, but where is that? Architectural design metaphors in the electronic library. In *Finding common ground: Creating a library of the future without diminishing the library of the past*, ed. C. LaGuardia, 58-67. New York: Neal-Schuman.

Langford, D. 1993. Evaluating a hypertext document. *ASLIB Proceedings* 45(9):221-226.

Lester, D. 1995. The Web goes prime time; libraries can, too. *Technicalities* 15(4):6-7.

Levine, R. 1996. *Guide to Web style (Sun Microsystems)*. Available from World Wide Web: (http://www.sun.com/styleguide/).

Levy, D. M., and C. C. Marshall. 1995. Going digital: A look at assumptions underlying digital libraries. *Communications of the ACM* 38(4):77-84.

Lowry, A., P. Soderdahl, and B. I. Dewey. 1996. Staffing a Web-based information system. *College and Research Libraries News* 57(10):640-643, 650.

Lynch, B. P. 1995. Editor's notes. In *Information technology and the remaking of the university library*, ed. B. P. Lynch, 1-4. San Francisco: Jossey-Bass.

Lynch, C. A. 1995. The technological framework for library planning in the next decade. In *Information technology and the remaking of the university library*, B. P. Lynch, 93-105. San Francisco: Jossey-Bass.

Lynch, C. A. 1996. Integrity issues in electronic publishing. In *Scholarly publishing: The electronic frontier,* In eds. R. P. Peek and G. B. Newby, 133-145. Cambridge, MA: MIT Press.

Lynch, P. J. 1995. Publishing on the World Wide Web: Organization and design. *Syllabus* 8(9):24-25.

Lynch, P. J., and S. Horton. 1999. *Web style guide: Basic design principles for creating Web sites.* New Haven, CT: Yale University Press.

Manoff, M. 1996. Revolutionary or regressive? The politics of electronic collection development. In *Scholarly publishing: The electronic frontier,* eds. R. P. Peek and G. B. Newby, 215-229. Cambridge, MA: MIT Press.

Marchionini, G. 1995. *Information seeking in electronic environments.* New York: Cambridge University Press.

Martin, S. K. 1996. Organizing collections within the Internet: A vision for access. *The Journal of Academic Librarianship* 22(4):291-292.

Martin, W. B. 1977. *Redefining service, research, and teaching.* San Francisco: Jossey-Bass.

Mason, R. O. 1990. What is an information professional? *Journal of Education for Library and Information Science* 31(2):122-138.

McCabe, G. B., and R. J. Person. 1995. *Academic libraries: Their rationale and role in American education.* Westport, CT: Greenwood Press.

McClements, N., and C. Becker. 1996. Writing Web page standards. *College and Research Libraries News* 57(1):16-17.

McClure, C. R., and Lopata, C. L. 1996. *Assessing the academic environment: Strategies and options.* Washington, DC: Coalition for Networked Information.

McConnell, J. C. 1993. Technology and teaching in academia. In *Modern library technology and reference services*, ed. S. Huang, 31-40. New York: The Haworth Press, Inc.

McGowan, J. J., and E. H. Dow. 1995. Faculty status and academic librarianship: Transformation to a clinical model. *Journal of Academic Librarianship* 21(5):345-350.

McLeod, J., and M. White. 1995. Building the virtual campus bit by bit: World Wide Web development at the University of Maine. *Computers in Libraries* 15(10):45-49.

Medeiros, N. 1999. Academic library Web sites. *College and Research Libraries News* 60(7):527-530.

Mellendorf, S. A. 1996. Working the Web with a no-frills work page. *Online* 20, 21-24.

Metz, R. E., and G. Junion-Metz. 1996. *Using the World Wide Web and creating home pages: A how-to-do-it manual for librarians.* New York: Neal-Schuman.

Mitchell, S., and M. Mooney. 1996. INFOMINE: A Model Web-based academic virtual library. *Information Technology and Libraries* 15(1):20-25.

Nanard, J., and M. Nanard. 1995. Hypertext design environments and the hypertext design process. *Communications of the ACM* 38(8):49-56.

Naroyan, S. 1996. Simplicity vs. functionality at heart of design debate: Leaner pages are in vogue, but new technology may change that. *Web Week* 2(1):39.

Neal, J. G. 1996. Academic libraries: 2000 and beyond. *Library Journal,* 121(12):74-76.

Nicotera, C. L. 1999. Information access by design: Electronic guidelines for librarians. *Information Technology and Libraries* 18(2):104-108.

Nielsen, J. 1995a. *Multimedia and hypertext: The Internet and beyond.* Boston: AP Professional.

Nielsen, J. 1995b. Guidelines for multimedia on the Web. *The Alertbox: Current Issues in User Interface Design.* Available from World Wide Web: (http://www. useit.com/alertbox/9512.html).

Nielsen, J. 1996. Top ten mistakes in Web design. *The Alertbox: Current Issues in User Interface Design.* Available from World Wide Web: (http://www.useit.com/ alertbox/9605.html).

Nielsen, J. 1999. Ten good deeds in Web design. *The Alertbox: Current Issues in User Interface Design.* Available from World Wide Web: (http://www.useit.com/ alertbox/991003.html).

Nielsen, J. 2000. *Designing Web usability.* Indianapolis, IN: New Riders Publishing.

Noam, E. M. 1996. Electronics and the dim future of the university. *Bulletin of the American Society for Information Science* 22(5):6-9.

Norman, D. A. 1988. *The design of everyday things.* New York: Doubleday.

Okerson, A. 1996. University libraries and scholarly communication. In *Scholarly publishing: The electronic frontier,* eds. R. P. Peek and G. B. Newby, 181-199. Cambridge, MA: MIT Press.

Park, S. M. 1996. Research, teaching, and service: Why shouldn't women's work count? *Journal of Higher Education* 67(1):46-84.

Pasicznyuk, R. W. 1996. Library Web construction 101. *Public Libraries* 35(3):168-171.

Paton, J. A. 1995. *Guide for Web providers at Yale.* Available from World Wide Web: (http://www.cis.yale.edu/webguide/index.html).

Peek, R. P., and G. B. Newby. 1996. *Scholarly publishing: The electronic frontier.* Cambridge, MA: MIT Press.

Petroski, H. 1993. How designs evolve. *Technology Review* 96(1):50-57.

Pitkow, J. E., and C. M. Kehoe. 1996. Emerging trends in the WWW user population. *Communications of the ACM* 39(6):106-108.

Powell, J. 1994. Adventures with the World Wide Web: Creating a hypertext library information system. *Database* 17(2):59-66.

Quinn, B. 1999. Missing links: A survey of library systems department Web pages. *Library Hi Tech* 17(3):304-316.

Rich, L. A., and J. L. Rabine. 1999. How libraries are providing access to electronic serials: A survey of academic library Web sites. *Serials Review* 25(2):35-47.

Riggs, D. E. 1996. The intellectual side of academic librarianship. *College and Research Libraries* 57(4):314-315.

Rosenfeld, L., and P. Morville. 1998. *Information architecture for the World Wide Web.* Sebastopol, CA: O'Reilly and Associates.

Rouse, V. 1999. Making the Web accessible. *Computers in Libraries* 19(6):49-54.

Rowland, L. M. 1994. Libraries and librarians on the Internet. *Communication Education* 43, 143-150.

Sandmann, L. R., and A. Gillespie. 1991. Land grant universities on trial. *Adult Learning* 3(2):23-25.

Saunders, L. M., and Mitchell, M. 1996. The evolving virtual library: An overview. In *The Evolving Virtual Library,* ed. L. M. Saunders, 1-16.

Schamber, L. 1996. What is a document? Rethinking the concept in uneasy times. *Journal of the American Society for Information Science* 47(9):669-671.

Schnell, E. H. 1995. The anatomy of a World Wide Web library service: The BONES demonstration project. *Bulletin of the Medical Library Association* 83(4): 440-444.

Schnell, E. H. 1996. *Writing for the Web: A primer for librarians.* Available from World Wide Web: (http://bones.med.ohio-state.edu/eric/papers/primer/).

Schuman, S. 1995. Small is . . . different. In *The academic's handbook,* eds. A. L. DeNeef and C. D. Goodwin, 17-28. Durham, NC: Duke University Press.

Schuyler, M. 2000. The future of Web design. *Computers in Libraries* 20(1):50-53.

Shneiderman, B. 1992. *Designing the user interface: Strategies for effective human-computer interaction.* New York: Addison-Wesley.

Slattery, C. E. 1994. Faculty status: Another 100 years of dialogue? Lessons from the library school closings. *Journal of Academic Librarianship* 20(4):193-199.

Snyder, J. 1996. Good, bad, and ugly pages. *Internet World* 7(4):26-27.

St. Clair, G. 1996. Poverty into wealth. *College and Research Libraries* 57(1):6-8.

St. Lifer, E. 1996. Net work: New roles, same mission. *Library Journal,* 121(19):26-30.

Stearns, S. 1996. The Internet-enabled virtual public library. *Computers in Libraries* 16(3):54-57.

Stern, D. 1995. Expert systems: HTML, the WWW, and the librarian. *Computers in Libraries* 15(4):56-58.

Stoffle, C. J., R. Renaud, and J. R. Veldof. 1996. Choosing our futures. *College and Research Libraries* 57(3):213-225.

Stoffle, C., and K. Williams, K. 1995. The instructional program and responsibilities of the teaching library. In *Information technology and the remaking of the university library,* ed. B. Lynch, 63-75. San Francisco: Jossey-Bass.

Stover, M. 1999. *Leading the wired organization: The information professional's guide to managing technological change.* New York: Neal-Schuman.

Stover, M., and S. D. Zink. 1996. World Wide Web home page design: Patterns and anomalies of higher education library home pages. *Reference Services Review* 24(3):7-20.

Strain, H. C., and P. M. Berry. 1996. Better page design for the World Wide Web. *Online and CD-ROM Review* 20(5):227-237.

Tenopir, C. 1996. Generations of online searching. *Library Journal* 121(14):128-130.

Thuring, M., J. Hannemann, and J. M. Haake. 1995. Hypermedia and cognition: Designing for comprehension. *Communications of the ACM* 38(8):57-66.

Tillman, H. N. 1995. *Evaluating the quality of information on the Internet.* Available from World Wide Web: (http://www.tiac.net/users/hope/findqual.html).

Tilton, E., C. Steadman, and T. Jones. 1996. *Web weaving: Designing and managing an effective Web site.* Reading, MA: Addison-Wesley Developers Press.

Tufte, E. R. 1990. *Envisioning information.* Cheshire, CT: Graphics Press.

Ubois, J. 1996. Ten essential steps for maintaining a Web site. *Web Week* 2(13):27-30.

Van Brakel, P. A. 1995. Electronic journals: Publishing via Internet's World Wide Web. *The Electronic Library* 13(4):389-395.

Van Brakel, P. A., C. Roeloffze, and A. Van Heerden. 1995. Some guidelines for creating World Wide Web home page files. *The Electronic Library* 13(4):383-387.

Vandergrift, K. E. 1996. Build a Web site with a brain. *School Library Journal* 42(4):26-29.

Vind, O. 2000. Make your Web site healthier with an HTML code checkup. *Computers in Libraries* 20(1):40-44.

Waters, C. 1996. *Web concept and design: A comprehensive guide for creating effective Web sites.* Indianapolis, IN: New Riders Publishing.

Welsch, E. K. 1992. Hypertext, hypermedia, and the humanities. *Library Trends* 40(4):614-646.

Wilkins, M. L., and K. Nantz. 1995. Faculty use of electronic communications before and after a LAN installation: A three-year analysis. *Journal of End User Computing* 7(1):4-11.

Wolff, R. A. 1995. Using the accreditation process to transform the mission of the library. In *Information technology and the remaking of the university library,* ed. B. Lynch, 77-91. San Francisco: Jossey-Bass.

Zhou, Y. 1994. From smart guesser to smart navigator: Changes in collection development for research libraries in a network environment. *Library Trends* 42(4):648-660.

Zhu, X. J. 1995. *Individual differences in the use of a hypermedia library information system.* Unpublished doctoral dissertation, Indiana University.

Virtually Jewish:
The Creation of a Jewish Internet Tutorial

Terren Ilana Wein
Juna Z. Snow

SUMMARY. The authors created a Web-based tutorial for novice-to-intermediate users of the World Wide Web using primarily Jewish content in order to encourage potential Jewish users of the World Wide Web. The lessons contain information on Jewish-themed Web sites and progressively complex information about how to use the Web. Tips and practice exercises are included. *[Article copies available for a fee from The Haworth Document Delivery Service: 1-800-342-9678. E-mail address: <getinfo@haworthpressinc.com> Website: <http://www.HaworthPress.com> © 2001 by The Haworth Press, Inc. All rights reserved.]*

KEYWORDS. Jewish, Internet, tutorial, Judaism, bibliographic assistance, online learning

BACKGROUND

"Virtually Jewish: An Internet Tutorial from a Jewish Perspective," was created by the authors as an assignment for a class in the Graduate School of Library and Information Science at the University of Illinois at Urbana-Champaign. The class, "Instruction and Assistance Sys-

Terren Ilana Wein, MFA (E-mail: wein@alexia.lis.uiuc.edu) is pursuing a Master of Library Science degree and Juna Z. Snow, MS (E-mail: j-snow2@students.uuc.edu) is pursuing a PhD in Curriculum and Instruction, both at the University of Illinois at Urbana-Champaign.

Address correspondence to the authors at: P.O. Box 201, Savoy, IL 61874.

[Haworth co-indexing entry note]: "Virtually Jewish: The Creation of a Jewish Internet Tutorial." Wein, Terren Ilana, and Juna Z. Snow. Co-published simultaneously in *Journal of Religious & Theological Information* (The Haworth Information Press, an imprint of The Haworth Press, Inc.) Vol. 3, No. 3/4, 2001, pp. 203-214; and: *Theological Librarians and the Internet: Implications for Practice* (ed: Mark Stover) The Haworth Information Press, an imprint of The Haworth Press, Inc., 2001, pp. 203-214. Single or multiple copies of this article are available for a fee from The Haworth Document Delivery Service [1-800-342-9678, 9:00 a.m. - 5:00 p.m. (EST). E-mail address: getinfo@haworthpressinc.com].

tems," (LIS 316) focuses on bibliographic instruction and includes semester-long study of online instruction. Class members, working in groups of two or three, were instructed to create an online tutorial on a subject of their choice. The original idea for this particular tutorial was generated by a query on Ha-Safran (Hebrew for "the librarian"), the online discussion list maintained by the Association of Jewish Libraries, which serves Judaica libraries and librarians.

During the time when the authors were brainstorming tutorial topics, Glenn Ferdman, MLS, the Director of the Asher Library at the Spertus Institute of Jewish Studies, posted this query: "Dear Colleagues: Do any of you know of the existence of a Web-based tutorial of Judaica sites for novice Web-users? What I'm thinking of is a guided introduction to the Web using Judaica sites as the points of reference. Many thanks!"[1] The community need for this type of tutorial was thus established.

The assignment had three components: creation of a Web-based tutorial, class presentation of the tutorial, and evaluation of the tutorial. The tutorial project will have been finalized for the purposes of the original class by the beginning of May 2000. Ongoing maintenance and growth will occur at the site. The permanent URL for the tutorial is <http://leep.lis.uiuc.edu/seworkspace/wein/tutorial/Default.htm>.

The authors faced two major challenges in this assignment: the overall tutorial design, including instruction, interactivity, and evaluation; and content choices. In order to make content decisions, the potential audience was determined; the authors' topical knowledge was examined; and the pre-existing Web information was reviewed.

METHODOLOGY

In the beginning of the project, the decision was made to limit the length of the individual lessons in order to avoid overwhelming and/or boring potential users. During the audience assessment phase, the authors decided the main audience for the tutorial would be novice-to-intermediate Web users who were fairly Jewishly literate or who had an interest in learning more about Jewish issues. Another audience would be more advanced Web users who were interested in garnering more information on Jewish or Judaica Web resources. In other words, two possible audiences exist, with overlap between them: (1) a "Jewish" audience with little knowledge of Web-based issues who want to learn more about how to use the Web and might feel more comfortable and in control with Jewish content, and (2) a "Web-based" audience who are more knowledgeable about Web technology but are interested in learning more about Jewish information on the Web. The decision was made, therefore, to keep Web jargon to a minimum and to provide clear definitions for any Web vocabulary used. Some vocabulary dealing with Jewish culture and religion might be unfamiliar to some readers, but for the most part the authors felt that vocabulary could stand, again because the audience was seen to be Jewishly literate or Jewishly oriented. Several links within the tutorial could lead the user to a glossary of Jewish terms if needed.

The authors also made a conscious decision to attempt to include links to all the Jewish denominations. A disclaimer was inserted into the lesson dealing with "Jewish learning" that the authors were not rabbis and that only a rabbi could definitively answer questions of practice for individual users. Although the Jewish denominations differ from each other sharply on many issues, both major and minor, the authors attempted not to privilege any one denomination over another within the tutorial. Further, many Jews consider themselves Jewish in a cultural or ethnic sense, without being affiliated or practicing their religion. The overall tenor of the tutorial is, in fact, that "Jewishness" is a religion, a culture, and an ethnicity, and the authors wanted to include all those facets in order to increase the potential audience. A long period of time was devoted to negotiating lesson topics and lesson titles within the tutorial and what the authors wanted those topics and titles to reflect. The individual lessons were given the following names:

> Lesson 1: Getting Started
> Lesson 2: Reference Desk
> Lesson 3: Search Strategies
> Lesson 4: Community Center
> Lesson 5: Jewish Learning
> Lesson 6: Lists & Links

Home Page and Template

The home page provides the design and layout template for following pages. One-sentence overviews of each lesson are included. Navigation is provided both on the left side of the screen and at the bottom of the page. (See Figure 1.)

Lesson 1: Getting Started

Lesson One presents basic information for using the World Wide Web. The main goal is to acclimate the user to the Web–who is on it and what it can be used for. In addition, a mini-glossary of basic Internet terms that are used within the tutorial is provided, as well as a link to "NetDictionary" so users can easily look up any other unfamiliar terms. A practice exercise is provided: the user is asked to sign up for a free e-mail address in order to facilitate use of further lessons in the tutorial.

FIGURE 1

Virtually JEWISH

An Internet Tutorial from a Jewish Perspective

Lesson 1:
Internet Basics

Lesson 2:
Reference Tools

Lesson 3:
Search Strategies

Lesson 4:
Community

Lesson 5:
Jewish Learning

Lesson 6:
Links & Lists

Evaluation
& About Authors

Welcome to **Virtually Jewish**, an introduction to the Internet with a Jewish emphasis. The goal of this tutorial collection is to introduce the skills necessary to effectively use the Internet by illustrating Jewish websites as examples. The lessons are progressive with concepts building on each other, but you may start wherever you feel comfortable.

- Lessons 1 & 2 provide skills for beginning Internet use to find basic information.
- Lesson 3 demonstrates strategies for successful searching.
- Lesson 4 illustrates how to use the Internet to keep in touch -- or get in touch -- with family, friends, and community.
- Lesson 5 presents the world of Jewish learning available on the Internet.
- Lastly, Lesson 6 demonstrates the breadth of Jewish information on the 'Net.

Each lesson includes information on the topic, links to sites of interest, and a quick practice exercise.

To navigate through the site, click on a lesson in the navigation bar on the left of each page or on the bottom of each page. To return to this opening page, click on the "Virtually Jewish" header at the top of each page. If a link is broken or you have any comments, go to "Evaluation and About Authors."

Note to Educators: If you would like to use this site but object to certain content please contact the authors. A mirror site may be provided.

Lesson 2: Reference Desk

Lesson Two discusses how the Web can be used to answer reference questions. This topic was chosen for its general application to all potential users. This is a quick and easy way to show novice users who may be resistant to using the Web a real application that can immediately be put into effect. The Web topic of the lesson is bookmarking. Users can build their own "reference desk" through creating and editing bookmarks, a simple but important task. To emphasize the utility of bookmarking, links are provided to sites of Jewish reference interest, such as a calendar of holidays and glossaries of religious terminology, and to sites of general reference interest, such as a site which searches several dictionaries for the entered word and the *CIA Worldbook,* which provides very specific statistical and geographical information about the entire world. The practice exercise is to go to the Jewish calendar page, find out when Purim will fall in 2002, and bookmark the site. (See Figure 2.)

Lesson 3: Search Strategies

Lesson Three presents information on how to search the Internet, explains the basic differences between search engines and directories, and lists tips to help decide when to use a directory and when to use a search engine, as well as tips to get useful search results. Links are provided to several Jewish portals/gateways and search engines, such as Shamash, Virtual Jerusalem, and Maven (Yiddish for "expert"). In addition, the authors felt it was important to include information on anti-Semitism on the Web. Novice users especially might be prone to accidentally entering anti-Semitic sites brought up by search engines or might be shocked and offended and thus discouraged from further Web use. The practice exercise for this lesson was to run searches in a directory and a search engine and compare results. Specific search queries were suggested. (See Figure 3.)

Lesson 4: Community Center

Lesson Four discusses how the Web can be used to build and maintain community with Jewish family, friends, and 'tribe.' A variety of topics are covered under this general rubric: personal

FIGURE 2

Virtually JEWISH

An Internet Tutorial from a Jewish Perspective

Lesson 1:
Internet Basics

Lesson 2:
Reference Desk

Lesson 3:
Search Strategies

Lesson 4:
Community Center

Lesson 5:
Jewish Learning

Lesson 6:
Links & Lists

*Evaluation
& About Authors*

Lesson Two: Reference Desk

The Internet is a great place for finding the answer to basic questions -- questions like "what day will Passover fall on next year?" or "What's the weather like where my friend is vacationing today?" The easiest way to get these answers is to build your own reference "library" by bookmarking sites or by filing sites under "favorites," according to your browser type.

To bookmark a site, just bring your cursor up to "bookmark" in the ruler. Click on it, and then click on "add bookmark." When you've got several bookmarks in a similar category, you can make folders to keep your bookmarked sites categorized.

There are many Internet sites where the authors have prepared the answers to Jewish questions so that the information you need is only a click away. If you're thinking about going to Israel, for instance, you can find out how much the shekel is worth today. Or if you need to know the parsha (Torah portion) for a particular week, you can find it -- in fact, you can find the parsha with transliteration and Hebrew!

You can also read today's news (or past issues, as most online newspapers and magazines keep searchable archives) on the Internet. Many Jewish and Israeli newsources, such as *The Jerusalem Post* have webpages, as do mainstream publications such as *The New York Times*. The online version may not be as complete as the paper copy. Some sites, like the *Times*, have a special, more complete version for subscribers -- in this case, an online subscription just takes an email address and filling out a form. In the future we will bring you a list of Jewish and Israeli newspapers online.

Jewish Reference	**General Reference**
Z'manim (candle-lighting)	Dictionary
Holiday Calendar	Currency Converter
Torah/Haftorah Portion Information	Statistical/Geographical Information
A Folksy Glossary: religious/cultural terms	Weather Website
Academic Glossary: religious terms	Worldwide Government Information

Tip: please note that information you find on Jewish questions of religion will vary widely according to the denomination or affiliation of the

FIGURE 3

Virtually JEWISH

An Internet Tutorial from a Jewish Perspective

Lesson 1:
Internet Basics

Lesson 2:
Reference Desk

Lesson 3:
Search Strategies

Lesson 4:
Community Center

Lesson 5:
Jewish Learning

Lesson 6:
Links & Lists

*Evaluation
& About Authors*

Lesson Three: Search Strategies

Before we begin, we want to mention that surfing the Internet can sometimes lead to unexpected results. That is because some of the information on the web is compiled by computers. If you're looking for information on "Jewish history," for instance, you might find yourself looking at an Anti-Semitic site about "the history of Jewish domination of the world." Just be aware that Anti-Semitic sites do exist. There are also many sites put up by evangelicals or fundamentalists of other religions, some of which may have content that offends Jews. Read them if you want. Otherwise, just hit your "back" button.

How to Search

Out of the millions of sites on the Internet, how can you possibly find something you want? There are four basic ways to navigate the Internet. If you know exactly where you want to go, you can type the URL into the location bar. If you find yourself on an interesting page and you want to find out more, you can surf by clicking on hotlinks that link you to another page. Or for more organized searching, you can use a directory or a search engine.

What is the difference between directories and search engines?

There are two main differences. A directory is put together by people, and search engines are put together by computers. A search engine compiles sites to put in its database by searching for key words in the document. That's why, when you type in something "Jewish," you can sometimes get an Anti-Semitic site in which the word "Jewish" appears. In other words, the search engine doesn't edit for categories. A directory, on the other hand, is organized into categories by human editors.

That makes it sound like you would want to only use directories, but that's not the case. Directories tend to be smaller than search engines, and search engines are very powerful for running specific searches. They're both useful tools. There are also "second-generation search engines" like Google or Ask Jeeves that combine some of the features of directories and search engines, and "metasearch engines," like Dogpile, which search several search engines at once!

There's also the Open Directory Project, a free, open content, volunteer-maintained directory. There are many categories collected under Judaism, including Yiddish, Communities and Congregations, and History. If you come across an interesting site while surfing the Internet and you want to let others know about it, you can submit the URL.

homepages; list-servs, bulletin boards, and Internet Relay Chat; and organizations and institutions on the Web. Genealogy, a hot Web topic, is mentioned. The authors offered some examples of institutions on the Web, including links to the homepages for the major Jewish denominations. Obviously it is not possible to link every Jewish organization or institution on the Web. The authors chose to mention the homepages of some "special-interest" groups in order to show the diversity of Web-based information: the Jewish Deaf Community Center, the World Congress of Jewish Gay, Lesbian, and Bisexual Organizations, Hillel (the national Jewish college student's organization), Hadassah (a women's Zionist organization), and the Jewish Vegetarian and Ecological Union. These diverse organizations seemed to suggest how "Jewishness" is an umbrella under which many people can stand and spoke to what was suggested in the "Methodology" section–that "Jewish" needs are ethnic and cultural as well as religious.

There are two suggested practice exercises on this page. The first is to go to "Jewhoo," a light-hearted search engine of Jewish celebrities and notables, and find out how many "Star Trek" cast members are Jewish. The second is to browse list-servs, find one the user likes, and sign up. (See Figure 4.)

Lesson 5: Jewish Learning

Lesson Five introduces users to online Jewish Learning. The Web-use component of the lesson is to learn about plug-ins for audio and video. The practice exercise asks the user to listen to audio on the Web, downloading a plug-in if necessary. The user then is sent to "Navigating the Bible," a beautiful site from ORT where listeners can read and listen to Torah, Haftorah, and Maftir portions as well as blessings. Users can read the portion in Hebrew and in English; also available is cantillation for singing the Torah portions.

Lesson 6: Links & Lists (The Jewish World on the World Wide Web)

As of this writing the authors are still determining what exactly the final lesson should consist of. Planned is a tabular format organizing categories of information and collecting links in various categories, such as museums, libraries, arts, science, Yiddish, the Holocaust, and

FIGURE 4

Virtually JEWISH
An Internet Tutorial from a Jewish Perspective

Lesson Four: Community Center

The Internet is a wonderful tool for keeping in touch with friends and family and for making new connections. Many people have home pages where they show off family pictures. For example, one of the authors of this tutorial has a page dedicated to her nephew so that family across the United States and Canada can keep up with his development.

If you've been thinking of looking up *your* family tree, you're not alone. Genealogy is a growing area of the Web. An excellent site with many helpful features and great links is Distant Cousin. Another good place for Jews to do genealogy is JewishGen. This site has an interesting feature ("family finder") that puts you in touch with others looking up the same name or placename. It also uses "soundex," a phonetic searcher, so don't worry if you can't spell that Ukrainian shtetl name.

Shmoozing is important to all of us, and the Internet is a prime place to find good shmoozing through list-serves, live chat, and bulletin boards. (Go back to our first lesson if you've forgotten those definitions.) Whatever it is you're interested in you can connect with others who have that same interest. Some list-serves, BBSs, or IRCs are for people of a certain age, others are for people in a certain profession or organization, and some are organized through interest in a topic. At Shamash, you can see there are Jewish-themed list-serves for every denomination and interest, from "Star Trek from a Jewish Cultural/Religious Perspective" to "Grandchildren of Holocaust Survivors." There's even a website called www.shmooze.org.

Another good place to find a list-serve is at Liszt, the mailing list directory. You can try "religion" or "culture" -- or try searching for whatever you're interested in. There is also jewishgroups or athens at Geocites, both of which have many Jewish-themed list-serves to choose from.

The Internet will also help you keep in touch with the tribe -- the Jewish family. You can learn more about the different denominations at their home pages, or locate a synagogue near you or wherever you are travelling. If you're in college, you can hook up with a Hillel, the national organization for Jewish college students. You can find Hadassah, or B'nai B'rith, or any number of organizations to help you build community, such as the Jewish Vegetarian and Ecological Society or the Jewish Deaf Community Center.

Finally, a fun place to learn more about who in our world is Jewish: Jewhoo. This is a light-hearted site where you can discover which actors, writers, Congresspeople, sports players, scientists, and other notable figures are Jewish.

Virtual Headquarters for Jewish Denominations

food. Because pages where individuals have collected their favorite or recommended links to Jewish topics are already numerous, the authors decided not to recreate this work, but rather to create their own "collected link to pages of links." The intent of the lesson will be to demonstrate the breadth of Jewish information of all types and levels of sophistication on the World Wide Web. Refining and re-categorizing this information into more specific pages within the tutorial will be an ongoing task.

End Page: About Authors and Evaluation Form

The end page has two components: authors' footnotes and contact information, and an evaluation form.

DESIGN CHOICES

The tutorial was started using an html (hyper-text markup language) editor. After working on the tutorial for approximately one month, it was moved onto the Graduate School of Library and Information Science server. From that point, the work was performed by hand-coding in html.

The intent was to create a Web site with a clean, professional look but a warm feel. Jewish-themed icons and backgrounds were chosen, starting with a blue Mogen David tile for the background. The color of the background tile led to the creation of a unique complementary blue color for the navigation bar and text. Three different Mogen David icons (other than the background tile) are incorporated into the pages: (1) in the navigation bar, (2) to indicate tips, and (3) to mark practice exercises. The particular icons were chosen for their small size, color match, and general unobtrusiveness with the design.

A font with serifs is used to maximize ease of reading. No blinking or moving animations or text are included because of potential distractibility and/or irritation to the user. Alternate text are assigned to all images to address possible accessibility issues for any special-needs users. Because the main audience was seen as novice-to-intermediate users, the authors included two ways to navigate and were careful to maintain consistency with icons and general layout.

PRE-EXISTING WEB INFORMATION

In order to determine if similar tutorials already exist, searches were run in the major Jewish directories. The search results revealed many sites that collected links to Jewish-themed Web pages, and many sites that contain extensive Jewish information. The results yielded no existing site that presents an Internet tutorial from a Jewish perspective. No search was conducted through Israeli/Hebrew-language Web sites because neither of the authors read Hebrew proficiently. Of course, there are many sites of collected links by both individuals and institutions that provide invaluable assistance.

EVALUATIVE COMPONENTS

After the final lesson, users are directed to a page containing an evaluation form and author information. The authors presented an early, unfinished version of the site to classmates for feedback (this was a required component of the class). Classmates helpfully pointed out some vocabulary inconsistencies and potentially confusing design issues. Preliminary feedback regarding the site was also conducted informally by family, friends, and community members, who were helpful in highlighting style and language inconsistencies and submitting Web sites to possibly include. A request to evaluate the site was submitted to the e-mail list of the M'vakshe Derekh ("seekers of a way") minyan at Sinai Temple in Champaign-Urbana, of which one of the authors is the coordinator. Members of M'vakshe Derekh were seen as good preliminary evaluators due to their level of Jewish literacy.

One preliminary evaluator, an advanced user and Jewish Professional, stated that not enough links were included in the individual lessons, and volunteered to export all the "thousands" of his bookmarks to the authors.[2] A novice user alerted the authors that she did not realize that the links would take her outside the tutorial and suggested more information on navigation and technology requirements.[3] Another novice user and Jewish Professional who took the tutorial had this to say: "I have now been addicted for the past 45 minutes and at this point in time I can ill afford to do that . . . but what it tells you is there is so much interesting stuff to learn and do on your Web site."[4] This user may have been slightly biased, being the aunt of one of the authors.

Further evaluation, yet to take place as of this writing, will occur in the authors' class when the tutorial is presented. For the purposes of the course, the authors will be preparing a thirty-minute presentation of the tutorial for fellow students. The presentation will include interacting with the tutorial, a hand-out on the goals, content, and potential uses of the tutorial, and an evaluation sheet for fellow students to complete.

By the time this article reaches publication, the evaluation results will have been incorporated into the tutorial. Comments, queries, and suggestions from future users are encouraged.

CONCLUSION

This site will continue to be maintained after its submission as a course project. The intention is to continue to expand the site, possibly by creating additional lessons and continuing to update links. Users will continue to be able to submit comments or questions. Perhaps an "Ask the Librarian" query will also be added after one of the authors has received her Master of Library Science degree.

The site will be submitted to Ha-Safran for dissemination. It will also be submitted to the major directories, including the Jewish directories mentioned within the tutorial. The authors hope that dissemination by word-of-mouth will be extensive, as a community need for a Jewish Internet tutorial has been demonstrated.

Readers of this volume are invited and encouraged to visit *Virtually Jewish* at <http://leep.lis.uiuc.edu/seworkspace/wein/tutorial/Default. htm> and leave their comments.

NOTES

1. Glenn Ferdman, "Web-based Judaica tutorial?" in Ha-Safran [online discussion list], 23 February 2000 [cited 17 April 2000].

2. Rob Silverman, e-mail communication with T. I. Wein, 18 April, 2000.

3. Annette Buckmaster, e-mail communication with T. I. Wein, 18 April, 2000.

4. Ruthan Wein, e-mail communication with T. I. Wein, 17 April, 2000.

Index